Muttering of a Madman 3

Letters to my Family
on
Understanding Islam, Health Care, Demographics

And

Other Things of Interest

J.T. Oney *Regimen? Best wishes J.T.O*

i

Also by J.T. Oney

Mutterings of a Madman 1

Letters to my family on War and Politics

Mutterings of a Madman 2

Letters to my family on Science and Religion

Murder on Thornton Mountain

Betrayal at Saint-Etienne

Morgan's Mountain

Logan County Justice

Bloody Logan County

Logan County War

ISBN-13: 978-1507802755

ISBN-10: 1507802757

This book is dedicated to my wife, Anita Honeycutt Oney, who gave me the time, support and patience to attempt another career.

J.T. Oney

Table of Contents

Part 2 – Health Care and the Affordable Health Care Act (ACA)

Part 3 – Demographics in America

Mutterings of a Madman 3

Part 1

Understanding Islam

Part 1 – Understanding Islam

Context for the Islam Letters

In the next series of letters I intend to take a look at Islam. As many of you may now know I have always had an interest in Christianity and as an extension an interest in Judaism and other religions such as Taoism, Buddhism, etc.

When I was younger, much younger, one of the organizations I belonged to had as one if it's doctrines to "**Know Your Enemy.**" In many exercises that meant creating an Area Study which had as one of its components taking a close look at the culture and the religion of the area of interest and in many cases that was Islam since the Islamic community is world-wide

To be truthful, however, I have never had much of an interest in Islam but the rise of Islamic extremism has dictated that I now take a close look at it. Well, why now?

We are now fighting and for the foreseeable future will continue to fight Islam extremist both here and abroad and, of course, I would rather fight them abroad than in the hills of Kentucky. Islamic extremist are a small but growing segment of the Islamic community that has been gaining in strength over the past few years.

I believe it was inevitable for the simple reason that Islamic extremism is winning the battle within the world Islamic community which is now taking place between the Islamic moderates and the Islamic extremists.

The problem in this on-going battle is to distinguish between the extreme Islamist and the moderate Islamist for we will need the help of the Islamic moderates if we are to prevail in this conflict. Unfortunately, we as westerners seem to paint all Muslims with the same brush and use stereotypes to exclaim, for example, "that all Muslims are terrorists."

Nothing of course is farther from the truth. Westerners still feel antipathy toward Islam that extends back to the Crusades of the middle ages which were military campaigns sanctioned by the Roman Catholic Church. Some westerners still talk in terms of a 'Great Crusade' against Muslims.

On the other hand Muslims are suspicious of our understanding of Islam. This also goes back to the Crusades when westerners vilified Islam, denigrated the Prophet Muhammad and attempted to wipe Islam from the face of the earth.

Religious wars are always brutal affairs. Just look at the Thirty Years war between the Catholic and the Protestants in the 1600s. This was one of the most devastating wars in European history that in many cases reduced state populations by as much as forty percent.

I must put a caveat here for as a Christian I will be writing about Islam through the eyes of a Christian. I will attempt in so far as possible to present Islam through Islamic eyes but we both know that is going to be impossible. Nevertheless, these are my letters so I will attempt it anyway.

Another caveat, I have not lived in a Muslim country but I do realize, like all religions, that Islam is exceptionally complex and has been interpreted differently by many Islamic cultures yet it has a few simple tenets shared across those cultures so rather then look at each individual cultural interpretation of Islam I will concentrate on its common tenets.

As you read these letters and attempt to understand Islam I would encourage you to put aside any preconceived notions that you may have about Islam and approach it with a "Beginners Mind."

There is a famous story about a Zen master who receives a college professor who wishes to talk about Zen. The professor sits down at the table for tea with the Zen master and begins to pontificate about the teachings of Zen. The master begins pouring the tea and keeps pouring until the cup begins to overflow.

The professor exclaims, "The cup is full. No more will go in!"

The Zen master says, "Like this cup you are full of your own opinions and speculations. How can I show you Zen unless you first empty your cup."

Well, in order to understand Islam, like the college professor, you must first empty your cup and begin with no preconceived notions.

J.T. Oney

Letter 1 - Islamic Overview

"In the name of Allah, the Most Compassionate, the Most Merciful. All praise is due be to Allah, Lord of the Worlds, The Most Compassionate, the Most Merciful. Sovereign of the Day of Judgement. You alone we worship, and to You alone we turn for help. Guide us to the straight way; The way of those whom You have favoured, Not of those who have incurred Your wrath, Nor of those who have gone astray."

Thus begins the **Quran**, the revealed word of God to the Prophet, **Muhammad**. The Quran is a document recited to Muhammad for the purpose of revealing the final word of God to the people of the world. The Quran is believed by Muslims to be the final revealed word of God and contains guidance on how Muslims are to conduct their lives.

A Muslim is one who has professed Islam, that is, one who has submitted to the **"Will of God."** There are about 1.5 billion Muslins in the world of all nationalities who practice Islam. Islam is the second largest religion in the world (Christianity is the largest) and is expected to soon be the second largest religion in the United States. About 20-24% of the world's population is Muslim with between 3-7 million in the United States. South Asia (India, Pakistan and Bangladesh) contain the highest proportion of Muslims by area. Indonesia contains the highest percentage of Muslims of any nation. Only about 20% of the world's Muslims live in the Middle East.

Muslims represent the majority population in fifty-seven countries to include Iran, Iraq, Pakistan, Egypt, Indonesia, Bangladesh, and Nigeria. In addition there is a significant Muslim population in India, China, the Central Asian Republics and Russia.

Surprisingly, and contrary to popular belief, the majority of Muslims are not Arabs. Only about 20% of the of the world's 1.5 billion Muslims come from Arab countries. The largest Muslim communities are to be found in Indonesia, Pakistan, Bangladesh, and India.

Christianity expresses itself in many forms, Baptist, Methodist, Presbyterians, etc. Just as there is a great diversity in Christianity so there is a great diversity in Islam. Muslims maintain there is only one divinely revealed and mandated Islam but there are many Muslim interpretations of Islam just as there are many interpretations of Christianity.

The two primary branches of Islam are Sunni and Shii. Sunni accounts for about 85% of the 1.5 billion Muslims. The Sunni Muslims make up the majority in most Muslim countries to include Saudi Arabia, Turkey and Egypt. The Shii account for about 15% of the Muslim population with the majority located in Iran, Iraq, Bahrain, and Azerbaijan and, according to some estimates, Yemen. Later, in another letter, I will discuss the Sunni-Shii split which has torn apart the Islamic community for hundreds of years and continues to tear it apart today.

All Muslims share, to include the Sunni and Shii, a limited number of articles of faith. These are summarized as:

1. **There is only one God and that is Allah.** All Muslims believe there is only one God in the Universe. Islam is similar to Christianity and Judaism in that it is a **Monotheistic** religion. That is, the belief there is only one God and he is all powerful. Allah is the name of the Muslim God but He is the same as the God of Christianity and Judaism.

2. **There are Angels**. God, Allah, created unseen beings called angels who work tirelessly to administer the kingdom of God in full obedience to his will. The angels surround us at all times, and each has a duty with some recording our words and deeds.

3. **There are Prophets of God**. Muslims believe that God communicates His guidance through human prophets sent to every nation. These prophets, from a Muslim perspective, start with Adam and include Noah, Abraham, Moses, Jesus and Muhammad. The main message of all the prophets is that there is only One true God and He alone is worthy of being worshipped.

4. **There is a Final Day of Judgment**. God created man for a special purpose and inherent in the Islamic belief is that there will be a final judgment in which all men will be judged by God. They will be judged as to whether or not they led their lives in accordance with God's will. According to Islamic teachings, those who believe in God and perform good deeds will be eternally rewarded in Heaven. Those who reject faith

in God and do not follow the will of God will be eternally punished in the fires of Hell.

5. **There is Predestination**. Muslims believe that since God is the Sustainer of all life that nothing happens except by His Will and with His full knowledge, that is, events are predestined. This belief does not contradict the idea of free will. God does not force us to do anything but our choices are known to God beforehand because His knowledge is complete. Everything is God's will, therefore, this belief helps the Muslim through life's difficulties. Muslims express this belief in the word *Inshallah*.

6. **There is a Final Book of God**. God intervened in human history in a specific place at a specific time to reveal to man an authoritative and final guide to God's Will. Between 610 and 632 AD in the western part of Arabia, God intervened to provide mankind a guide, **the Quran** (Koran). This guide takes the form of a document that was recited to the Prophet Muhammad by the Angel Gabriel. The Quran is a divine message to mankind with the Prophet Muhammad serving as God's Messenger. Muslims believe the Quran is God's final revelation revealed to the Prophet Muhammad and is the authoritative guide to what God expects of men and women.

All Muslims share these six essential tenets. Muslims are not interested in the nature of God because they believe this is simply a waste of time because man will never know God because God is unknowable. God has no Gender and, if he does, we can never know it even though we commonly use a masculine article in describing Him.

Religious Similarities

Strange for many, I'm sure, is that Islam has many similarities with Christianity and Judaism. For example, both are monotheistic religions, that is, all three religions believe there is only one God who is the creator, ruler and judge of the universe.

Another interesting similarity is between the founders of Judaism, Christianity and Islam. For example, Moses was a slave, Jesus was a carpenter while Muhammad was an illiterate caravan manager but yet each founded a large monotheistic religion.

Muslims, like Christians and Jews, believe in Prophets to include not only Muhammad but also the prophets of the Old Testament to include Abraham, Moses and Jesus. Where they differ in this area is that Muslims believe that Jesus is a Prophet but not the Son of God.

Muslims believe, as do Christians and Jews, in angels, heaven, hell and the final Day of Judgment. For example, Muslims believe that angels are part of God's creation and are used by Him to protect humans and to relay his messages. For example, Gabriel bought God's divine revelations to Muhammad; Michael provides nourishment for human bodies and souls; while Raphael will sound the trumpet twice signaling the Day of Final Judgment. Many Muslims believe angels are created from light and that two angels attend each human and record their words and actions until the moment of death when that account is presented to God for a Final Judgment.

Muslims, like Christians and Jews, believe in the Day of Judgment in which a cataclysmic event will destroy the world and all creatures will receive their reward in heaven or punishment in hell based upon the account recorded by the two angels assigned to each Muslim. The signs of the Day of Judgment will include the return of the great deceiver, **al-Dajjal**, who will spread corruption and evil across the earth; the return of **Mahdi**, a Muslim messianic figure; and the Second Coming of **Jesus Christ**.

Some Muslims believe the coming of Mahdi will bring justice and truth before the Day of Judgment while other Muslims believe the Second Coming of Jesus Christ will fulfill that role as foretold in the Quran, Chapter 43, Verse 61: *"An he Jesus shall be a Sign that the coming of the Hour of Judgment therefore have no doubt about the Hour but follow ye Me: this is a Straight Way."* The Prophet Muhammad is expected to be the first to rise and arrive at the place of assembly.

Muslims, like Jews and Christians, believe in Heaven and Hell for the Quran emphasizes the ultimate responsibility and accountability of each Muslim believer and that their actions will be judged accordingly and rewarded with either eternal Heaven or an eternal Hell based upon the recording of their actions in the **Book of Deeds**. The Quran, Chapter 23, Verses 102-103 states: *"Then those whose* *balance of good deeds is heavy will attain salvation, but those whose balance is light will have lost their souls and abide in Hell forever.*" The Quran's version of the afterlife describes the Garden of Paradise as a heavenly mansion of bliss with gently flowing rivers, beautiful gardens and cool streams of water for drinking.

Islamic tradition elaborates on the role of *houris*, sometimes translated as beautiful companions or virgins. However, the Quran makes no mention of the sexual role of *houris* and most Muslims understand *houris* as virgins but only in the sense of pure or purified souls. The Quran, Chapter 56, Verses 35-38 states that "*Indeed, We have produced the women of Paradise in a new creation And made them virgins, Devoted to their husband and of equal age, For the companions of the right.*" However, with that said, the *hadith* (the teaching, deeds and sayings of Muhammad), by various scholars, does mention the seventy-two virgins as being given to Islamic males who enter Paradise.

Muslims also believe that God's revelation was received in the Old Testament and the Quran. They, therefore, believe Jews and Christians are "**People of the Book**" who also belong to the "**Religion of Abraham**" and received revelations through prophets which form the scriptures. They differ, however, in that Muslims believe the Prophet Muhammad received the final and complete revelation from God through the angel Gabriel in order to correct the human errors that had made their way into the scriptures of Christianity. For example, one of the errors Muhammad believed had crept into the scripture was that Jesus was the Son of God and not just a Prophet.

Muslims, like Christians and Jews, believe themselves to be '**Children of Abraham**' but descended from a different branch of the family. Both the Old Testament and the Quran tell the story of Abraham, Sarah and Sarah's slave, Hagar. Sarah was old, barren and could no longer bear a child so she encouraged Abraham to conceive a child with Hagar. They called this son Ismail. After the birth of Ismail, Sarah became pregnant and bore a son called Issac. Sarah soon pressured Abraham to send Hagar and Ismail away so that her son Issac would inherit from Abraham. Abraham was reluctant to do this until God promised that He would make Ismail the father of a great nation. The Muslims believe that Hagar and Ismail settled near Mecca and that they, Muslims, are descended from Abraham through Ismail while Christians believe they are descended from Abraham through Issac.

Since Muslims do not believe Jesus is divine they do not believe in the Christian doctrine of the Trinity, that is, one God in three persons. Muslims fail to understand how one can believe in three Gods and still be monotheistic.

Muslims recognize Jesus as a prophet but not the Son of God. It must be remembered that for Muslims associating anyone or anything with God is idolatry and a sin against God. Remember Salman Rushdi and the Satanic Verses?

Muslims do not believe in the doctrine of inherited sin. Although Muslims believe in Adam and Eve in the Garden of Eden, there is no doctrine of an inherited Original Sin in Islam. Consequently, in contrast to Christianity, there is no belief in suffering or atonement for mankind. The punishment of Adam and Eve is solely due to their disobedience of God's Will.

In Islam there is no emphasis on shame, disgrace, or guilt instead the emphasis on the ongoing human struggle, *jihad*, to do what is just and right in obeying the Will of God.

A Broader View of Islam

Islam has been viewed in many ways by westerners. For example, one way to view Islam is through **Islamic Law**. This is a term, however, that is often misunderstood and wrongly used by western press. Islamic law is simply the dos and don'ts that all Muslim are to act in accordance with to satisfy God's Will. I will discuss Islamic law in a later letter.

Islam can also be understood as a **community of believers** but because cultures differ on how each interprets the Quran, the dos and don'ts varies considerably depending upon their culture. A woman's dress code is an example of this. The Quran simply says a woman must dress properly or modestly. The difference in interpretation can be seen in the fact that some cultures stress full body cover while other cultures may simply stress a head scarf. From the Muslims perspective this does not affect their core beliefs but is simply interpreted that there is diversity in unity.

Islam can also be treated as **a civilization**. From the 7th through the 15th century the most vital part of western civilization was centered around the Mediterranean. While all Europe was in the Dark Ages the Islamic civilization was advancing in terms of medicine, law, mathematics, etc. The Islamic civilization of that time assisted in bringing Europe out of the Dark Ages into a period of enlightenment. I will also discuss more on this in a later letter.

Islam can also be seen as **a movement**, a living force in the world today. Westerners believe that Islam is now in a revival stage and is viewed as a threat to Modernity – whatever that is? I will discuss Muslim extremism in a later letter.

American Islam

An overview of Islam would not be complete without a few words related to Islam in America. It is estimated that Islam is the second most popular religion in America and may have as many as 7 million followers. It is also estimated that as many as 20,000 Americans convert to Islam annually. Muslims have been in America since the settling of the country with some of the oldest and most well-stablished communities in the midwest in locations such as Dearborn, Michigan and Cedar Rapids, Iowa.

Muslims are well integrated into American society unlike those in Europe, particularly those in France and England where Muslims seem to have settled in poor neighborhoods. Recent surveys have shown that over 60 percent of American Muslims have a bachelor degree or higher; 44 percent are in professional positions and 60 percent earn over $50,000 annually. However, they still face several challenges such as opposition to building mosques, finding time and space to pray, and the problem of Muslim women wearing headscarves at work.

African-Americans present an interesting story in American Islam. As much as 30 percent of Muslims in America are African-American. This should not be surprising for it is estimated that up to 20 percent of African slaves brought to America were Muslims who were forced to convert to Christianity. Many African-Americans are, therefore, drawn to Islam because they feel they are returning to a tradition that was taken from them. When an African-American converts to Islam they often drop their given name and embrace a Muslim name because they feel the given name had been forced on them by slave owners. For example, Cassius Clay became Muhammad Ali.

The Nation of Islam is the organization most responsible for bringing African-Americans to Islam. This organization began in the 1930s when a man named Wallace D. Fard began preaching in Detroit. He preached a philosophy of understanding that was connected to Islam. His most important follower was Elijah

Muhammad who took leadership of the organization and preached that Fard was divine and that he, Elijah Muhammad, was a prophet. He also advocated racial separation, forbade intermarriage and wanted blacks to only support black businesses. His most famous follower was Malcolm X who continued to preach the separatist philosophy.

Elijah Muhammad's son, Warith Dean Muhammad, saw that the Nation of Islam philosophy was inconsistent with the Quran and broke away to form the more moderate *American Society of Islam* which was more closely aligned with Sunni Islam. The Nation of Islam continued under Louis Farrakhan who has since moderated their philosophy.

In my next letter I will discuss the Prophet, Muhammad.

References:

1. *What everyone Needs to Know About Islam*, John L. Esposito
2. *A History of God*, Karen Armstrong
3. *Islam*, Karen Armstrong
4. *God and his Prophet: The Religion of Islam*, The Great Courses, John Swanson
5. *Cultural Literacy for Religion,* The Great Courses, Mark Bergson
6. *Great World Religions: Islam*, The Great courses, John L. Esposito
7. The Wikipedia, Various newspaper, and Magazine Articles

Letter 2 – The Prophet Muhammad

Information related to Muhammad, the Muslim Prophet and God's messenger, is found in the *Quran*, early biographies and the *hadith* which is tradition literature about what the Prophet said and did. Therefore, more is known about Muhammad than perhaps any other prophet.

Before looking at the Prophet, however, it is necessary to look at the time in which Muhammad lived and Islam was formed and emerged for like all religions, Islam was not created in a vacuum but was a result of and a response to the political and social conditions of the time.

The time of the Prophet was dominated by two great superpowers: the **Christian Byzantine Holy Roman Empire** and the **Sasanian Persian Empire** (the last Iranian Empire) which competed for world domination. The Byzantine Empire dominated the Mediterranean while the Persian Empire encompassed Egypt, Judea, Syria, Iraq and Iran. Arabia, the land of Muhammad, was just on the periphery and to the south of the struggle between the two empires and for all practical purposes was outside their influence.

The peoples located in the Arabian Peninsula were organized into a kinship structure which was organized by tribes, then by clans, then by families. Many were Bedouins who lived along the great desert while others lived and traded along the Red Sea coast.

Pre-Islamic religion was polytheistic and reflected the tribal social structure. In addition, Arabia was the home of a variety of religious practices to include Judaism, Christianity and Zoroastrianism. As the Arab tribes struggled for survival they developed the culture of *muruwah* which is normally translated as manliness but implies such things as courage in battle, patience, and endurance and, above all dedication to the tribe. That is, manliness, courage in battle and upholding the tribal and family honor were central family and tribal virtues. The tribe was headed by a *sayyid* (chief) who shared his wealth equally with the other tribe members and was responsible for avenging the killing of a tribe member by killing a member of the other tribe. This vendetta (blood feud) was the only way of ensuring the security of the tribe in a region with no central authority. This was a very violent time and vendettas of this type could easily get out of hand if the killing was thought to be disproportionate to the original offense. For example, they did not kill five for one for that would be disproportionate. It was always one for one.

There were two major prosperous cities located on the Eastern slope of the Hijaz Mountains which paralleled the Red Sea. The northernmost city was named **Rathrib** (later renamed Medina). The southernmost city was **Mecca** which prospered by taking advantage of the caravan routes. It was most famous as the home of the **Kabah** which at this time was a pagan shrine thought by Arabs to be built by Abraham and Ismail.

Mecca was the main site of a great annual pilgrimage by the various tribes to honor the tribal patron deities. The annual pilgrimage was centered on the Kabah which contained the representations of the 360 different tribal gods and goddesses. The head of the gods and goddesses was a supreme god called *al-lah*, creator of the Universe. The pilgrimage of the tribes to the Kabah was sponsored by the Meccans and was a very profitable enterprise. Violence was forbidden in the sanctuary around the Kabah. The was enforced by the Quraysh tribe who were the guardians of the Kabah and who had grown wealthy due to the mercantile trade and the annual pilgrimage.

The Arabs of that time had never been favored with a Prophet and felt a sense of spiritual inferiority. The Jews and Christian with whom the Arabs traded taunted them because they had not received a revelation from God and had no Prophet similar to Moses and Jesus.

The Birth of Muhammad

Muhammad ibn Abdallah was born into this culture in 570 AD in Mecca in what is now Saudi Arabia. He was born into the Hashimite family of the Quraysh tribe which was the most prominent and powerful in Mecca. The Hashimites are still honored today as the family of Muhammad. For example, the King of Jordan belongs to the Hashimite family and is revered as such.

Muhammad lived in Mecca for the first 52 years of his life from 570 to 622 AD. Historically, Muhammad's life in Mecca is divided into two periods: the period before his prophetic vision (570-610 AD) and the period after declaring his prophetic visions (610-622 AD).

The Mecca in which Muhammad lived was a city of continual strife exemplified by caravan raids and continual vendettas. At this time raiding was an integral part of tribal life and was undertaken to increase property and goods such as camels, cattle, and slaves. The raiders attempted to avoid bloodshed lest it lead to a vendetta and further bloodshed.

Muhammad earned his living acting as a manager for the caravans of a wealthy widow named *Khadija*. He married Khadijah (her full name was Khadijah bint Khuwaylid) when he was 25 and she was 40. They had six children, two sons who died in infancy, and four daughters, Zainab, Ruqayyah, Umm, and Fatima (more on her later). Until 610 AD, he lived the uneventful life of a prosperous merchant and a good husband.

The Prophet of God

Muhammad was known in Mecca for his integrity, trustworthiness and reflective nature and on a regular basis retreated to a desert hilltop, Mount Hira, to reflect on the meaning of life. In 610 AD, on a dark night on Mount Hira, a night known in Islam as the *"The Night of Power and Excellence"*, he was called to be a Prophet of God. Muhammad was enveloped in an overpowering presence and heard the voice of the Angel Gabriel commanding him to 'recite', *Iqra!*. He protested that he was unlettered but the words nevertheless poured forth. He received these recitations and revelations from God over the next 22 years until his death in 632 AD at the age of 62.

These recitations were preserved orally, then eventually written down by scribes and then collected to become the Quran (Koran). With the encouragement of his wife, Khadija, perhaps his first convert, Muhammad began to preach his revelation to the citizens of Mecca repeating the divine verses that had been recited to him by the Angel Gabriel. Muhammad could neither read nor write so his followers listened and learned it by heart and those who were literate wrote it down. Twenty years after Muhammad's death the first compilations of the Quran were made

Like Jesus, he preached a **reformist message** that denounced the status quo and called for social justice for the poor, equality of women and protection for the most vulnerable. His message called for the people to engage in a *jihad* of the soul, to reform their communities and to live a good life based upon religious belief and not loyalty to the tribe. He preached that each person was personally accountable, not to the tribe, but to the **Will of Allah**, the one God. He rejected Arabian polytheism and insisted there was only one true God. This obviously did not endear him to the merchants of Mecca.

Muhammad condemned the unbridled materialism, avarice and corruption characterizing Meccan society of that time. He called this a *jahiliyya* society – a society ignorant of Islam. This term as used by Muhammad described pre-Islamic society but later began to be used by Muslim extremist to describe modern societies as anti-Islamic.

While in Mecca Muhammad continued to receive messages from God for the next ten years. These messages were short in length and were primarily warnings to the people. Muhammad, at first, did not think of himself as founding a new religion but as a Warner, a *nadbir*. These shorter messages are now in the back of the Quran while the messages Muhammad received in Medina are longer and are in the front of the Quran.

Eventually Muhammad's religious message became known as **Islam** which is thought of as the unconditional act of surrender to **aL-Lah** or God. By this act of unconditional surrender a Muslim was transformed and became a man or woman who had surrendered his or her whole being to Allah. Muhammad did not preach obligatory doctrines about God but instead presented Him as a moral imperative which some theologians think is the essence of monotheism.

Because of his reformist message Muhammad aroused the suspicion and animosity of the tribal leaders, the priests and the major merchants of the city and, as a result, he and his followers began to suffer persecution. Muhammad's claim to be a Prophet and the divine revelation he recited to the people posed a threat to tribal political authority and the revenue from the annual pilgrimage to the Kabah.

The real split with the leaders of Mecca came, however, when Muhammad forbade his followers from worshiping the pagan gods proclaiming there was only one true god worthy of worship.

Some Western historians, however, cite the incident with the **Satanic Verses** as holding the key to the final split between Muhammad and the leaders of Mecca resulting in his subsequent flight to Medina.

The Satanic Verses

The first mention of the Satanic Verses is by the tenth-century historian Abu Jafar at-Tabari. According to Tabari, Muhammad was distressed by the rift with most of his tribe after he had forbidden his followers to worship pagan gods and, inspired by Satan, allowed several pagan gods to be venerated. Later Gabriel came to Muhammad and told him these verses were of '**Satanic**' origin and should be stricken from the Quran and replaced by lines indicating these gods, **al-Lat** (the Goddess), **al-Uzza** (the Mighty) and **Manat** (the Fateful One) were simply figments of the imagination. After these verses were recited all chances of reconciliation between Muhammad and the leaders of Mecca were lost since, thereafter, Muhammad refused to make any concession to polytheism or idolatry. Henceforth, *"Allahu Akbar"* (God is Greater(est)) became the cry of the Muslim.

A brief note on the Satanic Verses: There are some individuals, and I am one of them, that doubt the occurrence of this incident since it was first mentioned over 400 years after the death of Muhammad and was not mentioned in the Quran or earlier Islamic literature

In 619 AD the Prophet's wife, Khadijah, died and about that same time his uncle, Abu Talib, also died and was, therefore, unable to protect Muhammad and his followers. His uncle, Abu Talib, had raised Muhammad after his parents had died and because of his standing in the community of Mecca had assured Muhammad's safety while he had preached his message from God. After the death of his uncle the persecution by the Meccan merchants increased and, fearing assassination, Muhamad was forced to leave Mecca.

It was in 621 AD, perhaps the lowest point in Muhammad's life, that he received a mystical experience called by Muslims the "*Night Journey*".

The Night Journey (or Ascension)

One night while sleeping near the Kabah Muhammad received a visit from the angel Gabriel. Muhammad mounted a mystical horse, *Al-Buraq* (Lightning), and flew from Mecca to Jerusalem, referred to in the Quran as the '*Further Mosque*'. In Jerusalem he climbed a ladder leading to the throne of God. It was on this journey that he met the other Prophets to include Abraham, Moses, and Jesus.

He met with God and received guidance on the fixing of the Muslim prayer for five times a day.

The Night Journey of Muhammad has made Jerusalem the third most important city to the Muslim community after Mecca and Medina. Muhammad climbed the ladder into heaven from what is now the **Al-Aqsa Mosque** which is the third holiest site in Islam and is located in the Old City of Jerusalem. Both the Al-Aqsa Mosque and the **Dome of the Rock** sit on the site of the **Temple Mount** which is the premier holy site in Judaism since it is the place where Solomon built the first Jewish Temple. Jordan has custodial rights over al-Aqsa and other holy sites in Jerusalem, most prominently the raised esplanade known to Muslims as the Noble Sanctuary and to Jews as the Temple Mount. This integrated Jewish and Islamic site has been contested since the end of the "Six Days War" when Israel gained control of the area. The site is viewed with emotion by both the Muslims and the Jews which has resulted in numerous killings.

The Hijra

In 622 AD Muhammad along with Abu Bakr (more on him later) and approximately two hundred of his followers migrated from Mecca to Yathrib. In Yathrib Muhammad accepted the position of binding arbiter between the warring clans. The migration from Mecca to Yathrib is called the *hijra* by Muslims and is one of the most important events in Islamic history. The Muslim calendar begins with the year of the *hijra* and the creation of the first Islamic community in Yathrib which was later named Medina, *Medinat al-Nabi*, "**City of the Prophet.**"

The year of the *hijra* marks the transformation of Islam from a religion to a political system – a combination of church and state. This stands in comparison to the belief in the United States of the separation between the state and the church. In Islam the church and the state are one and the same. This period also established the twin ideals of *hijra* (to emigrate from a hostile, anti-Islamic society) and *jihad* (to resist and fight against injustice) were established.

During Muhammad's time in Medina he served as a prophet, political ruler, military commander, chief judge and lawgiver for the Muslim community composed of both Muslims and non-Muslims such as Jews and Christians.

While in Medina Muhammad established a constitution, the **Charter of Medina**, which set the rights and duties of all its citizens. The Charter recognized the rights of Jews and Christians as "***People of the Book***" and as an allied community, entitled to coexist with Muslims in return for their loyalty and payment of a poll tax.

Muhammad's Battles

Muhammad had begun to threaten the economic viability of Mecca through a series of raids on their caravans resulting in numerous skirmishes and three major battles. Muhammad thought these raids were justified by his being exiled from Mecca. The three major battles he fought were the **Battle of Badr**, the **Battle of Uhud**, and finally, the **Battle of the Ditch**. These three battles changed the history of Islam and of the world.

The Battle of Badr

In 624 AD the Battle of Badr took place between Mecca and Medina. Prior to the battle, the Muslims and the Meccans had fought several smaller skirmishes in late 623 and early 624 AD.

The **<u>Battle of Badr</u>** was the first large-scale engagement between the two forces. Muhammad intended to attack a main caravan from Mecca and surrounded the wells at Badr, located on the caravan route midway between Mecca and Medina on 12 March, 624 AD. The caravan from Mecca arrived on 13 March and as was tradition among the Arabs of that time three champions from each side were chosen to do battle prior to the main engagement. The Champions from Medina were victorious and the Muslims immediately unleased their arrows and charged the Meccans who broke and ran assuring victory for Muhammad and with this victory he began his real ascent as a leader of Arab and the Muslim world.

The Muslims of Medina took special significance from this battle and viewed it as a victory of monotheism over polytheism. Even today it remains an important symbol to Muslims.

The Battle of Uhud

Approximately one year later the Battle of Uhud was fought on Saturday, March 19, 625 AD at the valley located in front of Mount Uhud, in what is now northwestern Arabia. This battle was the second major military encounter between Mecca and the Muslims of Medina. In the first major battle, The Battle of Badr, a small Muslim army had defeated a larger Meccan army. The Meccans were now intent on avenging their defeat at the Battle of Badr.

In the **Battle of Uhud**, Muhammad had positioned his archers on the forward slope of Mount Uhud and had gained an initial advantage by forcing the Meccan line to retreat thereby exposing their main camp. When this occurred the archers, in violation of Muhammad's orders, left their position to ransack the Meccan camp. This allowed a surprise attack from the Meccan cavalry which brought chaos to the Muslim ranks and, during this engagement, Muhammad was badly wounded. In order to save themselves and Muhammad from destruction, the Muslims withdrew up the slopes of Mount Uhud while the Meccans declared victory and marched back to Mecca.

There were three Jewish tribes in and around Medina, the Qaynuqa, Nadir and Qurayzah and, for one reason or another, these tribes became the chief casualties of Muslim success. Approximately two years after the Battle of Uhud, Muhammad, in 627 AD, expelled the **Jewish Banu Nadir and Banu Qaynuqa tribes** from Medina for violating the Charter of Medina. The Banu Nadir had attempted to assassinate Muhammad while the Banu Qaynuqa engaged in a vendetta with Muslims resulting from the stripping of a Muslim woman naked.

In order to seek vengeance on Muhammad for expelling them, the Jewish tribe leaders went to Mecca to enlist the help of the leaders in an attack on Medina. Mecca raised an army of over 10,000 foot soldiers and about 600 horsemen.

The Battle of the Ditch

Near the middle of March, 627 AD, the Meccan army, led by Abu Sufyan, marched on Medina. As the Meccan army departed for Medina, horsemen from the

Banu Khuza, a major Arab tribe near Mecca, left to warn Muhammad of the invading army.

In the **Battle of the Ditch**, Muhammad, at the urging of Salman, the Persian, decided to dig a ditch to act as a barrier to the cavalry on the north and east side of Medina. Every capable Muslim in Medina including Muhammad was enlisted in digging the massive trench line which was completed in six days. The other sides of Medina were protected by rocky mountains consisting of lava flows and trees both of which were impenetrable by cavalry.

The siege of Medina began on March 31, 627 AD and lasted for 27 days. Muhammad had approximately 3000 warriors against the 10,000 from Mecca. The trench was the difference. Sieges were uncommon in Arabian warfare and the Meccan army was unprepared to deal with the trench dug by the Muslims. The armies gathered on either side of the trench and exchanged insults backed up with occasional arrows fired from a safe distance.

After several unsuccessful attempts to breech the trench line, Abu Sufyan attempted to enlist the Jewish tribe, Banu Qurayza, to attack the Muslims from the rear (south). Muhammad had not fortified his position south of Medina because he had signed a defense pact with the Banu Qurayza. However, the massive army of Mecca made the Banu Quarayza feel safe enough to join in the attack on Medina.

Muhammad was in deep trouble and knew it but fortune intervened for about this time Muhammad received a visit from **Nuaym ibn Masud**, an Arab leader who was well respected by all the Meccan leaders but who had, unbeknownst to them, secretly converted to Islam. Muhammad asked him to end the siege by creating discord amongst various factions making up the Meccan army.

Nuaym ibn Masud was a brilliant strategist and did this by first going to the Banu Qurayza and warning them that if the siege failed they would be left to the mercy of Muhammad who would surely kill them. In order to prevent this he advised the Banu Qurayza to demand hostages from Abu Sufyan in return for cooperation.

Nuaym ibn Masud then went to Abu Sufyan and warned him that the Banu Qurayza had defected to Muhammad and intended to demand hostages which they intended to hand over to Muhammad. It was really a devious, brilliant strategy that ultimately resulted in the besieging army withdrawing back to Mecca.

After the Meccan army had withdrawn from Medina, Muhammad immediately besieged the Banu Qurayza who, after 25 days, surrendered unconditionally. After their surrender Muhammad went to the middle of the market place in Medina, dug trenches, then marched over 600 Banu Qurayza men into the market place and beheaded them for their betrayal then sold their women and children into slavery.

Scholars have various opinions as to why Muhammad killed the Banu Qurayza. One theory is that his previous clemency to his enemies was taken as a sign of weakness for the custom at that time was to kill your enemies. Another reason cited was that the punishment was in response to the perceived betrayal of the joint defense pact entered into by the Banu Qurayza with Muhammad.

Other scholars, however, cite Muhammad's treatment of the Jews of Banu Quarayza as a sign that he was anti-Semitic similar to other future Muslim extremist such as Osama bin Laden or ISIS.

I personally don't think that Muhammad was being anti-Semitic. His dealing with the Banu Quarayza, at least to me, was political in nature rather than theological or racial. He simply regarded them as traitors and a political threat to Medina, therefore, he dealt with them in accordance with the customs of the Arabs at that time. It must be remembered that this was a violent society and the chief of the tribe was not supposed to show mercy to traitors like the Quarayza. The stakes were simply too high because this was a fight to the death.

The remaining Jews and Christians continued to enjoy full religious liberty not only in Medina but in the Islamic empire. However, the Muslim hatred of Jews became rabid only with the creation of Israel in 1948 and the loss of Arab Palestine. In fact, the Muslims imported anti-Semitic myths such as those in the **Protocols of the Elders of Zion** because they had none of their own.

Regardless of Muhammad's rational for killing the Jewish men of Banu Quarayza it seems, unfortunately, to have set the stage for the coming conflict between the Jews and Muslims.

In 628 AD a truce was signed between Mecca and Medina allowing the Muslims to travel on a pilgrimage to Mecca but requiring Muhammad to end his raids on the caravans of Mecca. This truce continued to enhance the prestige of

Muhammad among the Arab tribes and began to rally the surrounding Arabian tribes to the protection of his banner.

In 630 AD there was a clash between the client tribes of Mecca and Medina and Muhammad declared the truce broken, raised an army of 10,000 and marched on Mecca. The Quarysh of Mecca surrendered and converted to Islam leaving Muhammad as the political and religious leader of both Mecca and Medina and since Muhammad thought of the Kabah as the true house of Allah his first act was to clear it of the 360 pagan idols leaving the Kabah as a symbol of the one and only true God.

From 630 to 632 AD Muhammad continued to expand Islamic domination until by 632 AD all of Arabia was under the Islamic banner creating one Islamic community on the Arabian Peninsula finally bringing peace and putting an end to the vendettas and raiding amongst the various Arab tribes for they all now belonged to one Islamic community.

In 632 AD, at the end of the tenth year after his migration to Medina, Muhammad completed his first true Islamic pilgrimage to the Kabah, and through this pilgrimage taught his followers the rites of the annual Great Pilgrimage, the *Hajra*. More on the Hajra pilgrimage in a later letter.

Several months after this pilgrimage, Muhammad fell ill and died on Monday, 8 June 632 AD, in Medina, at the age of 62 in the house of his wife Aisha. With his head resting on Aisha's lap, he is said to have murmured his final words: "***Rather, God on High and Paradise.***"

He was buried in Aisha's house but during the reign of the Umayyad caliph al-Walid I, the ***Al-Masjid an-Nabawi*** (the Mosque of the Prophet) in Medina was expanded to include the site of Muhammad's tomb in Aisha's house. The Green Dome above the tomb was built by the Mamluk sultan Al Mansur Qalawun in the 13th century. Among tombs adjacent to that of Muhammad are those of his companions (the ***Sahabah***), the first two Muslim caliphs, Abu Bakr and Umar, and an empty one that Muslims believe awaits the prophet, Jesus Christ.

Muhammad became revered by Muslims not as a divine man but as a Perfect Man. He surrendered fully to the Will of God and therefore set the standard for all Muslims to follow. Perhaps above all, as a messenger of God, he had created one of the three major religions of the world.

In my next letter I will discuss the Five Pillars of Islam.

References:

1. *What everyone Needs to Know About Islam*, John L. Esposito
2. *A History of God*, Karen Armstrong
3. *Islam*, Karen Armstrong
4. *God and his Prophet: The Religion of Islam*, The Great Courses, John Swanson
5. *Cultural Literacy in America,* The Great Courses, Mark Bergson
6. *Great World Religions: Islam*, The Great Courses, John L. Esposito
7. The Wikipedia, Various newspaper, and Magazine Articles

Letter 3 - The Five Pillars of Islam

There are five simple but essential observances that all practicing Muslims accept and follow. These **"Five Pillars of Islam"** represent the core that unites all Muslims no matter their culture and distinguishes Islam from all other world religions. In Islam, worship is part of daily life and is not limited to mere rituals. The formal acts of worship and meeting these five pillars of worship remind all Muslims that they are members of a worldwide community of believers.

The five pillars of Islam are: the declaration of faith, prayer, fasting, charity, and pilgrimage.

1.   **Declaration of Faith**: The first Pillar of Islam is the Declaration of Faith. The statement in Arabic is ***La ilaha illa Allah wa Muhammad Rasul-ullah***, meaning "There is no God except God, and Muhammad is the Messenger of God". This declaration of faith is known as the ***Shahada*** (to witness). To convert to the faith of Islam, a person has only to say this statement. However, this Declaration of Faith is more than just a statement; it must be shown with one's actions.

Allah is the Arabic name for God, just as ***Yahweh*** is the Hebrew name for God and ***Deus*** is the Latin word for God which has been used for centuries in the Roman Catholic Mass. From a Muslim's perspective they are all the same God although having different names.

The ***Shahada*** proclaims a Muslim's absolute belief in the oneness of God and His exclusive right to be worshipped. This is the doctrine of ***tawhid***, the oneness of God. For the Muslim associating anything with God is idolatry. The Quran, Chapter 4, Verse 48 states: "***God does not forgive anyone for associating something with Him, while He does forgive whomever He wishes to for anything else. Anyone who gives God partners has invented an awful sin***."

Because of this, in Islamic communities, you will not see an image of God or an image of Muhammad, instead they will be presented in the abstract. In addition, it is easy to see from this verse why Muslims do not believe in the Trinity. That is, since Islam is a monotheistic religion how can they believe in three Gods in One.

The second part of the *Shahada* states that Muhammad is a prophet of God just like Abraham, Moses and Jesus before him. He is not only a prophet but a Messenger of God who brought God's final revelation; that is, he brought the final and complete revelation from God as revealed to him in the Quran. Muslims believe that his prophecy confirms and fulfills all of the revealed messages, beginning with Adam. In addition, Muhammad serves as the role model through his exemplary life, therefore, a believer's effort to follow Muhammad's example reflects the emphasis of Islam on practice and action. The *Shadada* is so important that it is the ideal last words a Muslim should speak in his/her life.

2. **Daily Prayer** is the second Pillar of Islam. Muslims perform five formal prayers a day that provide them spiritual strength and peace of mind. The Muslims worship five times a day: at daybreak, noon, mid-afternoon, sunset, and evening. The prayers consist of standing, bowing, kneeling, putting the forehead on the ground, or sitting. The Prayer is a means by which the relationship between God and His creation is maintained.

The worship, *salat*, includes recitations in Arabic from the Quran, praises of God, prayers for forgiveness and other supplications. The prayer is an expression of submission, humility, and adoration of God. Prayers can be offered in any clean place, alone or together, in a mosque or at home, at work or on the road, inside or outside. However, it is preferable for Muslims to pray with others as one body united in the worship of God since this provides a sense of belonging to a common community.

As they prepare to pray, Muslims face Mecca, the holy city centered around the Kabah - the house of God built by Abraham and his son, Ishmael. At the end of prayer the Muslim will recite the *Shahada* and then twice repeat: "*Peace be upon all of you and the mercy and blessings of God.*"

Originally Muslims faced Jerusalem, however, when it became apparent to Muhammad that the Jews in Medina would not accept the message of Islam Muhammad received a revelation and changed the direction, the *qibla*, of prayer from Jerusalem to Mecca.

The Muslims reminder to pray is given by a call to prayer which is provided by a *muezzin*. This is the call that can be heard from the mosques announcing it is time to pray. According to tradition the African slave, Bilal, gave the first call to prayer when Muhammad marched into Mecca and rededicated the Kabah. The Muslim call to prayer follows a standard pattern: The first words are *Allaha Akbar*, "God is Great", and this is repeated four times. The next part of the call is an expression of witness, *Ashadhu an la ilaha illa'llah*, "I bear witness that there is no God but God, and Muhammad is his messenger". This is followed by the formal call to prayer, *Hay 'ala al-salah*, "Come to Prayer" which is repeated twice. This is followed by, *Hay 'ala-falah*, "Come to Flourishing" which is a reminder of how important prayer is to the Muslim. At the end of the call to prayer, *Allaha Akbar,* is again proclaimed followed by another affirmation of oneness of God, *la ilaha illa'llah.*

Once a week Muslims have a congregation prayer, the *juma,* "Friday" prayer, at a mosque or an Islamic center. Inside the mosque is a niche, a *mihrab*, that indicates the direction of Mecca. Near this is a pulpit, a *minbar*, from which the Friday sermon is given. Each mosque will have a courtyard where the faithful can wash or perform their ritual purifications before prayer. Muslims will wash their hands, mouth, nose, face, arms, head, ears and feet. Since the mosque is a sacred place, Muslims remove their shoes before entering.

All mosques will separate the sexes. Generally the women will be in a separate room or if a separate room is not available they will be in back of the men or to one side of the men but never in front of the men since they will also need to prostrate themselves during prayer. The Friday prayer service will be composed of a *khutbah*, a sermon by the Iman followed by the prayer. The khutbah will generally consist of a reading from the Quran followed by an application of the message to the lives of the congregation. During prayer the Iman will chant from the Quran but he will always include the *Al Fatiha*, the first sura in the Quran, in his chant.

3. **Charity** is the third Pillar of Islam. It reminds Muslims that all wealth is a blessing from God, and, because of this, Muslims are required to share their wealth with others, therefore, in Islam, it is the duty of the wealthy to help the poor and needy. This almsgiving is called *zakat*, or, literally, purification. It is a common Muslim saying that, *"prayer carries us halfway to God; fasting brings us to His door; almsgiving procures for us admission."*

In Islam, the true owner of everything is God, not man. People are given wealth as a trust from God. Zakat is worship and thanksgiving to God by supporting the poor, and through it one's wealth is purified. It requires an annual contribution of 2.5 percent of an individual's wealth and assets. Therefore, Zakat is not mere "charity", it is an obligation on those who have received their wealth from God to meet the needs of less fortunate members of the community. Zakat is used to support the poor and the needy, help those in debt, and, in olden times, to free slaves. It basically serves as a form of social security in Muslim countries.

In early Islam the Zakat was collected by the government, held in a central treasury and used to help the needy, to build schools, hospitals, hostels and to defray government expense. The Quran, Chapter 9, Verse 60 states: "***The alms are for the poor, the needy, and those who collect and distribute them, and for redeeming slaves and captives, repaying debtors, and in the cause of God, and for traveler. Thus God commands. God is All-Knowing and Wise.***"

In modern Islam Zakat is left to the conscience of individuals and is not controlled by the government.

4. The **Fast of Ramadan** is the fourth Pillar of Islam. Once each year, Muslims are commanded, if their health permits, to fast for an entire month from dawn to sunset. Those who are sick, pregnant, or weakened by old age are exempt from fasting. In addition, Muslims on a journey may postpone and make it up later. Ramadan is the ninth month of the Muslim calendar which coincides with the month in which the first revelation of the Quran came to Muhammad. However, because Muslims use a lunar calendar the time of Ramadan shifts by eleven days each year so that a Muslim, during his lifetime, will experience fasting during every season. This month is a period of intense spiritual devotion in which no food, drink or sex is allowed during the fast. Families will rise before sunrise and have their first meal of the day which must last them until sunset. After sunset the fast is broken by a light meal popularly called *iftar*, "breakfast", which often begins with the eating of three dates, which is how Muhammad ended his fast. Muslim children do not begin fasting until after puberty and then they may gradually work up to full fasting.

During this month Muslims practice self-control and focus on prayers and devotion. During the fast, Muslims learn to sympathize with those in the world who have little to eat.

Ramadan is also a special time to listen to or recite the entire Quran. This is done by dividing the Quran into 30 sections to be recited each day of the month. On the 27th day of the month Muslims will commemorate the "*Night of Power and Excellence*" which is the night in which Muhammad received the first of God's revelations.

Fasting, for the Muslim, develops spirituality and dependence upon God. A special evening prayer is also held in mosques in which recitations of the Quran are heard. The month of Ramadan ends with one of the major Islamic celebrations, *Eid al-Fitr,* the Feast of the Breaking of the Fast, which is marked by joyfulness, family visits, and the exchanging of gifts.

5. The **Hajj Pilgrimage** to Mecca is the fifth Pillar of Islam and is the most well-known among westerners. Every Muslim strives to make this pilgrimage to the sacred sites in Mecca, in present-day Saudi Arabia. The pilgrimage occurs about sixty days after the end of Ramadan, between the 8th and 12th day of the last month of the Islamic calendar. It is the most intense spiritual experience for a Muslim.

At least once in a lifetime, every adult Muslim who is physically and financially able is required to sacrifice time, wealth, status, and ordinary comforts of life to make the *Hajj* pilgrimage, putting himself totally at God's service. Every year over two million believers from over 100 countries and different cultures and languages travel to the sacred city of Mecca to respond to God's call. The pilgrimage commemorates and reenacts events from the life of Abraham, Hager, Ismail and Muhammad.

During the pilgrimage men wear two pieces of white cloth to symbolize purity and the equality of all believers. One cloth is tied around their waist while the other is draped over the shoulder. It is interesting to note that the Hajj clothing is saved and used as a final shroud when they die. The women wear modest dress or modest clothes; that is, their bodies should be covered with the exception of their faces, hands and feet. Throughout the pilgrimage Muslim pilgrims chant, "*I am here, O my God! You are without any association. I am here! I am here! I am here!"*

Muslim tradition teaches that if they perform the *hajj* with great devotion they will be forgiven their sins; therefore, many of the elderly and the sick hope they will die on the *hajj* since they have been cleansed of their sins.

The *hajj* pilgrims circle, counterclockwise, seven times around the **Kabah**. This symbolizes the pilgrim's entry into the divine presence of God and reenacts the movement of angels around the heavenly throne of God. The late Iranian philosopher Ali Shariati captured the essence of this rite when he wrote, *"As you circumambulate around the Kabah, you feel like a small river merging with a big river. Carried by a wave you lose touch with the ground. Suddenly you are floating, carried on by the flood. As you approach the center, the pressure of the crown squeezes you so hard that you are given a new life..."* For Muslim the hajj is the height of spirituality.

The Kabah is about 40 feet long, 33 feet wide and 50 feet high and is covered with a black cloth embroidered with gold thread of Quranic verses. It is the most sacred space in the Muslim world. In the right corner is a Black Stone about 12 inches in diameter symbolizing God's covenant with mankind. The stone was placed there by Abraham and Ismail as a symbol of God's covenant with them and by extension with the Muslim community. The Kabah is located in the compound of the Grand Mosque in Mecca. The original Kabah is thought by Muslims to have been built by Adam as a replication of the heavenly House of God which contained the divine throne around which the angels circled. However, it was believed by Muslims to have been destroyed by the neglect of unbelievers and the great flood. According to the Quran, Chapter 2, Verse 127 Abraham and his son, Ismail, rebuilt the holy house: *"And when Abraham, and Ishmael with him, raised up the foundations of the House: 'Our Lord, receive this from us; Thou art the All-hearing, the All-knowing."* At the time of Muhammad the Kabah was under the control of the Quraysh who were using it as shrine to the tribal gods. When Muhammad returned from exile in Medina and assumed control of Mecca he cleansed the Kabah of the 360 idols and returned the shrine back to the worship of the one true God.

Another ritual of the *hajj* is the **casting of seven stones** at three pillars which stand at the place where Satan met Abraham and Ismail. This stoning symbolizes

Abraham's rejection of Satan's temptation that he not follow God's command and sacrifice his son.

The climax to the pilgrimage is the assembling of over two million Muslims at the **Plain of Arafat** which is the location where Muhammad delivered his farewell sermon from the **Mount of Mercy**. Tents are constructed on the hills and valleys to house the pilgrims while they reflect on God and Muhammad's sermon.

The hajj ends with the *Eid–al-Adha*, the Feast of Sacrifice, which is a feast that comes at the end of the *hajj* and is celebrated by not only those on the pilgrimage but also by Muslims around the world. During this time Muslims sacrifice an animal to commemorate God's substitution of a ram for sacrifice instead of Abraham's son Ishmael. Many Muslims on the Hajj will not sacrifice their own animal but will hire a butcher to sacrifice the animal which is then given to the poor.

Those Muslims who have made the *hajj* can now put the prefix of '*al*' before their name such as "*al-hajj*" or "*hajii*" to designate they have made the pilgrimage.

The five pillars of Islam is what all Muslims share in common no matter their difference in culture or politics. These five things: the confession of faith, prayer, almsgiving, fasting and pilgrimage are what makes a Muslim, a Muslim.

Muslims throughout the centuries have attempted to add *jihad* as the sixth pillar of Islam but it has never gained official status.

I will cover the **Quran** and *Jihad* in the next letter.

References:

1. *What everyone Needs to Know About Islam*, John L. Esposito
2. *A History of God*, Karen Armstrong
3. *Islam*, Karen Armstrong
4. *God and his Prophet: The Religion of Islam*, The Great Courses, John Swanson
5. *Cultural Literacy in America,* The Great Courses, Mark Bergson
6. *Great World Religions: Islam*, The Great Courses, John L. Esposito
7. The Wikipedia, Various newspaper, and Magazine Articles

Letter 4 - The Quran

The Quran for Muslims is the literal Word of God sent from heaven to the Prophet Muhammad as a guide for all mankind. It confirms the Torah (the Old Testament) and the New Testament as revelations from God but revelations that, over time, have been corrupted. Muslims believe that after the death of the prophet Jesus that wrong or non-biblical beliefs were incorporated into both the Torah and the New Testament thereby corrupting their original pure revelations. For example, corruptions as viewed by Muslims are the elevation of Jesus from that of a prophet to the Son of God and the subsequent fabrication of the Trinity at the Council of Nicaea. Muslims, therefore, believe these types of fabrications distort God's original message.

The Quran, for Muslims, was sent as a correction to the Torah and the New Testament and because of this they believe that Islam is the oldest monotheistic religion since it represents the original and final revelations of God.

Westerners, from an historical standpoint, believe Islam is the youngest of the monotheistic religions because Islam was created after the Jewish and Christian communities. Islam, however, as viewed by the Muslims, is the original religion of God because it can be traced back through the prophets to God; therefore, the Quran embodies the original revelation and, because of this, they feel Islam is the oldest of the Monotheistic religions since it is the final and complete word of God.

Muslims use the ***Quran***, the ***Sunnah*** (the example of Muhammad's life) and the ***Hadith*** (the narrative traditions of Muhammad's sayings and deeds) as a guide to daily life. These three items represent the foundation stones upon which Islam and the Islamic civilization is built.

The Quran was revealed to Muhammad in two stages over a 22 year period, starting in Mecca (610-622 AD) and later in Medina (622-632 AD). The revelations of God through Muhammad making up the Quran was preserved both orally and in written form during the life of Muhammad. During the reign of the third **caliph** (successor), Uthman (644-658 AD), the revelations were compiled into its current format.

The Quran is composed of 114 chapters or **Surahs,** which means "enclosure". Each Surah is composed of *Ayya's* which means "sign" indicating they are signs from God. The 600 verses, or Ayyas, was collected but not edited by theme or by chronology. The **Surahs** are assembled according to length with the shorter Mecca verses appearing at the end of the Quran and the longer Medina verses appearing at the front of the Quran. The shorter Mecca verses are primarily concerned with religious belief and practices while the longer Medina verses are primarily concerned with the problems of the Islamic community.

The one main them that emerges from the Quran is *Tawhid,* or the oneness of God. Muslims, like Jews and Christians, are monotheistic and for them the oneness of God means the oneness of creation and, since God's domain extends in all areas, life cannot be divided into secular and sacred spheres as we do in the west. For a Muslim every aspect of life, family, economics. politics, etc., must accord with the will of God, therefore, for a Muslim the state and church are one.

The Quran was written in Arabic which is viewed by Muslims as a sacred language, therefore, all Muslims recite Quranic verses in Arabic and pray in Arabic no matter their county, culture or language. Recitation of the Quran is central to Muslim life since for them hearing the Quran verses is hearing the Word of God recited by a human voice, therefore, recitations of the Quran is an art form and Muslims derive great pleasure in listening to its rhythmic, rhyming, repetitive prose. It is as if the Quran was not made for private reading but for oral recitation.

For an example of the most famous Quran reciters Google '*Qurani reciters*', listen to the recitations and see what you think. I have always thought the same of the King James Version of the Bible; that is, the Quran was written to be heard.

As an aside, I have always thought this one of the difficulties for people to understand the Quran whose primary language is other than Arabic. For example, suppose I am a Muslim and only spoke Pashtun and memorized the Quranic verses perhaps with no real understanding of their true meaning. Because of this I can easily be influenced by radicals who have deliberately misinterpreted the Quranic verses for their benefit.

Until recently translations of the Quran into other languages was resisted and in many cases forbidden for fear that the original text and meaning would be corrupted. Muslims believed that the Quran is a miraculous text that was divinely inspired and that its ideas, language, and style as expressed in Arabic cannot be imitated or duplicated.

Umar ibn al-Khattab

According to a story written by ibn Ishaq, a noted biographer of Muhammad, Umar ibn al-Khattab, the second Rashidun Caliphate, was so moved upon hearing the Quran recited for the first time that he converted to Islam. There are two stories of his conversion, here is the one I like best. In this version Umar heard his sister reciting from the Quran and knocked her to the ground because he was opposed to the preaching of Muhammad. Upon seeing his sister bleeding on the floor, Umar felt ashamed and picked up the manuscript and began to recite aloud. Umar, an acknowledged authority of Arabic oral poetry, was struck by the beauty of the language and exclaimed, *"How fine and noble this speech."* and immediately converted to Islam. It is as if Muhammad had created a new literary form without which Islam would not have taken root.

Westerners tend to find the Quran a difficult book to understand. I suppose because of the difficulty in properly translating the Quran into English because it is written in a repetitive, highly illusory manner. Many Muslims claim that when they read a translation of the Quran in another language they are reading a different book because none of the beauty of the Arabic language comes through.

I have always found it interesting that Hebrew, Sanskrit and Arabic languages are sacred to the Jews, Hindus and Muslims. Christians do not have a sacred language for they accept Jesus as the Word of God. I have always found that interesting for it does make Islam difficult to understand for so much of its meaning and beauty is in the language.

I personally believe there is some justification to this fear of Quranic translation. For example, type into Google, Quran, Chapter 9, Verse 60, and see how many English interpretations you get. Can you determine which is the one that most closely follows the original Arabic text? Or for that matter how it sounds to a Muslim.

God is viewed by Muslims as merciful and compassionate. Every recital of the Quran begins with "***Bismallah al-Rahan al-Rahan***" or "In the name of God the Merciful and the Compassionate." This phrase is also used by Muslims at the beginning of letters and speeches. Muslims will also say *Bismallah al-Rahan* before they begin almost any task such as driving a car or eating a meal.

The Quran mentions two beings, Humans and Spirits, residing in three places; Heaven, Hell and Earth. I have mentioned Heaven and Hell in previous letters so here I will only discuss spirits which include angels, ***jinns*** and devils.

Angels, as mentioned previously, function as guardians, recorders and messengers of God. ***Jinns*** are between angels and humans and can be either good or bad. ***Jinns*** are thought of as magical and are known in the west as Genies; think of Aladdin and his lamp or better yet, "I Dream of Jeannie." I have always thought that title an interesting play on words.

Devils are fallen angels that tempt human beings in their moral struggle thus we have ***jihad,*** which is thought of by Muslms as a continuous, individual, morale struggle. The leader of the devils is Satan, ***Shaytan,*** who represents evil or disobedience to God's Will. Satan was ejected from Heaven because he failed to obey God and prostrate himself before Adam. The fall of Satan led to the human struggle between good and evil - a ***jihad*** for the soul of man.

Humans were created by God to be his representative here on earth. God gave the earth to humankind and it is their duty to carry out God's will. Muslims believe in Adam and Eve and the Garden of Eden but do not believe in the concept of Original Sin. For Muslims, sin is the act of disobedience to God's will rather than a state of being. Islam emphasizes the need to repent by returning to the straight path of God. For Muslims there is no emphasis on shame, disgrace or guilt. The emphasis, however, is on ***jihad***, the ongoing struggle of humans "***to do what is right and just according to God's Will.***"

Social Justice

Among the most prominent themes of the Quran is that of social justice for the poor, the children and the women. Muhammad's emphasis on social justice was a direct threat to the tribal power structure of Mecca since his emphasis was on the responsibility of Muslims to care for each other regardless of their status in the community. The Quran institutionalized this by means of the *zakat*, an alms tax and one of the Five Pillars of Islam, which was a voluntary charity for the poor. In addition, *usury*, the collection of interest on a loan, and false contracts was also discouraged and condemned. The Quran makes specific mention, Chapter 4, Verse 74-76, that Muslims should make every effort to struggle, a *jihad*, for the rights of the oppressed among men, women and children.

Equality

Another major theme in the Quran is that men and women are equal and complementary. The Quran, Chapter 9, Verse 71 states: "***The believing men and believing women are protectors of one another. They enjoin what is right and forbid what is wrong and establish prayer and give zakat and obey Allah and His Messenger. Those - Allah will have mercy upon them. Indeed, Allah is Exalted in Might and Wise.***"

The Quranic revelations prohibited female infanticide, abolished women as property, established their legal rights and allowed women to retain control of their property. The current status of women in Islamic society is under some debate and their status, by western standards, has long been viewed as oppressive. As I have looked at Islamic society I have found that not to be true as an Islamic community but is certainly true when looked at from the perspective of individual countries and cultures. For example, women in Egypt have access to the best education and hold responsible positions on both the private and public sector, yet, until recently, needed a male family's permission to travel. In Saudi Arabia women own over seventy percent of the bank savings yet are sexually segregated and forbidden to drive a car. In some sectors of Pakistan the Taliban have prohibited girls from attending school.

The Quran specifically states that men and women are equally responsible for adhering to the Five Pillars of Islam. In addition, God makes no difference between genders. I suspect the status of women in the Islamic Community will continually be debated since interpretations of the *Quran*, *Hadith* and *Sunnah* are made primarily by males. In many Muslim countries, however, this is changing as more women begin to interpret the Quran.

Religious Tolerance

Another major theme in the Quran is religious tolerance. The Quran, Chapter 2, Verse 256 states: "***Let there be no compulsion in religion: Truth stands out clear from Error: whoever rejects evil and believes in Allah hath grasped the most trustworthy hand hold, that never breaks. And Allah heareth and knoweth all things***." According to the Quran God created a world of human diversity with Jews and Christians regarded as **People of the Book** who also received a revelation from God. Because of this, Jews, Christians and Muslims share a common belief in one God and as Islam expanded Muslims did not attempt to impose their religion on them but regarded the Jews and Christians as a protected people (***dhimmi***) who were permitted to retain and practice their religion. For that time - the 7th century - it was a very enlightened view.

There are, however, some extremist Muslim groups who preach an exclusivist philosophy; fortunately there are also a number of Muslim moderates who challenge that view. However, that does not prevent the extremist Islamic leaders from their new interpretation of Islam and a subsequent attempt to impose their hatred on others.

Jihad – To Struggle

Another major theme of the Quran is ***Jihad***. There are two basic meanings to jihad: violent and non-violent. Muhammad, in a prophetic tradition, said after returning from a battle, "***We return from the lesser jihad to the greater jihad***." The lesser jihad is viewed as an obligation of all Muslims to defend their community. The greater jihad is viewed by Muslims as the struggle against oneself in terms of selfishness, greed, and evil. This greater jihad is viewed by Muslims as the more difficult struggle.

In modern times the call to *jihad* has rung like a clarion call across Islamic lands to rise and defend Islam. The cry of jihad has been used in wars of liberation, wars of independence and wars of terror. We have only to hear the names of

Afghanistan, Palestine, Kosovo, Kashmir, Chechnya, Osama bin Laden and ISIL to visualize the image of a Muslim carrying an AK-47 in the name of *jihad*.

The earliest mention of jihad to engage in defensive warfare was just after the flight of Muhammad to Medina. The Quran, Chapter 22, Verses 39-40, states ***"Leave is given to those who fight because they were wronged (surely God is able to help them) who were expelled from their homes wrongfully, for saying, 'Our Lord is God'."*** Sometimes this is taken out of context by Muslim extremists to provide a rationale for indiscriminate slaughter. This verse specifically refers to the wrongful flight from Mecca and provides a justification for Muslims to fight the Meccans.

The purely defensive nature of jihad is stressed by Muhammad in the Quran, Chapter 2, Verse 190, by saying, ***"And fight in the way of God with those who fight you, but aggress not: God loves not the aggressor."***

As I indicated previously there are Five Pillars (duties) of Islam which are the bedrock upon which Islam stands such as the **shahada**, **hijra** and **zakat**. Early Muslim leaders wanted *jihad* to be the sixth unofficial pillar of the Islamic faith such that it would become an instrument of Islam expansion but that was not to be. As a result, for Muslims, there seem to be five major categories of *jihad*:

(1) *Jihad* against one's own self,
(2) *Jihad* of the tongue,
(3) *Jihad* of the hand and
(4) *Jihad* for the oppressed
(5) *Jihad* of the sword.

Islamic jurisprudence focuses on regulating the conditions and practice of ***Jihad of the sword***. As the Muslim community grew, questions arose as to the proper conduct or behavior in war. This is nothing new for even Christians have struggled with the question of what is a ***just war***. The Quran, Chapter 2, Verse 295 states that violence and aggression of war ***must be proportional***. In addition, Muhammad stressed that it was forbidden to kill noncombatants such as women, children, monks, and rabbis as well as not damaging cultivated or residential areas.

Unfortunately Muslim extremist such as Al Qaeda and ISIL have used the pattern of ***jihad*** for their own purposes. Terrorist attacks like that of September 11, 2001, which was planned and executed by bin Laden (and other radical Islamic fundamentalists) were not sanctioned by more moderate Muslims and, in fact, was condemned by Muslims all around the world as a violation of the teachings of the Quran.

It is true that in the Quran there are verses commonly called the "***sword verses***" that call for the killing of non-Muslims or unbelievers. For example, in Chapter 9, Verse 5 the Quran states "***When the sacred month have passed, slay the idolaters wherever you find them, and take them and confine them, and lie in wait for them at every place and ambush.***" The problem with this Quran verse, like similar Quran verses, is that Muslim extremists take the quotes out of context. This verse, for example, was directed at Mecca who the Muslims in Medina were fighting.

In my opinion, the radical Islamic fundamentalists, such as Al Qaeda and ISIL, are attempting to redefine traditional interpretation of the Quran, such as the ones shown above, to support their violation of its tenets through the issuance of Fatwas by themselves or friendly mullahs.

The word of God found in both the Quran, Torah and New Testament have been interpreted by human beings from different social contexts and have yielded multiple meanings and practices resulting in a struggle not only for the soul of the Islamic community but for the soul of the Christian community.

In my next letter I will cover the Sunni and the Shii split that has devastated the middle-east for millennia.

References:

1. *What everyone Needs to Know About Islam*, John L. Esposito
2. *A History of God*, Karen Armstrong
3. *Islam*, Karen Armstrong
4. *God and his Prophet: The Religion of Islam*, The Great Courses, John Swanson
5. *Cultural Literacy in America,* The Great Courses, Mark Bergson
6. *Great World Religions: Islam*, The Great Courses, John L. Esposito
7. The Wikipedia, Various newspaper, and Magazine Articles

Letter 5 - The Sunni and Shii

As we read the daily newspaper or listen to the news we learn of fighting throughout length and breadth of the middle-east. There seems to be multiple reasons for the fighting: the so-called Arab Spring in which Muslims strive for democracy against autocratic tyrants which unfortunately, like most rebellions, is being hijacked by extremists; the conflict resulting from the US invasion of Iraq that continues to play out as Iran and ISIL attempt to exert their influence in Iraq; the debacle of the Afghanistan War as Pakistan attempts to use the Taliban to exert their political influence in Afghanistan; Moderate Muslims continually battle Extremist Muslims over control of the Islamic community (which may turn out to be the major overarching battle); finally, you have the Sunni versus Shii, a never ending battle which has gone on for centuries and seems to be in the mix of all the middle-east conflicts.

There are no denominations in Islam as there are in Christianity such as Catholic, Baptist, Methodist, Presbyterian, etc. However, despite the fact that all Muslims share a common belief such as the Five Pillars of Islam there are divisions over the questions of such things as leadership, theology, interpretations of Islamic Law and how best to respond to modernity and the West.

The division about the political and religious leadership in Islam is perhaps the most violent and the longest. This division began just after the death of Muhammad and resulted in two major branches of Islam: the Sunni and the Shii.

The Sunni account for about 85 percent of all Muslims while the Shii account for about 15 percent of all Muslims; however, they do account for about 40 percent of the middle-east Muslim population. Shia majority countries are Iran, Iraq, Bahrain, Azerbaijan and, according to some estimates, Yemen. There are, however, significant Shii minorities in many countries throughout the world.

Sunni majority countries in the middle-east include Egypt, Saudi Arabia, Syria, Jordan, Palestine and the UAE. Although Turkey is a secular country about seventy-two percent of its population is Sunni Muslim.

The Sunni versus Shii conflict has been going on for over fifteen hundred years and appears to be an irresolvable dispute that will continue for another thousand years or until one side wipes out the other after all this is a religious conflict and religious conflicts are ruled by emotion and seem to have no boundaries or rules.

Well, what caused the Sunni-Shii split and the resulting conflict?

The original Islamic community founded by Muhammad in Medina was both a faith and a political order. That is, from a westerner's perspective there would be no difference between the church and the state. Islamic religion would inform the political community such that religion, power, civilization and culture would be intertwined.

The death of Muhammad in 632 AD ended the direct guidance from the Prophet to the Islamic community and Abu Bakr, the close companion and son-in-law to Muhammad, was elected the *Caliph* (Successor to the messenger of God). This election started the political split between Sunni and Shii Muslims.

The Sunni wanted a *Caliph* while the Shii wanted an *Imam*. The Caliph is not considered a prophet but is primarily a political leader. However, he does have considerable religious prestige as the leader of the religious community, the *ummah*. The Shii Imam, on the other hand, is considered both a religious and a political leader.

The Sunni Muslims were **the followers of *Sunnah***, or followers of the example set by Muhammad, and believed the leadership of Islam should pass to the most qualified person to be designated the caliph, or successor. The caliph would succeed Muhammad as the political leader of the Muslims and would serve as the protector of the faith but would not enjoy any special religious status.

The Shii Muslims, *shia-tu-Ali*, or followers of Ali, opposed the selection of Abu Bakr as caliph and believed that Muhammad's successor should be hereditary and be a male member of Muhammad's family. The male members would be descended through Muhammad's daughter, Fatima, and her husband, Ali. They believed that Ali, Muhammad's first cousin and husband of Fatima, should be the leader, or *Imam*, of the Islamic community. Shia Imams were the direct bloodline descendants of Muhammad and, therefore, had significant religious authority.

The *Imam,* although not a prophet, was an inspired individual and was both a religious and political leader and would serve as the final authoritative interpreter of God's will. The Shii believe that the sayings, deeds and writings of the Imam to be authoritative religious texts similar to the Quran and the Sunnah.

However, Ali was passed over and three Caliphs, Muhammad's companions, were elected prior to Ali finally being elected Caliph.

The first four caliphs are called the ***Rightly Guided Caliphs*** and ruled from 632 to 661 AD. Ali did not become caliph until after three intervening elections but he was finally elected caliph in 656 AD and established his capital at Kufu, in present day Iraq. He ruled from 656 until 661 when he was assassinated by Abdur

Rehman ibn Muljim, a Kharijite. At Ali's death, **Muawiyah**, a general in Damascus, asserted his authority and established the ***Umayyad Dynasty*** which lasted from 661 to 750 AD.

Upon Ali's death, Hasan, his oldest son, became his successor but agreed to cede the Caliphate to Muawiyah on several conditions. One of those was that Muawiyah would not appoint a successor. Hasan then retired to Medina where, at the urging of Muawiyah who wanted to pass his Caliphate to his son, Yazid, he was poisoned by his wife Ja'da bint al-Ash'ath ibn Qays. As an aside nine of the first twelve Imams were poisoned.

Ali's followers remained disaffected and in 680 AD Ali's son, Hussein, Muhammad's grandson and the younger brother of Hasan, refused to swear allegiance to Yazid, the son of Muawiyah, and led a revolt in an attempt to gain control of the Muslim community. This failed and Hussein and his followers were defeated at the Battle of Karbala.

The Battle of Karbala

There are a number of historical battles that I have always admired and the Battle of Karbala is one of those. Hussein and his followers were faced with overwhelming odds and knew it was sure death for them to engage in the battle yet they persisted anyway. You cannot help but admire that kind of courage

Muawiyah I died in 680 AD and appointed his son Yazid as his successor, thereby converting the caliphate into a dynasty. Yazid instructed his Governor of Medina, Walid, to force Hussein ibn Ali to pledge allegiance to Yazid. Hussein refused to make the pledge and since he was the Grandson of Muhammad he was viewed as a threat to the dynasty of Yazid.

On his way by caravan to Kufu, Yazid's army intercepted Hussein and his followers at Karbala, located in present day Iraq. Negotiation took place and it became obvious that the army of Yazid had been ordered to kill Hussein and his followers. Hussein asked that he and his men be allowed to pray the night of 9 October, 680 AD. After prayers that night Hussein asked that if any of his followers did not want to die with him they were free to leave that night. None left choosing instead to die with Hussein. Hussein and his followers prayed that night and the next day formed to battle the army of Yazid.

The battle took place on 10 October, 680 AD. This was not really a battle in the literal sense but more of a massacre since Hussein had only about 70 followers while the army of Yazid had over 5,000 horsemen. The battle began with assaults by the army of Yazid which were repulsed with the loss or wounding of many of Hussein's men. After being repulsed the Army of Yazid began to shoot flights of arrows which they had promised not to do. In order to prevent the women and children of the caravan from being killed or wounded, Hussein and his men chose to challenge the Yazid army to individual combat. One by one Hussein and his followers were killed by champions from the Yazdi army. After the battle the head of Hussein was sent to Yazid while the heads of his followers were sent to the various tribes to gain favor with Yazid.

Hussein and his followers, because of their bravery and courage, are regarded as martyrs by all Muslims and the Battle of Karbala is commemorated by both Shii and Sunni Muslims. Karbala is amongst the holiest cities for Shia Muslims.

Prior to the battle of Karbala the Shii had a political difference with the Sunnis. After the Battle of Karbala the Shii had a theological difference with the Sunnis. The Battle of Karbala resulted in a definitive split between the Sunnis and the Shii and the Shii came to view themselves as an oppressed minority and to view the Sunni as usurpers of Islamic power who had created an unjust society.

Over time, however, the Shii did enjoy some political power by creating the *Fatimid Dynasty* in Egypt which lasted from 909 through 1171 AD and the *Safavid Empire* in Iran from 1501 to 1722 AD. The Shii, since that time, have remained the dominant religion in Iran.

Shii Islam developed three main divisions as a result of a disagreement over the number of Imams who succeeded Muhammad: the **Fivers** (the Zaidi) who recognized five Imams, the **Seveners** (the Ismaili) who recognized seven Imams and the **Twelvers** (the Ithna Ashari) who recognized twelve Imams.

Twelvers are the most populous form of Shia and recognize twelve imams from the time of Ali down to the twelfth, who disappeared as a child. Twelver Shia believe he is hidden and will return in the future to bring about a perfect Islamic ummah, community. This seems to give Twelver Shiism a strong messianic dimension.

The Twelvers are the dominate Shii in Iran, Azerbaijan, Bahrain, Iraq and Lebanon. The Twelvers in Iran developed a religious hierarchy whose leader is acknowledged as an *Ayatollah,* a sign of God, because of their reputation for knowledge and piety. For example, Ayatollah Khomeini became the leader of Iran in 1979. Iranian Ayatollahs have become so powerful that many consider them infallible.

Some Background

The historical split between the Sunni and Shii has had a devastating effect. First, the Sunni have historically ruled over the Shii who have always viewed themselves as an oppressed and disinherited minority and because of this the Shii have always believed their struggle was to restore God's rule on earth. The dream of the Shii then is to restore a just social order led by their Imam. For them, the glorious history of the Sunni simply reinforces the belief of the Shii that the Sunni have illegitimately usurped Muslim power at the expense of a just society.

The twentieth century has seen a reinterpretation of Shii history to mobilize and actively fight against injustice. This has found expression by the Shii in Lebanon where they have struggled to achieve greater social, educational and economic opportunities during the 1970s and 1980s. Unfortunately, the continual conflict in Lebanon has left the country devastated.

More dangerous, however, is Iran, a Shii dominated country, that has awakened from a long slumber and during the Islamic revolution of 1978 and 1979 equated the Shaw with Yazid and Khomeini with Hussein and established an Islamic guided country. Of course that resulted in the slaughter of their own dissident citizens but from their perspective the slaughter was all in the name of social justice. In addition it must be remembered the Iranians are Persians who Churchill once called '*the Huns of the middle-east*'. Iranian desire seems to be to recreate the Persian Empire.

If I were a Sunni in the middle-east I would be very, very afraid of Iran for if they finally achieve the development of a nuclear weapon, I believe the religious zealots of Khomeini followers will not hesitate to threaten or possibly use it against the Sunnis. Unfortunately, the Israelis will be right in the middle of the conflict. Iran should rightly be viewed by both the Saudis and the Israelis as an existential threat. I will discuss this further in a letter on Islam Extremism.

In closing, let me say something about the *Kharijites* since they were one of the earliest examples of radical Islam. The Kharijites initially began as the followers of Ali but broke away because they felt Ali had disobeyed God's will when he compromised with the rebellious general, **Muawiyah,** rather than continue an all-out war. They formed a separate community which strictly followed the Quran and the Sunnah. The Kharijites world view is strictly black and white. For them there is no grey area. They believe in a literal interpretation of the Quran and the Sunnah and for them you are either a believer or a non-believer and non-believers are those people who do not accept the uncompromising world view of the Kharjities.

This ideology has been replicated in modern times in Osama bin Laden, who masterminded the Twin Towers disaster and created Al Qaeda. I thought about including ISIL in this list but realized that ISIL, although extremist, is really a criminal/terrorist enterprise.

In the next letter I will discuss Islam and the Crusades.

References:

1. *What everyone Needs to Know About Islam*, John L. Esposito
2. *A History of God*, Karen Armstrong
3. *Islam*, Karen Armstrong
4. *God and his Prophet: The Religion of Islam*, The Great Courses, John Swanson
5. *Cultural Literacy in America,* The Great Courses, Mark Bergson
6. *Great World Religions: Islam*, The Great Courses, John L. Esposito
7. The Wikipedia, Various newspaper, and Magazine Articles

Letter 6 – Islam and the Crusades

When Muhammad assumed control of both Mecca and Medina, he immediately began to expand Islamic influence and establish a Muslim community over the entire Arabian Peninsula by means of both force and diplomacy.

In 632 AD the Prophet died and over the next 100 years the Muslim empire continued to expand to include everything from North Africa to South Asia. It was a massive empire even greater than the Roman Empire at its height. Muhammad intended the new Islamic Empire to be a community of believers all worshiping a sovereign God and living according to Islamic law.

These conquests sought to spread the Muslim rule rather than gain converts to Islam. The rulers of the conquered lands were replaced but the government, bureaucracy, and culture of each country were preserved. Muslim rule seemed to have learned a lesson from the Byzantine and Persian Empires and rather than harshly subjugate their conquered territories they were more flexible in dealing with the inhabitants of the land they conquered.

The rule of Muhammad and the *rashidan*, the four Rightly Guided Caliphs (632-661 AD), are regarded by Muslims as an idealized past that serve as both guidance and inspiration. The Rightly Guided Caliphs were the first four successors who were all Muhammad's companions and were chosen by a process of consultation followed by an oath of allegiance by all Muslims. The first three caliphs, Abu Bakr, Umar and Uthman, conquered an empire that stretched from Spain to the Indus Valley in India. In 657 AD the Arab Army in Egypt marched on Medina and murdered Uthman, the reigning Caliph, and offered the Caliphate to Ali. This, however, was opposed by Muawiyah, the governor of Syria.

The selection of the fourth Caliph, Ali, husband of Fatima (the youngest daughter of Muhammad) resulted in two civil wars and the split between the Sunni, Shii and the Kharijites (an extremist Islamic group) that exists to this day.

The Umayyad Dynasty

The Kharijites assassinated Ali in 661 AD and the caliph was seized by Muawiyah who moved the capital of the Muslim Empire (Sunni) to Damascus. Muawiyah founded the **Umayyad Dynasty** and turned the Caliphate into an hereditary dynasty dominated by a military aristocracy. The Umayyad Dynasty lasted from 661 to 750 AD and completed the conquest of the Persian Empire and half the Byzantine Empire. The Umayyads gathered power and wealth to themselves and established a flourishing, cosmopolitan capital in Damascus. Their wealth and power, however, were thought by some Muslims to undermine the Arab way of life and became the seeds of their eventual destruction.

There were two major groups opposing the Umayyads. The first were the **Kharijites** who combined a religious fundamentalism with and exclusivist equality in social, political and economic affairs. That is, if you were a believer you were treated with equality but if you were a non-believer then you may be killed. The Kharijites opposed the Umayyads because of their lifestyle.

The second major group was the **Shii** who opposed the Umayyads because of their refusal to submit to Ali and the usurpation of the Caliphate.

The Abbasid Dynasty

The Umayyad Dynasty attempted to conquer Constantinople in 674 and 717 AD but were defeated both times resulting in the gradual decline of the dynasty. In 750 AD an Abbasid slave led a revolt that overthrew the Umayyad Caliphate and established the Abbasid Caliphate at Baghdad. This Caliphate lasted from 750 to 1258 AD and resulted in an Islamic community of great economic power and, from my perspective, one of the most remarkable civilizations in history. I suspect this was because the Abbasids aligned their government with Islam and became the patrons of the *Ulama* (religious scholars).

They built mosques, established madrasas (schools) and supported the development of Islamic scholarship. In addition, they established great urban cultural centers at Cordoba, Baghdad, Cairo, Nishapur and Palermo. These were centers for the translation of manuscripts from Sanskrit, Greek, Latin, Syriac, Coptic and Persian into Arabic. These translations included the literature from Aristotle, Plato, Galen, Hippocrates, Euclid and Ptolemy.

As an aside, Louis L'amour wrote a book, arguably his best book, about this era called "*The Walking Drum.*" If you have never read it, then I encourage you to do so for it is just a great adventure story.

The Abbasid support established a flourishing Islamic civilization that made original contributions in the area of law, theology, philosophy, literature, medicine, algebra, geometry, science, art, and architecture.

This amazing Islamic civilization flourished while Europe was mired in the Dark Ages. Fortunately, when Europe began to emerge from the Dark Ages the scholars of Europe turned their attention to these Islamic learning centers and rediscovered their lost heritage and through these Islamic centers Greek philosophy was retransmitted to Europe. The medieval Christian philosophers and theologians such as Albert the Great, Thomas Aquinas, Abelard, Roger Bacon and Duns Scotus readily acknowledged their debt to these Muslim learning centers and Muslim scholars.

Unfortunately, this golden age of Islamic civilization was threatened by both internal and external opposition which resulted in the Abbasid Dynasty beginning to fragment.

This fragmentation was the result of two factors: the **Shii Fatimid Dynasty** of Egypt and the **Crusades**.

The Fatima Dynasty

The Abbasids had started their dynasty by defeating the Shii and attempting to eliminate them. The Shii had dispersed to new Islamic cities in North Africa. One sect of the Shii was the Fatimids, named after Fatima, the wife of Ali and the daughter of Muhammad. In 909 AD the Fatimid leader, **Al-Mahdi**, rallied the Berbers in Morocco and swept across North Africa. In 962 AD the Fatimid forces established their seat of power in Cairo, took the holy cities of Medina and Mecca then began to push into Syria against the Abbasids

By the early 11th century the Fatima caliphs ruled the Shii from Cairo while the Abbasid caliphs ruled the Sunni from Baghdad. In mid 11th century this stalemate was broken by the arrival of the Seljuk Turks and the Crusaders.

Seljuk Turks and the Crusades

The Crusades lasted for almost 400 years from 1095 to 1453 AD and left a legacy that continues to this day by establishing a model for all subsequent conflicts between Islam and Christianity and between Islam and the West. The Christian west viewed Islam as both a religious and a political threat. These fears became a reality as Islam became a world power while Christianity stagnated in the Dark Ages.

The Crusades are viewed by many historians as the first thrust of European imperialism into the Middle East. Many westerners, on the other hand, view the Crusades as being motivated by a religious desire to liberate Jerusalem. Most scholars of the Crusades view these as myths. Why is that?

Well, first some more history.

In 636 AD the Muslims defeated the Byzantine forces at the Battle of Yarmouk and took control of Palestine. In the following years control of Palestine passed through the Umayyad Dynasty, the Abbasid Dynasty, to the Fatimid Dynasty.

After Jerusalem fell to the Muslims in 638 AD both Christians and Jews were allowed to live in and make Pilgrimages to Jerusalem now under Muslim rule. This peaceful coexistence existed for over 400 years until the arrival of the Seljuk Turks.

The Seljuk Turks

In 1001, Basil II, perhaps the greatest of the Byzantine emperors, concluded a formal treaty with the Fatimid caliph of Egypt, Al-Hikim, to protect Christian Pilgrims on their way to Jerusalem and Bethlehem. Basil II died in 1025 AD and after his death there was a rapid demise of Byzantium power due to inept rulers who drastically reduced military spending resulting in weakening their Eastern frontier which opened the way to the Turkomen.

In the late 1050s the Seljuk Turkomen burst out of Central Asia into the Near East and revived Muslim Sunni power. Earlier the Seljuk Turks had been converted to Sunni Islam by contacts with Muslim merchants of the Abbasid Dynasty. In 1055 AD Tuhgril Bey united the Turkomen tribes, invaded what is now Iraq, entered Baghdad and restored the Abbasid Caliph who appointed him as

Sultan (guardian) and entrusted him with the military power to wage war. The Sultan's aim was Cairo, the seat of the Fatimid Shia caliphate, but first he had to secure his northern flank against the Byzantine Empire which was a Fatimid ally.

In 1068 AD Romulus IV was appointed Emperor of Byzantine to stop the Seljuk Turks. He raised a large army and met the Seljuk Turks in 1071 at the Battle of Manzikert located in what is now Western Turkey. Alp Arslan had succeeded Tuhgril Bey as the Sultan of the Turkomen and his forces annihilated those of Romulus IV.

The defeat of Romulus IV had several major effects. First, it accelerated the decline of the Byzantine Empire, second, it started the gradual turkification (I guess this is a word) of Anatolia (the majority of present day Turkey) and, third, and most importantly from the Crusades perspective, it resulted in the carving out of states under Turkomen control which disrupted the long-established pilgrimage routes of the Western Europeans to the Holy Land.

The result was the Crusades. Even though the primary cause of the Crusades was the disruption of the Pilgrimage routes, the people could have only undertaken the Crusades because of the improved economic and social changes that had taken place in Western Europe over the last 400 years. That recovery which assisted in fostering the Crusades is too lengthy to cover.

Alexios I

In 1095 AD, after the Battle of Manzikert, the Byzantine emperor, Alexios I, following a tradition of hiring mercenaries from Western Europe, sent envoys to the West requesting military assistance against the Muslims. Simultaneously with the attempt to hire mercenaries he also played on the Pope's emotion to prevent the Seljuk Turks from disrupting pilgrimages. He needed to reinforce his army so his representatives, in order to recruit mercenaries, probably exaggerated the dangers facing the Eastern Empire in order to secure the needed troops.

Well, what Alexios I wanted was western mercenaries. What Alexios I got, to his misfortune and the misfortune of the Byzantine Empire, was the Crusades.

The message from Alexios was received by Pope Urban II who decided to assert his independence from the western European secular rulers and began to marshal various arguments for the proper use of armed force by Christians. His activity resulted in intense Christian piety, a renewed interest in religious affairs, and religious propaganda advocating a "*Just War*" in order to retake Palestine from the Muslims. As he proclaimed, "*Deus Vult*" (God wills it).

By these means Pope Urban II sought to reunite the Christian church under his leadership by providing the Byzantine Emperor with military support. In addition, the Crusades became a means by which he could harness the warlike nature of the nobles of Western Europe

Therefore, in 1095 AD, he proclaimed the **First Crusade** with the stated goal of restoring Christian access to holy places in and near Jerusalem. Pope Urban II promised forgiveness of all sins to whoever joined the Crusade. However, joining the Crusade for the participants was not all about religion. For them, especially the western nobles, there was the opportunity for economic or political gain, a desire for adventure, and the feudal obligation to one's lord. And, of course, there was gold to be had and kingdoms to gain so what mercenary can turn that down?

Pope Urban II speeches filled the crusaders with a religious fervor that would only be slacked when they washed their hands in Saracen blood.

The word "Crusade" was apparently taken from the French word "croisade" and the Spanish word "cruzada". The Crusades were never referred to as such by their participants. Instead the original crusaders referred to them by such Latin terms as "*fideles Sancti Petri*" (the faithful of Saint Peter) or "*milites Christi*" (knights of Christ).

Each crusader swore a *votus* (vow) to be fulfilled on successfully reaching Jerusalem. In addition, they were granted a white cloth cross (*crux*) to be sewn onto their clothes thus the "*taking of the cross*" became associated with the Crusades. The Crusaders saw themselves as undertaking an *iter*, a journey, or a *peregrinatio*, an armed pilgrimage. The crusaders referred to the Muslims as "**Saracens**" while the Muslims referred to the crusaders as "**Franks**" or "Latins".

Most historians consider that between 1096 and 1291 there were seven major Crusades and numerous minor ones. However, some historians divide the Fifth and Eighth Crusades into two distinct Crusades making a total of nine major crusades. I will briefly cover only two crusades, the First and Third, that I think had the most impact on Islam.

First Crusade (1095–1099)

As I indicated Pope Urban II used the appeal from Alexios to assert his spiritual authority over Western Europe. In 1095 the Pope traveled to northern Italy and held a preliminary council at Piacenza. He then traveled across the Alps into France where his trip climaxed in a dramatic speech delivered at Claremont on November 27, 1095, and there he pronounced a remission of sin for those who undertook a Crusade for, as he said, they were '***chosen by god***' to fight the '***accursed race of turks***' who had committed atrocities against Christian pilgrims. The pope encouraged detailed planning for those going on the Crusade and set the date of departure as August 15, 1096.

Not unexpectedly, the monarchies of Western Europe, King Rufus of England, King Philip I of France and Emperor Henry IV of the Holy Roman Empire did not respond to his call, however, their nobles did. The monarchies apparently did not fully trust the reason for Urban II calling the Crusade.

The People's Crusade

Some preachers, however, attracted poorly armed but pious people who set out in March and April, 1096. This was the so called ***People's Crusade***. These were little more than disorganized rabble that had little or no military training. When the People's Crusade crossed into Germany in the spring of 1096 AD, units of Crusaders massacred thousands of Jews in the cities of Speyer, Worms, Mainz and Cologne, despite the efforts by Catholic bishops to protect them. The crusaders apparently not only intended to wash their hands in Saracen blood but also Jewish blood as well. After all, from their perspective, the Jews had crucified Jesus Christ.

This was the first major outbreak of anti-Jewish violence in Christian Europe and is cited as one reason for creating the state of Israel. As an aside, there currently seems to be a resurgence of anti-Semitism in Europe particularly in France. Germany, the home of the Jewish holocaust, is surprisingly free of anti-Semitism. I suppose because of its history and the holocaust.

The first wave of the People's Crusade arrived in Byzantine territory and immediately began to loot and attack Byzantine subjects. Alexios restricted the People's Crusade from entering Constantinople and instead provided them transportation to Civetot in Asia Minor with instructions to await the main army.

The Crusaders making up the People's Crusade ignored his advice and advanced on Nicaea on October 21, 1096 where Turkish Cavalry slaughtered the crusaders with the exception of the women, children, and those who surrendered.

The survivors subsequently accused the Byzantines of treachery which may have had an impact on the subsequent sacking of Constantinople by a future Crusade.

The Main Crusade

The Pope appointed *Bishop Adhemar of Le Puy* to lead the First Crusade which set out on the day of the Feast of Assumption, 15 August, 1095 AD.

The heavily armed and highly disciplined crusader armies set off from France and Italy at different times in August and September 1096. They were led primarily by three brave and experienced knights, Count Bohemond of Taranto, Godfrey of Bouillon, and Raymond IV of Toulouse. Count Bohemond is arguably the most famous knight to come out of the 1st Crusade.

The bulk of the army was divided into four parts travelling separately to Constantinople. It is estimated by historians that the western forces may have totaled as many as 100,000 persons, counting both combatants and noncombatants. The armies journeyed eastward by land toward Constantinople, where they were welcomed warily by the Byzantine Emperor. Well, when you have about 100,000 armed men descending upon you it pays to be cautious.

In the spring of 1097 the crusaders were transported by the Byzantine Imperial Fleet to Asia Minor were they advanced against Nicaea. In mid-May 1097 the Crusaders bombarded Nicaea's walls in preparation for an assault. On the morning of June 19, 1097, the day fixed for the assault, the city capitulated to Alexios. Two days after the capitulation of Nicaea the crusaders set out for Antioch.

The crusaders won their first victory over the Turks at Bozuyuk pass. The crusader army had divided into three columns with an experienced Frankish Knight commanding each column. Bohemond, perhaps the greatest warrior of the first Crusade, led the first column, Godfrey the second, and Raymond the third. Bohemond led his column into the pass and was immediately ambushed by the Turks. Bohemond sent his knights forward while the infantry established a fortified camp. Bohemond was driven back to the fortified camp and sent word for Godfrey and Raymond to come to his assistance. The Turks mistakenly thought Bohemond's column represented the entire Crusade and failed to notice the columns of Godfrey and Raymond. Godfrey reinforced the right flank of Bohemond while Raymond slipped unnoticed through the pass and attacked the Turks from the rear. When that occurred Bohemond and Godfrey attacked and routed the Turks.

For the crusaders this was proof that God was on their side. The holy city of Antioch was now in their sights.

They marched across Asia Minor and by October, 1097, they stood before the walls of Antioch. The march across Asia Minor, however, had been an ordeal with a great loss of life. Some historians estimate the crusaders lost one-half of their combatants due to thirst and Turkish raids.

The fertile plain on which Antioch lay allowed the crusaders to recover from their journey and to blockade Antioch. The crusader armies assaulted the city of Antioch between October 1097 and June 1098 before finally capturing it.

Bohemond continued to demonstrate his military leadership by defeating two Turkish relief forces from Damascus and Aleppo. In addition, he devised a stratagem to capture Antioch. Bohemond bribed a disgruntled Armenian official named Firuz to allow them access to the city. On the evening of June 2, 1098, the crusaders broke off the siege and appeared to retreat from Antioch which tricked the city leaders into thinking the siege was over. At midnight the crusaders turned back toward Antioch and on a prearranged signal Firuz lowered a ladder and Bohemond and 60 knights climbed the ladder, captured the wall and opened the gates of the city to the crusader army. Once inside the city the Crusaders massacred the Muslim inhabitants and pillaged the city. This seems to have set the stage for future crusader attacks on cities resulting in the massacre of Muslims and the sacking of the city. Needless to say this was viewed as sacrilege by Muslims since it was against Islamic law to kill innocent civilians.

Bohemond decided to stay in Antioch as its ruler while the remainder of the crusaders under Godfrey and Raymond marched south, moving from town to town along the coast, before finally reaching the walls of Jerusalem on 7 June 1099.

Both Jews and Muslims fought together to defend Jerusalem against the invading Franks but on 15 July 1099 the crusaders entered the city and proceeded to massacre the remaining Jewish and Muslim civilians, to include the women and children, while pillaging or destroying mosques and the city itself.

Raymond D'Aguilers, a witness to the looting and pillaging, wrote this about the crusader sack of Jerusalem "... *Wonderful sights were to be seen. Some of our men (and this was more merciful) cut off the heads of their enemies; others shot them with arrows, so that they fell from the towers; others tortured them longer by casting them into the flames. Piles of heads, hands and feet were to be seen in the streets of the city. It was necessary to pick one's way over the bodies of men and horses. But these were small matters compared to what happened at the Temple of Solomon, a place where religious services are normally chanted ... in the temple and the porch of Solomon, men rode in blood up to their knees and bridle reins. Indeed it was a just and splendid judgment of God that this place should be filled with the blood of unbelievers since it had suffered so long from their blasphemies."*

The First Crusade was over and its success confirmed God's favor and set the stage for Western European Crusades and the massacre of Muslims for the next 200 years.

The Muslims had long fought among themselves, but they were finally united by **Salah al-Din** (Saladin), who created a single powerful state. Following his victory at the Battle of Hattin, Saladin easily overwhelmed the disunited crusaders in 1187 and retook Jerusalem on 29 September 1187. Terms were arranged and the city surrendered, with Saladin entering the city on 2 October 1187. Saladin was faithful to his word and spared the civilians and left the churches and shrines relatively intact. Compare this to the 1st Crusade where the Muslim inhabitants were slaughtered. Saladin from this day forward began to be admired by the Christian community as being chivalrous and in the same mold as a knight.

In the 3rd Crusade, Richard the Lionhearted and Saladin, after numerous battles, apparently came to admire and respect one another.

Third Crusade (1187–1192)

Saladin's victories shocked Europe and Pope Celestine III received an enthusiastic response to his call for a Third Crusade. This Crusade would be notable for its royal participants: Richard the Lionhearted of England; Philip II of France; and Frederic Barbarossa, the Holy Roman Emperor and a German national hero. The name Barbarossa may be familiar to you from WW2 when Hitler named his invasion of Russia, ***Operation Barbarossa***.

The Emperor Barbarossa raised an army in Germany and Italy, and in 1189 AD, marched overland to Constantinople accompanied by approximately 50,000 pilgrims and soldiers which was more than twice the number in Saladin's Army. In 1190 he marched into Asia Minor but was ignominiously drowned while crossing the River Calycadnus (Seleph). It is unclear from history whether he attempted to cross the river on horseback and was drowned or whether he cooled himself in the river and suffered a heart attack. Either way the result was that most of the German Army returned home. This would have been the largest and best trained army to have faced Saladin but the death of Barbarossa prevented that from occurring.

In the spring of 1190 Richard the Lionhearted's fleet set sail from Dartmouth and joined Philips II fleet at Marseilles and in July, 1190, they both set sail for Sicily. In Sicily they quarreled when Richard reneged on marrying Philips half-sister, Alys. Philip set off for March 30, 1191, and arrived at Acre on May 20, 1191. Richard, who was delayed by the pleasures of Sicily and his conquest of Cyprus, arrived at Acre on 8 June, 1191. Once at Acre Richard assumed command of the Crusade and recaptured the city of Acre on July 21, 1191. He then proceeded to slaughter all its Muslim inhabitants to include women and children despite his promises to the contrary. As a result Muslim memories of Christian heroes like Richard the Lionhearted are certainly more negative than in the West.

Richard apparently had an abrasive personality and seemed to want to have his way even if it dishonored other crusaders. Philip II, after the sack of Acre, sailed home in anger and immediately began to conspire with John, Richard's brother (remember Robin Hood?), to raise a rebellion in England in order for John to become King.

In addition, Richard also apparently offended Leopold of Austria by throwing his banner to the ground much to the dismay and anger of Leopold, This act would later have unforeseen ramifications for Richard.

Richard, now with sole command of the Third Crusade, began to advance down the coast toward Jaffe. Saladin unsuccessfully attempted to stop him. They apparently came to admire one another's fighting ability and in the winter of 1191-1192 negotiated a settlement to end the Third Crusade.

In 1192 an Armistice was declared for five years with the Christians keeping the Levantan ports while Saladin retained Jerusalem but guaranteed the safety of Christian pilgrims to the holy city.

On an historical note, Richard sailed triumphantly for Europe but was shipwrecked on the coast of Italy near Venice. He attempted to make his way through Germany but was captured in December 1192 and imprisoned by Leopold who still resented Richard's discourtesy at the Battle of Acre. He was given to Henry VII, the Holy Roman Emperor, and was ransomed for one hundred and fifty thousand marks in 1194 and returned to England. On 25 March, 1199 Richard was wounded in the left shoulder by a shaft from a crossbow and died of gangrene on 6 April, 1199.

The Crusades had begun to decline during the thirteenth century and finally degenerated into intra-Christian wars. For example, during the Fourth Crusade, Roman Catholic Crusaders sacked Constantinople and the Eastern Catholic church in 1204 AD. The Crusades had degenerated into Christian Sword against Christian Sword with the taking of Jerusalem forgotten.

The Crusades officially came to an end in 1453 when the Muslim Turks conquered Constantinople and renamed it Istanbul which became the seat of the Ottoman Empire. The Crusades had, however, forever changed Europe, the Muslim world and the future of each.

Crusade Results

There were a number of long lasting results from the Crusades, some results affected Muslims while others did not, but all are still being felt by both Muslims and Westerners to this day.

First, the Crusades left a lasting legacy of enmity between Muslims and Christians. Christians invaded a Muslim community under the pretext of freeing the Holy Land and in doing so indiscriminately slaughtered Muslim women and children. From a Muslim perspective this resulted in a Jihad against the Christian

Invaders to eject them from the Muslim homeland. This left an uneasy truce between both Muslims and Christians which lasts to this day.

Second, the persecution of Jews in the First Crusade began a thousand year tradition of organized attacks on the Jews of Europe ultimately leading to the Jewish Holocaust in which the Nazis killed over six million Jews. This led to the establishment of Israel, the ejection of Palestinians from their historic lands and the resulting continual conflict between Israel and Palestine.

Third, the crusades raised the power and prestige of the papal curia resulting in greater control over the entire western church and extended the system of papal taxation throughout the whole ecclesiastical structure of the West. The indulgence system grew significantly in late medieval Europe only to spark the Protestant Reformation in the early 1500s by Martin Luther. The result was the Protestant Reformation and the Thirty Years War, the most destructive war in European history.

Fourth, the Crusades resulted in the permanent split between the Eastern Orthodox Church and the Roman Catholic Church. Religious difference separated the two catholic churches but the final split resulted from the sacking of Constantinople by the Roman Catholic crusaders in 1204 AD during the Fourth Crusade.

Fifth, the Crusades influenced the attitude of the Western Church and people towards warfare. The frequent calling of crusades habituated the clergy to the use of violence which sparked a debate about the legitimacy of taking lands and possessions from pagans on purely religious grounds. This debate would rise again in the 1600, the Age of Discovery, as the banner of the church and slaughter was once more inflicted upon the Americas.

Sixth, the Crusades led to a dramatic increase in trade throughout Europe and between Europe and the Levant states established by the crusaders. In particular Genoa, Palermo, Marseilles and Barcelona became major ports for trading with the Levant. The long distance trade increased ship building, transformed banking practices and stimulated the growth of towns and cities across Europe. This had the effect of shifting the financial axis from Constantinople to Western Europe. (The Levant is the area encompassing the current countries of Syria, Lebanon, Israel and Jordan. These countries were subdivided during the Crusades into Kingdoms controlled by Crusader Knights.)

Seventh, the Crusades drew together the disparate civilizations of Western Europe, Byzantium, and the Islamic world. Each had been developing separately but the Crusades drew these worlds back together and the ensuing war, commerce and cultural exchanges decisively changed the future of Europe and the Middle–East. After the Crusades the European nation-state order emerged; the Byzantine Empire dissolved and the Islamic empire began to recede from its once proud and flourishing civilization.

The Crusades changed the world and many of the changes were disastrous, the ripples of which are still being felt today.

In my next letter I will discuss the Sharia and Islamic Law.

References:

1. *What everyone Needs to Know About Islam*, John L. Esposito
2. *A History of God*, Karen Armstrong
3. *Islam*, Karen Armstrong
4. *God and his Prophet: The Religion of Islam*, The Great Courses, John Swanson
5. *Cultural Literacy in America,* The Great Courses, Mark Bergson
6. *Great World Religions: Islam*, The Great Courses, John L. Esposito
7. *The Era of the Crusades*, The Great Courses, Kenneth W. Harl
8. The Wikipedia, Various newspaper, and Magazine Articles

Letter 7 - The Sharia and Islamic Law

Between the 7th and 10th centuries Muslim scholars began to formulate Islamic law. Islamic scholars of the Quran, during these three centuries, gradually developed into the *ulama* (learned ones), who were a professional class of religious scholars. The ulama developed Islamic jurisprudence, *fiqh,* or understanding, by attempting to interpret and apply the *Sharia*, God's guidance or law, as found in both *the Quran* and *the Sunnah,* the example set by the Prophet. Through their efforts Islamic law was formulated based upon three things: the Quran, the Sunnah and human interpretation by the ulama of the Quran and the Sunnah. *Sharia*, literally "a road leading to water' goes beyond narrow legal matters and encompasses all aspects of life. For most Muslims it means they want to live in accordance with God's will.

The development of Islamic law by the ulama came about as a response to the political and social concerns of these three centuries. That is, the ulama standardized Islamic law in order to limit the arbitrary judgments of the Umayyad Caliph and his judges.

During the Abbasid Dynasty in the 10th century, the development of Islamic jurisprudence took a major leap forward because of the patronage of the Abbasid Caliphs. It was during this time that the ulama became a separate class.

As Islamic Law developed, four major Sunni Law schools were created: the **Hanafi School** centered at Kufa, the **Malachi school** centered at Medina, The **Shafii School** centered at Cairo and Baghdad and the **Hanbali School** centered at Baghdad. The various schools were in general agreement on numerous issues; however, there were significant differences between the schools based primarily upon different textual interpretation of the Quran and the different geographic, social and cultural context in which the law was interpreted.

The major agreement between the various schools centered on the fact that Islamic law is based upon the fundamental requirement of Islam which is the submission to God's Will. The Quran stresses that Muslims must struggle in the right path, *Sharia*, in order to implement God's will on earth. In order to do this

Islam emphasizes *orthopraxy*, or **correct action**. This stands in contrast to Christianity which emphasizes doctrine or **correct belief**. While Muslims define themselves as an observer of Islamic law, Christians lean more toward doctrine and theology. my perspective, both religions engage in both doctrine and practice, so the difference between the two is simply a question of emphasis.

Islamic law is very dynamic because it is based not only upon *Sharia*, God's law or path, but upon the human interpretation, *fiqh*, of the law thus allowing for interpretation of the laws to meet specific cultural needs.

Westerners, for whatever reason, seem to equate Sharia with Islamic law. That is not the case for human interpretation greatly influences Islamic law. *Sharia* refers specifically to God as the Lawgiver whereas Islamic law is a broader category that encompasses both Sharia and its interpretation by man. This is important to Muslims because the development of Islamic law was the work of religious scholars rather than judges, courts and governments.

There are two major divisions within Islamic law. **First** is the Muslim's unchangeable duty to God by the observance of practices primarily involved in worship; for example, observance of the Five Pillars of Islam. **Second** is the Muslims duty to others which encompasses such things as the public law governing contractual law, international law and family law which governs marriage, divorce and inheritance. Both types of law play a prominent role in the Islamic community, however, there is a difference in how the Sunni and Shii community view the sources of the Islamic Law.

Sunni Muslims, for example, recognize four official sources of Islamic law. The **first** is the **Quran** which consists of approximately 80 instructions which were revealed to Muhammad when he established the first Islamic community in Medina. These chapters occupy the first part of the Quran and are directed toward the individual and the community.

The **second** is the **Sunnah,** the examples set by the Prophet. The Sunnah is what the Prophet said and did which are preserved in the stories and reports known as the **hadith,** the tradition of the prophet. The Sunnah are examples of the practice of Islamic faith and assist in explaining the principles found in the Quran.

The **third** is the *qiyas,* or analogical reasoning. If there is no text that exists in the Quran or Sunnah to address a situation then the ulama are free to use their independent reasoning, *ijtihad*, to look at similar situations and adapt those principles to the new situation. This is one of the reasons for the diversity of opinions between Islamic Law Schools. I was always struck by its similarity to common law used in the US which is based on past cases.

Fourth is the *ijma,* or consensus, of the Islamic community. This is interpreted to be the consensus of the ulama who are the interpreters of Islamic law. This source for Islamic law apparently originated when the prophet said, "*My community will never agree on an error.*" In this instance, a consensus of religious scholars can be used to determine the legality of an action.

The **Shii Muslims**, on the other hand, have a slightly different perspective on the sources of Islamic law. Both the Sunni and Shii agree on the Quran and Sunnah as sources of Islamic law, however, the Shii have their own collection of traditions from *Ali* and their *imams*, who are the Shii legal interpreters of God's law.

As I indicated previously, the different law schools agree on the basic essentials of Islamic law but differ in the interpretation of the law due to individual reasoning and social customs. The ulama at each law school can differ in their interpretation of text due to their individual social background and culture. There can also be a different interpretation based upon the geographical location of the law school. That is, each school has a particular orientation similar to political schools of thought here in the US. For example, the **Hanafi** School located in Kufu is more cosmopolitan while the **Malichi** School centered at Medina is more conservative.

Another major difference in schools is the issuance of an official interpretation of law called a *fatwa* which is a legal opinion written by an expert, a consultant or a *mufti* (a mufti is a legal scholar who advises judges and litigants). For example, it is not unusual for a Muslim to go to a legal scholar at a law school, ask for an opinion, and then use that opinion in an Islamic court.

Again, remember Salman Rushdie? The **Ayatollah Khomeini**, a Shii, wrote a fatwa that found Rushdie guilty of blasphemy and condemned him to death. However, another Shii Imam wrote an opinion that called for his trial by Islamic law rather than his death.

The Fatwa and Islamic Law

A *fatwa* is a legal opinion normally given by a **mufti** (a legal scholar) in response to request by an individual or an Islamic court. The authority of the fatwa is based upon three things: **one**, the perceived education of the mufti; **two**, his status in the Islamic community and, **three**, the persuasiveness of his argument.

Fatwas are historically independent of the Islamic judicial system and have recently been used to either support or to refute terrorism. For example, Osama bin Laden, prior to his 9/11 attack on the Twin Towers, issued two fatwas in which he declared war on the United States.

The **first fatwa** was issued in August 1996 and published in London in the *Al Quds al Arabi* newspaper. It was a 30 page uncompromising fatwa declaring war on the US and Israel. It was entitled "*Declaration of War Against the Americans Occupying the Land of the Two Holy Places.*" In this fatwa he chronicled the various injustices inflicted upon the Islamic community and called upon "*his Muslim brothers*" to concentrate on "*destroying, fighting and killing the enemy until, by the Grace of Allah, it is completely defeated.*" He then recommends a suitable means of fighting be adopted such as "*fast moving light forces that work under complete secrecy.*" Ben laden was particularly outraged that Americans were on Saudi Arabian soil, the location of Mecca and Medina, the two most holy sites in Islam and nothing but a war of Jihad would satisfy him.

The **second fatwa** issued by Osama bin Laden was published on February 23, 1998, also in the *Al Quds al Arabi* newspaper in London. Unlike the first fatwa, which was issued only by bin Laden, this fatwa was signed not only by bin Laden but also by Ayman al-Zawahiri (leader of Jihad group in Egypt and al Qaeda's second-in-command), Abu-Yasir Rafa'l Ahmad Taha (leader of the Islamic Group), Sheikh Mir Hamzah (leader of an jihad Islamic group in Pakistan), and Fazlul Rahman (leader of the Jihad Movement in Bangladesh).

This fatwa stated that "*three facts that are known to everyone*" compel war against the United States. First, the United States has been "*occupying the lands of Islam in the holiest of places.*" Second, the "*crusader-Zionist alliance*" has inflicted great devastation upon the Iraqi people. Third, the United States' goal is "*to serve the Jew's petty state and divert attention from its occupation of Jerusalem and murder of Muslims there.*"

It concludes with instructions to Muslims everywhere: *"...to kill the Americans and their allies -- civilians and military -- is an individual duty for every Muslim who can do it in any country in which it is possible to do it...."*

Well, he meant every word he said for he planned and launched his attack on the Twin Towers on September 11, 2001 killing over 3,000 Americans and continued to attack American interests until he was killed at approximately 1 AM on May 2, 2011.

There are a number of Muslim religious scholars who object to the use of terrorism by Muslims. For example, Muhammad Tahir-ul-Qadri, a well-known religious scholar and preacher in Pakistan, issued a 600 page fatwa on 2 March, 2010 condemning the use of terrorism and suicide bombers by declaring they had no place in Islamic teachings and that there is no justification for it. This fatwa was entitled *"Fatwa on Terrorism and Suicide Bombings"* and was a direct refutation of the ideology of Osama bin Laden, Al-Qaeda and the Taliban.

Islamic Law and the Family

A major area of study in Islamic law is Muslim family law of which there are three major areas: marriage, divorce and inheritance. Marriage in Islam is not a sacrament as it is in Christianity but is primarily a contract between families. That is, the traditional Islamic practice is for families to arrange marriages and be the contracting parties rather than the bride and groom. The preferred marriage is between Muslims within an extended family. For example, the marriage of first cousins is quiet common in arranged marriages.

The Quran, however, introduced reforms that recognize that a woman has the right to arrange her own marriage and receive the dower from her husband. For example, the Quran, Chapter 4, Verse 4 says, *"And give the women (on marriage) their dower as a free gift; but if they, of their own good pleasure, remit any part of it to you, Take it and enjoy it with right good cheer."* In addition, the Quran changed marriage obligations for a man. In pre-Islamic society there was no limitation on the number of women a man could marry. The Quran changed that and said a man could marry up to four wives provided he could support them. In the modern Islamic society, however, a monogamous marriage is the norm.

In Islamic society the relation between a man and a wife is complementary. That is, the public sphere is viewed as the primary area of man in the support and protection of his family while the primary role for a woman is as a mother and wife. That is, the woman is to manage the household and supervise the upbringing and religious training of their children. Regardless of their roles, in family matters and in society, women, as a practical matter, are viewed subordinate to men.

Divorce, the second leg of Islamic family law, is permissible in both Quran and the Sunnah, however, it is viewed very seriously since the family is at the heart of the Muslim community. In pre-Islamic society a man could have as many wives as he could support and divorce a wife at will while a woman had no grounds for divorce. The Quran and Islamic law introduced guidelines for greater equality between husband and wife. For example, a husband is required by law to pronounce, "I divorce you" three times, once each month for three months while at the same time pursuing reconciliation. In contrast, a woman must go to court and present grounds for a divorce. However, some Islamic communities have accepted the practice of the man saying "I divorce you" three times in rapid succession as satisfying this requirement.

The third leg of Islamic family law is inheritance. In pre-Islamic society all property passed to the nearest male relative of the deceased. The Quran, however, guaranteed the wives, daughters and sisters a 'fixed share' of the deceased property before it was passed to the nearest male relative. Don't get me wrong, the Islamic community is still male dominated, therefore, the male receives the dominant share of any inheritance.

In the twentieth century many western oriented Muslim governments implemented western style legal codes related to the family, however, with the exception of Turkey, family law was not replaced but reformed. For example, the minimum age for marriage was raised, man must obtain court permission before he can take a second wife, he must also obtain court permission to divorce, etc. However, more fundamental and conservative Muslim states reject these reforms as un-Islamic and western in nature. The momentum today in Islamic communities, however, seems to be toward gender equality and the growing empowerment of women.

Islamic law and Reforms

The advancement of technology, a changing culture, and political reforms in the Muslim community has brought about a tension between those religious scholars and communities who believe the Quranic law is unchangeable and those Islamic reformers and communities who believe the law must be interpreted not according to history but according to the present modern situation. That is, within the Islamic community there is a current struggle between reform minded Muslims and their desire to impose change from above and the **ulama** who see themselves as the guardians of Islam and the only qualified interpreters of Islamic law.

Therefore, within the Islamic community there is an ongoing battle that in many cases has broken out into actual conflict between those more conservative Muslims who equate God's divinely inspired laws with those found in legal manuals and those reformers who call for a change in laws more closely aligned with modern social customs. A conservative example is Afghanistan where fifty percent of the girls are married before they are sixteen and rape within marriage is legal. This custom is backed by Islamic law since in 2009 President Hamid Kharzi signed the *Shii Family Bill* requiring wives to submit to their husband's sexual advances.

On the other hand, some Muslim countries such as Egypt, Pakistan, Indonesia, etc., have adopted western legal codes and blended them with Islamic laws. For example, in 2001 Turkey established a new Civil Code which defined the family as a union based upon equal partnership with spouses having equal decision making powers.

Even with these reforms, family law remains at the heart of Sharia and has remained mostly intact in Muslim countries.

I will discuss Islam and women in the next letter.

References:

1. *What everyone Needs to Know About Islam*, John L. Esposito
2. *A History of God*, Karen Armstrong
3. *Islam*, Karen Armstrong
4. *God and his Prophet: The Religion of Islam*, The Great Courses, John Swanson
5. *Cultural Literacy in America,* The Great Courses, Mark Bergson
6. *Great World Religions: Islam*, The Great Courses, John L. Esposito
7. The Wikipedia, Various newspaper, and Magazine Articles

Letter 8 - Islam and Women

Background

The place of women in Islam remains a very sensitive and contested issue in Sharia, Islamic law and the Islamic community. The status of women in the pre-Islamic Arabia was the result of a male dominated society; however, the Quran introduced substantial reforms by stressing the equality of women while the development of Islamic law continues to bend toward greater equity for women. Nevertheless, despite these continuing reforms, the Islamic society remains essentially patriarchal and as a result the status of women is represented by great diversity in the Islamic community. For example, in some Muslim countries a woman can drive a car and hold professional positions while in other Muslim countries they need a male relative's permission to travel and a court will condemn them to death by stoning if found guilty of adultery. Some Muslim countries allow women to hold responsible political and business positions but, on the other hand, they are not able to vote. In Iran, for example, women must wear the chador (full body clothing) but yet women constitute a majority of students in the universities and serve in parliament.

In Pakistan, women can vote, serve as ambassadors but yet suffer under Islamic laws while in Afghanistan the Taliban prevent girls from attending school.

Yet, according to the Quran, men and women are equally responsible for adhering to the Five Pillars of Islam. The Quran outlines the ideal relationship between a man and a woman which is one of equality and complementarity. In addition to establishing the equity of sexes, the revelations in the Quran raised the status of women by prohibiting female infanticide, women were no longer property, and changed marriage to a contractual relationship.

Much of this equality between sexes came as a result of the Quran which declared that men and women are equal in the eyes of god and were created to be complementary. The Quran, Chapter 30, Verse 21 states, *"And of His signs is that He created for you from yourselves mates that you may find tranquility in them; and He placed between you affection and mercy. Indeed in that are signs for a people who give thought."*

Veiling of Islamic Women

The veiling of Islamic women represents one of the more interesting differences in how Islamic women are viewed and is much more complex than it first appears, or at least how it appears to westerners, and represents a major difference for woman across Islamic communities. Dressing or veiling for Islamic women can range from a simple headscarf to a dress covering the full body. For, example, the Taliban require a woman to wear a full body covering such as the chador or burqa while Egypt is more modern and woman pretty much dress western style.

The veiling of Islamic woman did not become widespread until well after the death of Muhammad. Veiling was originally a sign of honor and distinction and not a sign of oppression. Muhammad's wives and upper-class women did, however, wear the veil as a symbol of their status. Several generations after the death of Muhammad the practice of veiling for Muslim women became widespread which was apparently adopted from the upper class Persian and Byzantine women who wore the veil as a sign of their rank and to separate them from lower class women. However, the mingling of classes at Muslim prayer seemed to have encouraged the use of the veil across classes.

The perception of veiling by Islamic women seems to run in cycles. For example, as western ideology spread throughout the Islamic communities in the 1900s, Islamic women began to remove their veils and adopt western dress yet in the 1970s a significant number of modern Muslim women began to return to wearing Islamic dress. For them this was a voluntary movement led by middle class women who were well educated and cosmopolitan. These women chose to dress in modern Islamic styles and fashions and are viewed as agents of change within their community. They believe they are able to function more independently, command more respect and are not treated as sex objects.

On the other hand, critics of Islamic dress, particularly in western countries, question this free choice and see the woman as living in an oppressive culture and simply submitting to the dictates of their religion. I found this rather strange since Jews and Christian women, in a particular cultural context, have also covered their heads.

Some Muslims, however, look at Western women and say they only think they are free and do not see how their culture exploits them as they spend numerous hours on their appearance and allow themselves to be exploited as sexual objects.

Muslim women explain that proper Islamic dress is a symbol for them of religious devotion, discipline and freedom. They say, for example, that the hijab allows them to be valued for who they are and not how they look.

Different Quranic Interpretations

When discussing the status of women in the Islamic community it must be remembered that Muslim communities are basically patriarchal and that the Quran and the hadith are interpreted by men although women seem to be becoming more active in this area.

At the center of women's reformation is the different and conflicting Quranic interpretations by reformists and fundamentalists. In order to understand this it must be remembered that many Muslims believe there are two different types of verses in the Quran: the first are those verses that are universal and the second are those specific to a social context and, therefore, subject to interpretation. For example, the Quran, Chapter 2, Verse 228 states that *"... But the men have a degree over them [women] [in responsibility and authority]..."* this verse and several others in the Quran are open to interpretation. In this case the conservative Islamist interpret this verse as giving greater weight to a man whereas a reformist interpretation argue that rather than be interpreted literally the interpretation should be reformulated to reflect a changing culture based on economic conditions. However, Muslims who advocate a literal interpretation of the Quran believe that this verse expresses gender inequality that simply reflects God's revealed social order.

Another Quran verse open to interpretation is the Quran, Chapter 33, Verses 32/33, states that *"Wives of the Prophet, you are not like other women. If you have fear of God, do not be tender in your speech lest people whose hearts are sick may lust after you. And abide in your houses and do not display yourselves as [was] the display of the former times of ignorance."*

There has been much debate within the Islamic community as to how, in general, these verses should be applied to Muslim women. Islamic reformists have pointed out that these two verses address only the wives of the Prophet and not Islamic women in general. Ultraconservative Islamic leaders, on the other hand, maintain that these verses apply not only to the wives of the Prophet but to all Muslim women since they are to model their conduct after that of the wives of the Prophet.

One of the more interesting aspects of the modern Islamic women is the role she has begun to play in the mosque in an attempt to utilize religion to reclaim their historical role in Islamic life. I emphasize historical role because Islamic women of the Prophet's time were very active in the Islamic community. For example, Khadija, the prophet's wife, owned property, ran a caravan trade and provided educational instruction. Fatima, the Prophet's youngest daughter, was instructed in religious duties, enjoyed the active life as the wife of a caliph and the mother of Imams. She was exceptionally active in the Islamic community but is still viewed as the very embodiment of a virtuous Islamic women.

In the centuries after the death of Muhammad, Islamic women prayed regularly at the mosque with the men. In addition, they played a major role in the collection of the **hadith,** prophetic traditions. The Prophet's wife, Aeisha, played a major role in the first Islamic community as an authority on medicine and poetry as well as an important collector and communicator of **hadith**.

Honor Killing

While I was writing these articles on Islam, one of my daughters asked me about honor killings which had recently been in the news. I must confess that this is one area in Islam that I have had the most difficulty understanding and coming to grips with and so I find it very difficult, and perhaps this is a failing of mine, to not be dispassionate in writing about it.

An honor killing is the killing of a woman by her family for a perceived immoral conduct such as adultery, fornication of simply becoming too westernized.

In 2008 a sixteen year old German/Afghan girl was stabbed twenty-three times in Hamburg by her brother for '**impure moral conduct**.' In Pakistan alone it is estimated there are over 1000 women killed annually for immoral conduct, many by stoning. I really suspect this 1000 figure for Pakistan is grossly underestimated. A typical stoning occurs when the girl is buried up to her neck then stoned by her father, brothers, mother, sisters and other members of the community. The stones are not small but the size of bricks and if no stones of this size are available then actual bricks are used.

Studies indicate that honor killings accelerated during the period between the 1990s and 2010. This may be due to two major factors. First, this increase may be a function of jihadist extremism and Islamic fundamentalism and, secondly, the increase may simply reflect more accurate reporting.

For westerners the killing of a woman for immoral conduct seems like such a barbaric act that it is beyond our understanding yet when viewed from the context of a patriarchal society it seems understandable for honor killing is nothing new. In fact, it has been occurring for thousands of years starting in ancient civilizations such as Babylon, ancient Israel and even Rome.

Well, why do families engage in honor killings? They seem to be the result of a strong patriarchal society whose value systems reflect a deeply rooted social concept of honor and shame. In these societies a husband/father is responsible for safeguarding the safety and honor of his family. Immoral behavior on the part of a woman reflects adversely upon family honor, and to restore that honor a woman may be killed due to immoral conduct or simply because she has become too '**westernized**.'

A westerner may find this strange for by becoming too westernized it is meant a woman refuses to wear the hijab because she wants an education, to have a career, to have non-Muslim friends, refuses to marry first cousins and/or expresses a desire to marry someone of her own choosing. Because of the inability to comprehend Islamic extremism there are many westerners who view honor killings as a form of domestic terrorism, meant to ensure that Muslim women wear the Islamic veil, have Muslim babies, and mingle only with other Muslims. On the other hand Islamic fundamentalists think that only through the murder of an offending family member can honor be restored to the rest of the family. For them a female relative's sexual and reproductive activities are not seen as individual rights but rather as assets that belong to her father's family, her tribe, or her religion.

The punishment of a woman for immoral conduct has survived centuries through an interpretation of Sharia law, that say adultery is punishable by stoning. Supporters of stoning immoral women argue that it is legitimized by the acts and sayings of the Prophet Mohammad in the Hadith. For example, in the Hadith Sahih Muslim, Chapter 3: ***Prescribed Punishment For An Adulterer And An Adulteress***, Book 17, Number 4191, it states that"… ***And in case of married male committing adultery with a married female, they shall receive one hundred lashes and be stoned to death***."

Stoning is, therefore, set out as a specific punishment for adultery under several interpretations of Sharia. Unfortunately, in some instances, even a woman saying she has been raped can be considered an admission to the crime of *zina* (sex outside marriage) and she can be stoned.

In countries such as Iran, where stoning is legal and widespread, men often have significantly more legal rights than women. Iran has the world's highest rate of execution by stoning. No one knows how many people have been stoned in Iran but at least 11 people, as of 2013, are in prison under sentence of stoning.

Despite the Islamic Fundamentalist interpretation with regard to honor killings, it is not in the Quran or specifically called out by the Hadith nor is it sanctioned by Islamic law and, therefore, many Muslim scholars condemn honor killing as un-Islamic. For example, the Grand Ayatollah Mohammad Hussein Fadlallah, a prominent Lebanon Shii leader, has condemned honor killing in the strictest terms and issued a fatwa against honor killing. In an interview he stated that *"A woman is killed just for an accusation of having an illegal sexual relationship with another person. Even if this accusation has not been proven yet, the father, the bother, or the husband immediately kills her without resorting to the law in a public trial. I have issued a Fatwa prohibiting such acts."*

Despite creeping modernity, secular condemnation and the fact there's no reference to stoning in the Quran, honor killings still claim the lives of many women in Islamic communities around the world to include those in western countries.

Other Women Issues

There are a number of other issues related to Muslim women that I would like to address.

The first is **Marriage.** Marriage, under Islamic law, requires a woman's consent since it is viewed as a contract and not a sacrament. It is normally viewed as a contract between families rather than the bride and groom. The preferred marriage is between two Muslims preferable within the Islamic extended family.

The second is **marriage age**. The marriage age of a girl in Islam has become controversial in modern times. Traditionally, Islam has permitted the marriage of girls below the age of 10 because the practices of Muhammad, the Prophet, is considered a basis for Islamic law. According to Sahih Bukhari and Sahih Muslim, the two authentic hadiths, the Prophet married Aisha, his third wife when she was 6, and consummated the marriage before she reached the age of 10.

However, there is a debate among Islamic scholars about what this means. Some scholars suggest that it is not the calendar age that matters, rather it is the biological age of the girl that determines when she can be married under Islamic law. According to these Islamic scholars, marriageable age in Islam is when a girl has reached sexual maturity, as determined by her nearest male guardian. This age, they claim, can be any age depending on the girl. That is, some girls mature faster than others. There remains a strong belief among most Muslims and Muslim scholars that, based on Sharia, marrying a girl less than 15 years old is an acceptable practice for Muslims. For example, Muslim communities in Yemen, Saudi Arabia, India, Bangladesh, Pakistan, Indonesia, Egypt, and Nigeria have insisted that it is their Islamic right to marry girls below age 15.

Some Islamic scholars maintain that since, in Islamic Law, marriages cannot be forced, child marriages are implicitly forced marriages.

The third is **birth control**. There is no mention in the Quran of family planning, but there are Hadith interpretations that mention coitus interruptus. In present day Islam there are some ulama who oppose birth control because that challenges the will of God. However, the majority of ulama think that contraception is permissible as long as both the husband and wife agree since sex in marriage is also viewed as a form of communication and pleasure. Most Muslim religious leaders, however, oppose sterilization because it permanently alters god's creation.

The fourth is **abortion**. The Quran, Chapter 17, Verse 31 states that "*And kill not your children for fear of poverty. We provide for them and for you. Surely, the killing of them is a great sin.*" The Quranic tradition indicates that child bearing is one of the most important aspects of marriage for the Quran places a high value on the preservation of life. Muslim scholars seem to agree that the soul infuses the body at around 120 days of a woman's pregnancy and that abortion after that time constitutes murder and should be punished. However, if the woman's life is at risk then abortion is permitted because of her family duties and responsibilities.

The fifth is **divorce**. In contrast to the Western world where divorce was relatively uncommon until modern times, divorce, in the Islamic world was a more common occurrence in certain parts of the late medieval Muslim world. In the Mamluk Sultanate and Ottoman Empire, for example, the rate of divorce was high. In medieval Egypt, Al-Sakhawi recorded the marital history of 500 women, the largest sample of married women in the Middle Ages, and found that at least a third of all women in the Mamluk Sultanate of Egypt and Syria married more than once, with many marrying three or more times. According to Al-Sakhawi, as many as three out of ten marriages in 15th century Cairo ended in divorce. In the early 20th century, some villages in western Java and the Malay Peninsula had divorce rates as high as 70%.

The sixth is **marriage outside the faith**. In Islam, Muslim women may not marry non-Muslim men, a term that includes infidels, apostates, ex-Muslims, other monotheistic, non-theistic and polytheistic men. Further, a Muslim woman – either by birth or after conversion is not allowed to leave Islam to marry a non-Muslim, because leaving Islam is a religious *hudud* (a religious limitation) crime punishable with death. However, the Quran allows Muslim men to marry women of the *People of the Book* (Jews and Christians); however, any children from such marriage automatically belong to the Muslim father's faith. Many Islamic scholars explain this gender difference in gender marriage restrictions by explaining that Islam considers marriage an unequal relationship. That is, a wife is subservient to her husband and Islam forbids Muslim women, who are superior because of their religion, from placing themselves in a subservient position to a man with an inferior religion. Sharia stipulates severe punishment for non-Muslim and dhimmi men (a non-Muslim in an Islamic state) who marry and consummate their relationship with Muslim women. Hadud punishments are also stipulated for women who marry non-Muslims on their own accord. If after marriage, the husband leaves Islam or converts to another religion such as Christianity, Judaism, Hinduism or Buddhism, the marriage of the Muslim woman is automatically dissolved. This principle was established at the time of the Prophet. For example, when Ramla bint Abi Sufyan's husband converted to Christianity, her marriage was declared void by the Prophet because of the husband's decision to leave Islam.

The seventh is female **genital mutilation**. There is no mention of female or male circumcision in the Quran. Although its origins are pre-Islamic, female circumcision, also known as female genital mutilation (FGM) became associated with Islam because of the high value placed on female chastity, and is found only within or near Islamic communities. Muhammad did not subject any of his daughters to this practice. However, female circumcision is praised in several hadiths as noble, but not required. There is a widespread belief in several countries, particularly Mali, Eritrea, Mauritania, Guinea and Egypt, that female genital mutilation is a religious requirement. However, there is a concerted effort underway to end the practice of female genital mutilation. In Mauritania, "health campaigners estimate that more than 70 percent of Mauritanian girls undergo the partial or total removal of their external genitalia for non-medical reasons." In January 2010, 34 Islamic scholars signed a fatwa banning the practice.

In my next and final letter on Islam, I will discuss Islam Extremism.

References:

1. *What everyone Needs to Know About Islam*, John L. Esposito
2. *A History of God*, Karen Armstrong
3. *Islam*, Karen Armstrong
4. *God and his Prophet: The Religion of Islam*, The Great Courses, John Swanson
5. *Cultural Literacy in America,* The Great Courses, Mark Bergson
6. *Great World Religions: Islam*, The Great Courses, John L. Esposito
7. The Wikipedia, Various newspaper, and Magazine Articles

Letter 9 – Islam Extremism

Religious fundamentalism is the father of extremism and, unfortunately, there is no shortage of religious fundamentalism for it exists in Judaism, Christianity, Hinduism, and Buddhism. In fact, it exists in all religions since it seems to arise as a result of the conflict between modernity and the adherence to specific religious beliefs such as the literal interpretation of the Bible or the Quran.

Islam is the youngest religion and the rise of fundamentalism in Islam seems to have parallel issues that mirror Christianity's conflict with modernity. Initially fundamentalist, when confronted with modernity attempt to reform their religion but soon realize they can only go so far in accommodating modernity and then they begin to resort to more extreme measures. Well, why is this?

First, there is a deep feeling of disappointment with certain factors of modernity such as pornography, abortion, women's liberation, sex films, etc.; second, there is a growing fear that secular elements of the population intend to wipe out their religion; third, as their fear rises they become more extreme in their interpretation of their religion and begin to overstress those elements that are opposed to modernity; and, last, for whatever reason, they begin to stress the value of women in more traditional home oriented role. I suspect this may be because a woman is expected to educate the children thereby assuring the retention of the cultural values related to that religion. On the other hand, it may be because most religions are interpreted within the context of a patriarchal society.

All fundamentalists, to include Muslim fundamentalists, seem to share these common characteristics. Fundamentalism and fear of secularism seem to have a symbiotic relationship for fundamentalists views and behavior seem to become more extreme the greater the felt pressure to modernize. This, in turn, exposes the deep polarization in society between those who enjoy and benefit from secularism and those who are afraid of change and, as time passes, the coercive differences between modernity and fundamental religious beliefs become so great that for all practical purposes secularists and fundamentalists become two distinct elements of the same society. Because of this it is easy for the very religious to become an isolated community and feel they need to begin to use religion as a political tool and rebel against the secularist tendency to exclude religion from society.

In the United States we can see this in the desire for the Christian right to create a high wall between the state and the church but a low wall between the church and the state.

The use of religion as a political tool can, in turn, lead to violent extremism. It should be noted, however, that Islam neither supports nor condones the use of illegitimate violence and the Quran does not advocate or encourage terrorism.

So how did certain elements of Islam become extreme and begin to use violence as a political tool in their desire to combat secularism by creating an Islamic state?

Maududi – The Birth of Islamic Extremism

Abul Ala Maududi was perhaps the earliest Islamic fundamentalist who preached violence and the creation of an Islamic state. He viewed the rise of the western powers in the 20th century in Islamic countries as a potential threat to Islam. This, he felt, was a threat that might possibly crush Islam and, because of this, thought that Muslims must band together to counter this encroaching western secularism. He felt that God alone was supreme and no one need take orders from another human being and that revolution against the western powers was the duty of all Muslims and so he called for a *universal jihad* against the west because his fear of cultural annihilation led him to include jihad with the Five Pillars of Islam. In 1941, Maududi founded *Jamaat-i-Islami* (the Islamic Society) in British India where he proposed forming an Islamic state based upon Sharia law. Maududi, after its creation, moved to Pakistan in 1947 and worked to turn it into an Islamic state under Sharia law. For example, Maududi supported the complete veiling and segregation of women since he believed a Muslim society could not be Islamic without Sharia law. He was also the first to conceptualize the "*Islamic state*" and the idea of the "*Islamic revolution.*" Maududi believed that *jihad* should be used to create a world-wide Islamic community and allied his organization with the *Muslim Brotherhood* of Egypt which also believed in strict Sharia law.

Sayyid Qutb

Maududi may have taken the first step toward Islamic Fundamentalism and the creation of an Islamic state but most scholars view *Sayyid Qutb* as the founder of Sunni Fundamentalism although greatly influenced by Maududi. Qutb joined the Muslim Brotherhood in 1953 and was imprisoned by Nassar in 1956. While imprisoned he became convinced that religion and secularism could not exist peacefully in the same society. The violent secularism of Nassar led him to espouse a form of Islam that distorted the message of both the Quran and the Hadith. Qutb believed in religious tolerance but only after the political victory of Islam and the creation of an Islamic state. Nassar had Qutb executed in 1966 but not before he had influenced the Taliban, Al Queda, ISIL, and the Iranian Revolution.

The Taliban

The *Taliban* (translated as *students* in Pashtun) are fundamentalists who interpret the Quran and Hadith based upon the narrow education they received in the *Madrasas* of Pakistan.

Madrasas are a place of learning and studying and is currently used to describe an Islamic School. Madrasas became a contentious issue after 9/11 because western politicians and the western media began to associate them with terrorist training and jihadist breeding grounds. It is true that some madrasas, particularly those in the northwest territories of Pakistan, have become radicalized; nevertheless, Madrasas do have a long history as mainstream educational institutions. For example, the Indonesian *pesantens* (residential schools) have long been noted for their teaching of moderate Islam.

Mohammed Omar is the founder and spiritual leader of the Taliban since its founding in 1994. The Taliban came to power in Afghanistan in 1996 and were determined to return Afghanistan to their view of the original Islamic community. They began by making religion a tool of oppression and violence especially against women.

Their strict interpretation of Sharia has included the repression of women by their religious police. For example, under their interpretation of Islamic law women were not allowed to be treated by male doctors unless accompanied by a male chaperone; they faced public flogging and execution for violations of the Taliban's laws. In addition, the Taliban allowed and, in some cases, encouraged marriage for girls under the age of 16. It is estimated by some analysts that, under the Taliban, as high as 80% of Afghan marriages were forced.

Other Taliban restriction on women included wearing the Burqa, not wearing high heels, not speaking loudly in pubic, painting over windows in the ground floor dwellings to prevent women from being seen, banning women from being filmed, and banning women from radio, television, or public gatherings. Just from these laws alone it is obvious that the Taliban were very strict in their views of women.

The Taliban movement traces its origin to the Pakistani-trained mujahideen in northern Pakistan, during the Soviet war in Afghanistan (1979-1989). About 90,000 Afghans, including Mohammad Omar, were trained by Pakistan's Inter-Services Intelligence (ISI) during the 1980s. After the fall of the Soviet-backed regime of Mohammad Najibullah in 1992, several Afghan political parties agreed on a peace and power-sharing agreement known as the *Peshawar Accord*. This, however, was not in Pakistan's interests for they wanted to expand their sphere of influence in Central Asia, and did not expect the new Afghanistan leaders to subordinate their own nationalist objectives in order to help Pakistan realize its regional ambitions.

In 1991, the Taliban, a movement originating from *Jamiat Ulema-e-Islam* (Assembly of Islamic Clergy) which organized and ran religious Madrasa schools for Afghan refugees in Pakistan, began to develop in Afghanistan as a combined political-religious force. **Mullah Omar** started the Taliban movement with fewer than 50 armed madrasah students in his hometown of Kandahar, Iraq. Within months, however, 15,000 students arrived from the Pashtun madrassas in Pakistan. With the military support of the ISI and financial support from Saudi Arabia, the Taliban assumed control of Afghanistan in 1996.

That same year the Sudanese made it clear that Osama bin Laden, the leader of Al Qaeda, was no longer welcome so he moved his operation to Afghanistan now under the control of the Taliban. From there he began to plan the destruction of the Twin Towers on 9/11.

From 1995 to 2001, the Pakistani Inter-Services Intelligence (ISI) agency and military provided support to the Taliban. In addition, Al-Qaeda also supported the Taliban with regiments of imported fighters from Arab countries and Central Asia.

Toward the end of the Soviet military mission in Afghanistan, some mujahideen began to expand their operations to include Islamist struggles in other parts of the world, such as Palestine and Kashmir.

After the attacks of September 11, 2001, the Taliban were overthrown by the American-led invasion of Afghanistan but have since continued a low level insurgency aimed again at the overthrow of the Afghanistan government with continued support from the ISI. However, recent conflicts between the Pakistan Taliban in the Northwestern territories and the Pakistan government may lead the ISI to rethink their support for the Taliban. As far as I could determine, the Taliban ambitions and activities are restricted to only Afghanistan and Pakistan.

Al Gaeda

Al Qaeda (the Base) was formed by Osama bin Laden in 1988 in Afghanistan also during the Soviet/Afghanistan war. It got its name from the fact that bin Laden had established a 'base' for the training of Mujahedeen to fight the soviet invasion of Afghanistan. bin Laden and Ayman al-Zawahiri were particularly influenced by the teaching and writing of Sayyid Qutb. Based upon his teaching they began to envision the creation of a new world-wide Islamic caliphate. They also came to believe that the killing of civilians, particularly other fellow Muslims, was religiously sanctioned. This included the killing of the leaders of Muslim countries because they had failed to enforce Sharia law. They, therefore, ignored any aspect of the Quran which might be interpreted as forbidding the murder of civilians and other fellow Muslims. Al-Qaeda also opposed what it regarded as man-made laws and desired to replace them with a stricter form of Sharia law. Al-Qaeda leaders regard liberal Muslims, Shias, Sufis and other sects as Muslim heretics and attacked and killed them mercilessly. Above all, they felt that a Christian/Jewish alliance was conspiring to destroy Islam and needed to be combated.

The 1979-1989 Soviet/Afghanistan conflict was a turning point in the development of global jihad and the march by extremist toward an Islamic State. The Soviet/Afghanistan war had become globalized because of its many participants particularly those in the west. The US, and many Muslim governments, viewed the war as a ***good jihad*** against the soviets and because it could be followed across the world Muslim community on a daily basis it reinforced a sense of Islamic community thereby allowing the mujahidin to draw fighters from many parts of the world.

After the Soviet/Afghanistan war the global jihad became a rallying cry for bin Laden and Al Qaeda as they moved their battle to other countries claiming to be waging a holy war against the west and corrupt Muslim governments. As a result Al Qaeda became transnational in its identity, increased its ability to recruit fighters, increased its ability to formulate and attack strategic targets, and to better organize attack networks throughout the world.

Following the Soviet Union's withdrawal from Afghanistan in February 1989, bin Laden returned to Saudi Arabia just in time for the Iraqi invasion of Kuwait in 1990 that put the Saudi Kingdom and the House of Saud at risk. The world's most valuable oil fields were now within easy striking distance of Iraqi forces in Kuwait. At this time bin Laden offered the services of his mujahideen to King Fahd but the Saudi monarch refused his offer and decided instead to allow US and allied forces to deploy troops onto Saudi territory.

This deployment infuriated bin Laden for he believed the presence of foreign troops in the "***land of the two mosques***" (Mecca and Medina) profaned sacred soil. After speaking publicly against the Saudi government for harboring American troops, he was banished and forced to live in exile in Sudan.

From around 1992 to 1996, al-Qaeda and bin Laden were based in Sudan, however, due to bin Laden's continuous verbal assault on King Fahd, the Saudi government demanded his passport and revoked his citizenship. In addition, his family was persuaded to cut off his yearly stipend of $7 million dollars, his Saudi assets were frozen and his family publicly disowned him. There is, however, been a continuing controversy over whether or not he continued to receive support from his family and/or the Saudi government.

In 1996 the Sudanese government made it clear, perhaps because of Saudi pressure, that bin Laden was not welcome so he moved his operation to Taliban controlled Afghanistan which provided a perfect location for al-Qaeda headquarters since it was largely isolated from American political influence and military power. It was from this location that bin Laden began to plan and finally execute the 9/11 attack.

It was in 1996, that bin Laden announced a jihad by al-Qaeda to expel foreign troops and interests from Islamic lands. He issued a fatwa declaring jihad against the US and its allies and began to focus on planning attacks against the US and the West. The fatwa called upon Muslims to kill Americans and their allies when and where they could. This was met with some resistance by the *ulama* because they felt bin Laden did not possess the traditional Islamic scholarly qualifications to issue a fatwa. That, like most things, did not stop bin Laden because, just as he had rejected Quranic teaching not in his favor so he rejected the authority of the *ulama* since he considered them the paid employees of heretic Muslim leaders. To bin Laden, the presence of any infidel soldiers in the homeland of the prophet was sacrilege. He fancied himself a modern-day Saladin intent on liberating the Muslim lands from the infidels and in the process killing as many of them as possible. To us, that does not make a lot of sense, but to him it made perfect sense to kill and humiliate the "great Satan" because his (bin Laden) only audience was Allah.

The long term strategy of Al Qaeda was to collapse the US economy leading to global political instability which, in turn, would lead to a global jihad led by al-Qaeda resulting in the installation of a *Wahhabi Caliphate* across the world. This is obviously a long term strategy that I'm not sure was ever viable; however, it has caused and will continue to cause a tremendous amount of destruction and death around the world.

Osama bin Laden was a member of the *Wahhabi sect of Sunni Saudi Arabia*. As mentioned previously there are many interpretation of Islam but Wahhabi Islam is among the most ultraconservative. Wahhabi takes its name from *Muhammad Ibn Abd al-Wahhab* (1703-1791) who rejected the normal practice of Islam and called for a return to the "fundamentals" of Islam, the Quran and the Sunnah. Al Wahhab joined forces with *Muhammad ibn Saud* (the House of Saud) to subdue and unite the tribes of Arabia and convert them to a fundamental view of Islam. Unfortunately, in this view you are either a Muslim or a non-Muslim, you believe or you do not, you are either in the realm of Islam or the realm of warfare. Wahhabism is so extreme that it resulted in the destruction of the Karbala tomb of Hussein, the son of Ali, which is a venerated site and pilgrimage by the Shiite. This has become a major source of conflict between **Shii Iran** and **Sunni Wahhabi Saudi Arabia**. I believe their conflict is viewed by both states as existential.

Al-Qaeda has carried out a total of six major terrorist attacks, four of them in its jihad against America. In each case their leadership planned the attack years in advance, arranging for the shipment of weapons and explosives and using its privatized businesses to provide operatives with safe houses and false identities. These attacks included Yemen, the World Trade Center, the Nairobi Embassy, the destroyer USS Cole, and the 911 attack that destroyed the Twin Towers and killed approximately 3000 American civilians.

The loss of key leaders and the death of Osama bin Laden has, however, resulted in al-Qaeda's operations being reduced from actions that were controlled from the top down, to actions by franchise associated groups, to actions of lone-wolf, individual operators. Some experts argue that al-Qaeda has fragmented into a variety of regional movements that have little connection with one another. Others, however, argue that al-Qaeda is still an integrated network that is strongly led from the Pakistani tribal areas and has a powerful strategic purpose.

There are some, however, who believe Al Qaeda has no epicenter, but is simply an idea that has spread to other countries where terrorist cells, unique to each country, have been formed although driven by a common ideology.

I do not subscribe to this theory. From my perspective, the terrorist ideas and ideology associated with Al Qaeda are still formulated in the northwest territories of Pakistan and overlapping Afghanistan area. This epicenter, in turn, serves as an inspiration to other terrorists around the world and as long as this epicenter exists, the spread of this terrorist ideology will continue, therefore, they must be eliminated. This does not mean that eliminating the epicenter eliminates the threat. It simply means that we lower the risk of attacks to our homeland. I suspect there will continue to be offshore attacks to our national interest because Al Qaeda will remain a second order threat. Certainly, it has been forced to evolve and adapt in the aftermath of 9/11 and the subsequent killing of bin Laden, and there are some analysts who no longer consider them a serious threat especially when compared to ISIL. Of the two, certainly ISIL is the more extreme and dangerous.

ISIL

The *Islamic State of Iraq and the Levant* (ISIL) also called the *Islamic State of Iraq and Syria* (ISIS) is a Sunni, extremist, jihadist rebel group based in Iraq and Syria that is intent on forming an Islamic State, a Caliphat. Make no mistake this is a combined criminal/terrorist organization that follows an extreme interpretation of Islam, promotes religious violence, and regards those who do not agree with its interpretations of the Quran and the Sunnah as infidels and will gladly kill them.

Its philosophy is represented by a Black Standard variant of Muhammad's battle flag. The flag shows the seal of the Muhammad within a white circle, with the phrase above it, "*There is no God but Allah*".

The group was founded by Abu Musab al-Zarqawi under the name *Jama'at al-Tawhid wal-Jihad* (the Organization of Monotheism and Jihad) in 1999, and after Zarqawi swore allegiance to bin Laden in 2004, the organization was renamed *Tanzim Qaidat al-Jihad fi Bilad al-Rafidayn* (the Organization of Jihad's Base in Mesopotamia) better known as *al-Qaeda in Iraq* (AQI). In 2006, it joined other Sunni insurgent groups which consolidated into the *Islamic State of Iraq* (ISI). Some analysts trace its roots back to the Muslim Brotherhood in Egypt while others trace it back to Wahhabism.

The ISIL gained a significant presence in Anbar province and other areas, but proved so violent in attacking civilians, killing prisone, and executing suicide attack, that Sunni Iraqis and other insurgent groups soon rose up against them. In 2011 al-Baghdadi began sending Syrian and Iraqi ISIL members experienced in guerilla warfare across the border into Syria in order to establish an organization inside the country. They were led by a Syrian known as *Abu Muhammad al-Jawlani* and immediately began to recruit fighters and establish cells throughout the country.

In 2013, the group changed its name to the *Islamic State of Iraq and the Levant* (ISIL) because of its more inclusivist term. It grew significantly during the Syrian Civil war under the leadership of Abu Bakr al-Baghdadi. However, after an eight-month power struggle, al-Qaeda found they could not control ISIL and cut all ties with it. The original aim of ISIL was to establish an Islamic state in Sunni regions of Iraq and, after it joined the Syrian Civil War, this came to also include the Sunni areas of Syria.

In 2014, ISIL proclaimed a ***worldwide caliphate*** with ***Abu Bakr al-Baghdadi*** as its ***caliph*** who claimed to be a descendant and the successor to Muhammad. The group then renamed itself simply the ***Islamic State*** (IS). As a caliphate, it claims religious, political, and military authority over all Muslims no matter where they may be. It rejected the political divisions in the Middle East that were established by the Western powers during World War I in the Sykes–Picot Agreement and took as its immediate goal the establishment of a Sunni Islamic state in Iraq and the Levant region, which covers Syria, Jordan, Israel, Palestine, Lebanon, Cyprus, and Hatay province in southern Turkey.

Abu Bakr al-Baghdadi was named head of the Islamic State of Iraq (ISI) in 2010 after its leaders, Abu Abdullah al-Rashid al-Baghdadi and Abu Ayyub al-Masri, were killed by a US–Iraqi operation in April 2010. He is an Iraqui national who has a reward of $10 million dollars on his head. The only higher reward is for the head of Ayman al-Zawahiri, the head of Al Qaeda, who has a reward of $25 Million on his head.

Little is known of Al-Baghdadi and what is known is very sketchy. It is known that Al-Baghdadi was imprisoned at Camp Bucca along with other future leaders of ISIL from 2005 to 2009. Between March and April 2011, the ISI claimed 23 attacks south of Baghdad, all allegedly carried out under al-Baghdadi's command. Al-Baghdadi remained leader of ISIL until its formal expansion into Syria in 2013, when he announced the formation of the **Islamic State of Iraq and the Levant (ISIL)**.

In order to accomplish, this ISIL began a campaign of '**ethnic cleansing**' and internet propaganda based upon beheadings, mass executions, sexual violence against women, persecution against minority groups, and the destruction of cultural artifacts. As terrorists go these guys have proved themselves to be the most vicious in the desert and have struck fear in the hearts of everyone.

As of September 2014, there is estimated to be about eight million Iraqis and Syrians living in areas controlled by ISIL In this area former government workers maintain their jobs and are paid by the states after pledging allegiance to ISIL, welfare services are provided, price controls established, and taxes imposed on the wealthy while the captured dams continues to provide electricity and water. In this area only the police and soldiers are paid by ISIL.

Most of the people in this region have acquiesced to the presence of ISIL, therefore, its future looks promising. They have become well entrenched and most analysts believe the ineffective Syrian or Iraqi forces cannot dislodge them even with the help of American air power. The controlled population is not expected to rise against them since, from one analytical point of view, there appears to be adequate supplies of water and oil. In addition, ISIL controls about 40% of Iraq's wheat production and continues to support adequate food supplies which is crucial to popular support.

From another analytical point of view ISIL's attempt at nation building is a failure. In Mosul, the water has become undrinkable because there is no chlorine. Hepatitis is spreading and flour is scarce. In all the territories controlled by ISIL there is growing deprivation and disorganized, erratic leadership. In Raqqa, Syria, the ISIL capital, water and electricity are available only three to four hours per day while garbage lies uncollected on the streets. Sharia law, if anything, has grown even harsher. Shop keepers close their store five times daily for prayer, there are public executions for theft, blasphemy, and dissent. Homosexuals, under a new law, are thrown from tall buildings.

Despite these contrasting views, Western-backed intervention, "boots on the ground", is unlikely, therefore, ISIL is expected for the foreseeable future to continue to control an area the size of Pennsylvania.

The Iranian Theocracy

I want to close this letter, the last in this series on Understanding Islam, by discussing Iran and its theocratic government, for the future main actor in middle-east Islam will be the Islamic Republic of Iran. In 1979, the autocratic rule of the Shah was overthrown and a unique political system was installed in Iran which was part parliament and part religious theocracy, but under the leadership of a Supreme

Ayatollah and a government dominated by clerics belonging to the Twelver Shia branch of Islam.

The Shii theocracy of Iran is intent on developing a nuclear weapon as part of its security against its surrounding Sunni neighbors, particularly the Saudis, who along with Israel, view the clerics of Iran armed with a nuclear weapon as an existential threat.

The United States hopes that the imposition of crippling economic sanctions on the Islamic Republic of Iran will persuade the mullah led regime to cease their pursuit of nuclear weapons and to temper its ideological extremism. In addition to the economic sanctions, President Obama, in coordination with Israel, authorized the use of a computer worm called Stuxnet to sabotage Iran's uranium enrichment facility at Natanz (this action is denied by both the US and Israel). The power of Stuxnet gambit is that the Iranians can't know what other malware may have been planted in their computers or what new computer attacks the U.S. may unleash. I simply do not think that economic sanctions or cyberattacks against Iran will detract them from their pursuit of nuclear weapons. The Iranian Shii clerics hate the surrounding Sunnis and intend to dominate them through nuclear power. Perhaps even more important to the Iranian clerics is their theologically motivated desire to see the Jewish state entirely eliminated.

The smaller Sunni dominated countries surrounding Iran are scared to death that Iran will develop nuclear weapons for they know they will be threatened to either capitulate or be annihilated. Iranians are Persians and the surrounding Arabs have lived with the Persians for centuries and realize, as Churchill said, they are the "**Huns of the Middle East**" and will attempt to recreate the Persian empire through threats or, if necessary, violence.

The general consensus seems to be that if Israel or America allows Iran to cross the nuclear threshold then the Arab countries of the Gulf, out of self-protection, would have no choice but to leave the American sphere of influence and ally themselves with Iran. In addition, they will see the potential need to also obtain nuclear weapons. Arab leaders simply do not believe that Obama really understands the dimensions of the regional ambitions of the Persians and, for them, the weak Obama foreign affairs management and a lack of understanding Iranian ambitions is a toxic witch's brew.

Iran and Israel are sworn enemies and Israel believes that Iran will, without hesitation, use a nuclear weapon on them. For Israel, this is an existential threat and they will, without hesitation, attempt to destroy the nuclear manufacturing facilities of Iran by any means possible. The overriding national security tenet of Israel is that no regional adversary should be allowed to achieve nuclear parity with Israel. Israel learned a lesson in the crematoriums of the Holocaust and do not intend to relive that experience. The wounds of the Holocaust, for the Israelis, will never heal. In addition, they believe that an Obama policy toward a nuclear Iran will be one of containment rather than attacking it even though Obama has said a nuclear Iran would be unacceptable. Because of this belief, Israel, in my opinion, will undertake a unilateral attack on Iran if and when it feels it is necessary. This, in my opinion, will be within one month of Iran acquiring a nuclear weapon and nothing the US or anyone else can do will dissuade them from that attack

The Shia Mullahs leading Iran view the Jews as being contaminated because of their treason against Muhammad when Mecca attacked Medina during the *Battle of the Ditch* in 627 AD. The Shia clerics of the 17th and 18th century viewed the Jews as "*the leprosy of creation*" and "*the most unclean of the human race*." The Iranians deny the Holocaust and label it as an invented story. The Iranian leadership believes that the use of an atomic weapon against Israel would destroy Israel completely, while a nuclear attack against the Islamic countries would only cause damages. From their perspective, since they believe they could not be destroyed, there is nothing to prevent them from attacking Israel once they have a nuclear weapon. They simply do not subscribe to the theory of mutually assured destruction, however dangerous that may be.

Here, we have the makings of Armageddon in the Middle East and this is the reason why the US has been attempting to slow down the rate, or hopefully curtail, the development of the nuclear program in Iran. I hope diplomacy will succeed but, unfortunately, because of the extremism of the Iranian theocratic government and the perceived weak leadership of Obama, I do not think it can or will.

Iran is intent on developing a nuclear capability despite their protests that their nuclear facilities are only for peaceful purposes. Israel simply does not believe that is the case and is prepared to defend themselves with nuclear weapons which reportedly consists of more than 100 weapons, mainly two-stage thermonuclear devices, capable of being delivered by missile, fighter-bomber, and the two Israeli submarines on station in the Persian Gulf.

If Israel attacks Iran, and I believe they will if Iran develops a nuclear capability, it will be a combined submarine missile attack and an air attack most likely carried out by between 75 and 100 F-15s and F-16s. Prior to the attack the Israelis can be expected to go on a pre attack alert several times just to condition everyone without divulging which alert will be the actual attack. The aircraft will cross Saudi Arabia, most likely refueling in the desert with Saudi secret help, before proceeding to attack the uranium-enrichment facility at Natanz, the enrichment site at Qom, the nuclear research center at Esfahan, the Bushehr reactor site and other main sites of the Iranian nuclear program. This attack, whether it succeeds or fails will change the Middle East and Islam forever for it will result in a full blown regional war with thousands of Christian, Israeli, Sunni and Shii deaths.

If Israel succeeds in their attack, I suspect they will be roundly condemned by the moderate Arab regimes while receiving their secret thanks. If they fail it will simply reinforce the theocratic regime in Iran. Either way the Hezbollah will unleash a firestorm of missiles against Israel which will need to be combated.

Whether Israel succeeds or fails, the US, because our interests are aligned with Israel, will once again be at war because we will need to defend both Israel and Saudi Arabia.

I find it disappointing to end my last letter on Understanding Islam in such an alarmist fashion but feel I would be remiss in my duty to the family if I did not give my truthful analysis of what I expect to happen.

References:

1. *What everyone Needs to Know About Islam*, John L. Esposito
2. *A History of God*, Karen Armstrong
3. *Islam*, Karen Armstrong
4. *God and his Prophet: The Religion of Islam*, The Great Courses, John Swanson
5. *Cultural Literacy in America,* The Great Courses, Mark Bergson

6. *Great World Religions: Islam*, The Great Courses, John L. Esposito
7. The Wikipedia, Various newspaper, and Magazine Articles

Part 2

Health Care

And

The Affordable Care Act

-The ACA-

Part 2 – Health Care and the ACA

Context for the Health Care Letters

In the past I have written several missives related to the status of the Affordable Care Act (ACA) in which I summarized the objectives and selected parts of the Act. I wrote selectively about the ACA because of its complexity. Although I have studied and read extensively on the ACA ,nevertheless, I still do not fully understand each and every part of it. I ended my summary by indicating that I do not think the Republicans will be able to kill the Act despite their extraordinary effort to deny insurance to the poor. I still maintain, though, that it is a work in progress because it was passed in such haste that many things were done poorly or not at all. I suspect it will need several more revisions to make it as effective as it should be.

When I had completed the missives on the ACA, or at least completed those missives I had planned, I realized that I had not really said anything about the American health care system prior to the ACA and the necessity for the ACA. That is, what did the American health care system look like from around the turn of the century, 1900, until around 2014 when the ACA began to be implemented and why exactly did we need the ACA? My first letter in this series is an attempt to remedy that oversight for without this background the letters about the ACA will not make sense.

During the period prior to the ACA there were several attempts by both Republicans and Democrats to improve the health care system and, except for Medicare and Medicaid, none succeeded. Well, why were there so many attempts to improve the American health care system by both Republicans and Democrats? Since both parties agreed upon the necessity for change they must have known something was wrong with the current healthcare system.

Hopefully the first letter of this series will highlight for you some of the concerns of both Republicans and Democrats with that system. Do not be put off by the length of the first letter which is around eighteen pages. Just wade through it for only then will you truly have some insight into why our current health care system needed improving and the necessity for the Affordable Care Act (ACA).

J.T. Oney

Letter 1 - Healthcare Before the ACA

In order to provide some historical context for the ACA, I thought it would be both interesting and beneficial to review the American health care system prior to the ACA in order to provide some logic for its introduction. In order to do that some basic questions need answering. For example: Why is there a health care system at all? What caused it? Why do we need it? How does it operate?

In order to answer these questions we have to review the various haphazard implementations of the health care system over the last 100 years starting around 1900. That is, how did the hospitals, physicians and the private insurance companies interact to develop the American Health care system over the last 100 years?

Hospitals and Physicians

Currently hospitals are the dominant player in our health care system. There are currently approximately 4,985 acute care hospitals in the US and, as of 2012, there was roughly $970 billion spent on hospital care and that is more than Social Security ($730 billion) and defense ($650 billon). Obviously, it is currently a major industry but that was not always the case.

The early hospitals, prior to the 1900s, were mainly for the poor with the wealthy being treated at home. The treatments had very little physical intervention and mainly concentrated on religious exhortations. The Greek physician, Galen, who served the Romans as a physician around 170 AD, apparently had a more modern practice and for this reason physicians around 1900 were in disrepute because of their incompetence. Most medical students were enrolled in medical school for two years and attended only six months per year and then repeated the same classes the second year. Obviously medical school left a lot to be desired, and because of that most medical knowledge was acquired in practice most often in a hospital.

The early hospitals were largely funded by the leading citizens with the physicians volunteering their services. The extensive introduction, in the early 1900s, of radiology, sterile techniques and anesthesia allowed the hospitals to begin to change from body warehouses, for the poor to providing advanced surgical procedures and patient care. They came to depend less on charity and more on payments from those people who could afford it.

The Flexor Report

The American Medical Association, in 1904, established the Council on Medical Education and based upon the 1910 **Flexor Report** finally established a standard for medical education: a college degree, two years of preclinical work and two years of clinical instructions in hospitals. Simultaneous with the Flexor Report the Physicians began to campaign for licensing laws to drive out the quacks and poorly trained physicians who were bringing the medical profession into disrepute.

Over the next twenty-five years the Flexor Report had three major results. **First**, clinical training moved away from the doctor's office and the patients' homes to the hospital ward where the hospital became the site for medical training. **Second**, by extending the training period to eight years, a four year degree plus four years of medical school, physician training excluded students from poorer families. **Third**, Generalist where eased out of medical school faculty in favor of Specialist.

It should be noted at this time that Alice Lloyd, of whom I am great admirer, recognized the need for physicians, particularly from the poorer families in Eastern Kentucky, and began to fund the last two years of college normally at the University of Kentucky. For those students still showing promise she would also see to it that funds were made available for selected students to complete a medical degree at Louisville if they promised to return to serve their mountain community.

Despite these changes, the hospitals continued to operate with their own standards and procedures and were not subject to either federal or state guidelines.

In some places, primarily the east, voluntary and municipal hospitals dominated and were funded primarily by wealthy citizens. In the South and West physician owned for-profit hospitals dominated. Tension over money, still existing today, arose between the physicians and the hospitals. Hospitals needed physicians to refer patients to the hospital but yet hospitals did not pay the physicians and had little or no control over how they practiced in the hospitals. On the other hand, physicians needed hospitals for surgeries and diagnostic procedures and admitting privileges; that is, the privilege to admit and treat patients in a particular hospital.

Not only did the hospitals resist any external oversight but so did the physicians. Physician, since they worked singly or in small groups, resisted any attempt to organize patient care calling this "**corporate control of medicine**." Through the AMA they vigorously defended the value of small practices and fee-for-service medicine.

However, remote geographical locations for the railroad, mining, and lumber industry required the hiring of physicians to attend to the workers in these remote areas. In addition to hiring the remote physicians, the companies also controlled the medical care of their workers.

If you have difficulty visualizing this, think of Doctor Dempsey and the practice he had at the end of the swinging bridge located in the Bottom (West Garrett, Ky). He was basically a mining camp doctor whose medical practice was controlled by the mining company that hired him. He initially practiced out of his house but eventually built himself a block office that still stands. Deke and Shade Napier hauled most of his sand from the creek bank to build his office. While not practicing medicine, he carved the stones for the building himself.

Physicians came to distrust any intermediary whether the hospital or the company that threatened the physicians income and power. They even carried this distrust over to health insurance companies that might pay physicians; after all, they were corporations that might threaten the physician's control over their patients care.

World War 1 to World War 2

During WW1 the US established veteran's benefits and disability compensation. In 1930 the **Veterans Administration** (VA) was established to consolidate veteran's programs into one department. At that time there were 54 veterans hospitals all generally located in rural areas with low pay and a poorly trained staff. The advent of WW2 changed that. Congress recognized the need for additional hospitals and passed the *Hill Burton Act* in 1946. This was the first major health care act funded by the federal government and provided federal support for hospital construction throughout the country. It required communities to provide two-thirds of the construction cost, which meant that the poorer communities could not participate, which, in turn, meant that federally funded hospitals ended up in prosperous communities. In addition, even though federal funds were provided there was limited federal oversight and involvement in hospital policies and practices.

The Rise of Health Insurance

Between WW1 and WW2 health insurance arrived on the scene. The start of health insurance is fixed at 1929 in Dallas, Texas and was really prepaid hospital coverage in which Baylor University Hospital provided Dallas school teachers up to 21 days of hospital care for six dollars per teacher.

This type of arrangement quickly spread to other areas. The American Hospital Association strongly supported this type plan and in 1939 used the **Blue Cross** symbol for these types of hospital insurance plans. Twenty-five states had laws permitting the Blue Cross plans to be tax exempt, charitable organizations which were a significant advantage to these types of plans. They charged the same rate for all insured patients regardless of whether sick, healthy, old or young, and regardless of gender. These plans were primarily sold to large organizations.

During this time large commercial insurance companies avoided selling health insurance because of four primary reasons:

First, they feared sick people would buy health insurance leading to **adverse selection**;

Second, the company would have to **assess the risk** of each applicant which would be very expensive;

Third, the terms "sickness and health" were vague and hard to define which could potentially lead to abuse and lawsuits and;

Four, people used hospitals so rarely that they simply paid cash and there was no need for insurance.

However, the success of the Blue Cross plans were encouraging so commercial insurance companies jumped into the market since they began to realize that by insuring all the workers in a large organization that the problem of adverse selection and high assessment cost could be overcome. That is, if **the pool of patients was large enough** then the risk could be shared across all patients in that pool.

In the 1930s and 1940s the commercial market for health insurance exploded primarily because the physicians and the American Medical Association (AMA) softened their resistance to health insurance for three primary reasons:

First, the Great Depression reduced the utilization of everything to include physicians' services resulting in less income;

Second, there was increasing calls for government sponsored health insurance programs and the AMA favored private versus public programs;

Third, physicians began to worry that the Blue Cross plans might include payment for physician services in hospitals cutting them entirely out of the market.

Beginning in 1929 state medical societies began to offer coverage for office visits, house calls, and in-hospital physician services. These became known as the **Blue Shield** Plans.

World War 2 and Beyond

In 1940 over 20 million Americans had some form of health insurance but things were about to change not only for the insurance companies, but also for physicians and hospitals. WW2 was looming on the horizon and millions of men were in uniform and because labor was in short supply the industrial workers wanted higher wages and employers intended to pay it. But hold on, President Roosevelt, with the *Stabilization Act* of 1942, required prices and wages be stabilized at September 15, 1942 levels. However, his executive order implementing the act **excluded insurance benefits** from controls. In addition, the **National War Labor Board** ruled that health insurance did not constitute the wages or salaries specifically limited by the Stabilization Act.

Therefore, one way to reward American laborers was not through increased pay but by providing them health insurance so by 1950 two-thirds of the American work force had health insurance for hospital stays. This, of course, impacted both the hospitals and the physicians. In addition, in 1954, the IRS issued a *tax exclusion* which declared that the monetary value of the employer sponsored health insurance was not part of the workers income.

The combination of exempting health insurance from the Wage Stabilization Act and the IRS health insurance tax break of 1954 firmly institutionalized employer sponsored health insurance in the US

Another postwar transformation in health care grew from the creation of *Medicare* in 1965. Aime Forand of the House Ways and Means Committee sponsored a bill that linked health insurance with Social Security and called it Medicare. This act had two major impacts on the US health care system:

First, the hospitals now had the funds to expand and upgrade their technology and

Second, the hospitals no longer needed to provide free or subsidized care to the elderly poor which took away from their bottom line. In addition, the Medicare payment was generous because it **paid hospitals cost plus a percentage** to compensate for capital expansion. This inflated payment system lasted until the introduction of *prospective payments* in 1983 (more on this later).

In the 1950s hospitals began establishing separate Intensive Care Units (ICU). The monitoring of heart rhythms became routine in the 1960s. In addition, the treatment of health problems through a heart catheter and long term dialysis also became possible. Previously fatal cases of leukemia in children began to be cured. In the late 1970s chemotherapy could also cure several different cancers. Throughout the 1970s, 80s and 90s high technology medical care advanced in the US Hospitals enabling physicians to work miracles.

Unfortunately, miracles come at a cost, which simply increased the need for health insurance.

As an aside the 1990s also brought hospital acquired infections such as MRSA, *Staphylococcus aureu,s* and super bugs. One out of every 20 hospital patients was subject to a hospital infection (Yes, I was one of those!). It is estimated that 100,000 people die a year from these infections.

As the number and variety of conditions physicians are able to treat increased, there has also been a growing number of disturbing medical errors. It is estimated that between 44,000 and 98,000 people die in hospitals as a result of medical errors.

In addition, as hospitals grew in technical complexity, so did impersonal treatment. Patients' personal physicians stopped making rounds and, instead, hospitals began to rely upon *Hospitalists* (in house physicians) to care for the patient. Inevitably, with the explosive growth of technology available to treat patients, so did the patient's bill and the need for health insurance.

Why Health Insurance

Insurance is one way people deal with uncertainties (risk). For example, this is how one deals with the potential or unexpected damage to homes, cars, and other property. In the absence of a national health system, like the U.K.'s National Health Service, insurance companies use **the market place** to implement health insurance.

However, there are practical problems with the market place. For example, not everyone (or their employer) can afford insurance, so **people are left uninsured**, some of whom will become sick and if they become sick, and everyone usually does, then this means that the uninsured can end up:

1. Either dying of treatable illnesses,
2. Seeking treatment for chronic conditions in emergency rooms,
3. Amassing large quantities of medical debt and ultimately going bankrupt.

Medical charity may cover some of the shortfall but it still does not cover all the uninsured. This means that the government tends to end up in the market - even if it doesn't want to directly run a national health care system - through subsidizing insurance for the uninsured poor. Think Medicare, Medicaid and the Affordable Care Act. In addition, for us Oney boys, think Tricare.

Republicans, for whatever reason, seem to ignore the costs to the economy of having large numbers of people dropping out of the workforce either due to chronic illness or death. From my perspective, these costs are just too high to ignore; therefore, people need medical insurance just as they need auto insurance, home insurance, etc. For them, there are three primary reasons for procuring health insurance.

The **First** reason is to protect the individual and large families from the large, unexpected financial losses when they get sick, and people do get sick on a random basis, which may result in large, unpredictable financial losses. In many cases, if the losses are high enough, it may even result in bankruptcy. In order to reduce the risk of a large financial loss people pay a small predictable amount of money to the insurance companies who, in turn, promise to pay a large amount of money if a random illness occurs. Sometimes this works, sometimes it doesn't.

One author gave this example. In 2008 Oregon ran out of funds to pay its portion of the Medicaid bills which left 90,000 people on its waiting list. Those managing the state Medicaid funds decided to conduct a lottery to enroll 30,000 people in Medicare (the amount of money it had) leaving 60,000 uninsured (More on Medicaid later).
Well, I did say there was a certain amount of uncertainty with regard to health but a lottery to see who lives and who dies? Now that is interesting!

Secondly, health insurance reduces the financial and psychological barriers to using health care services. Most people weigh risk versus rewards in any decision. With an illness an individual weighs the cost of pain relief against the cost of medical service. In this fashion, health insurance reduces the perceived cost, leading more people to utilize health service, which ultimately increases the need for health service. By the way, Actuarial science calls this "***insurance induced demand***." I love these made up terms!

Recently I had an abscessed tooth; however, my insurance (Medicare (Part A/B) and Tricare) does not cover dental care and, because of the excruciating pain, I decided that my out of pocket expense was worth the pain relief. At that time I could only imagine what a financially strapped individual might have done. Indeed, I did imagine them tying their tooth to a door knob then closing the door or reaching for a pair of pliers and pulling it themselves. Those seemed to be favorite remedies in the mountains when I was growing up.

Third, health insurance, through pooling, spreads the risk across a large number of people. I might have mentioned the unpredictability of sickness, well, that was not quite an accurate statement. In any given year 50% of the population hardly use health services while 10% of population use 66% of the health care service. In providing health, insurance companies, through *Actuarial Science*, determine in which group you belong. This allows then to determine (underwrite) how much to charge for a health service premium. For example, older people are more likely to get sick than younger people and, therefore, will be charged more.

Fortunately, the health of a pool of a larger population of people is more easily predicted than a smaller pool of people. The larger pool of people will contain more young and healthy adults, who will not take advantage of the medical services, but yet pay for the medical service of a smaller percentage of people in the pool who do get sick. That is, a larger group of people operating in this fashion (think ACA) can be insured more cheaply than a smaller group because there is less risk of a large unpredictable loss, therefore, big businesses are charged less to insure than a small business. Go figure!

Problems Providing Health Insurance

The insurance company must face and resolve two problems when providing health insurance. These are moral hazarding and adverse selection.

<u>**Moral hazarding**</u> means the selection of a more expensive test or procedure than is necessary. For example, ***Insurance Induced Demand*** leads to the increased use of health service. On the whole, this is good; however, it can also lead to a demand for a health service that is not necessary or lead a patient or physician to choose a more expensive test or procedure when a less expensive test or procedure might accomplish the same end. In order to counter moral hazarding, insurance companies employ a number of strategies.

One counter is to make people pay part of their health cost through a *deductible* which may range as high as $5,000 dollars. That is, high deductible plans may mean that the patient may have to pay as much as $5,000 dollars before the insurance company covers any health cost. **Another counter** is to have an individual pay a portion of the cost each time they use a service. This is generally in the form of a *co-payment* at the time a service is provided. This can be anywhere between $5 and $20 dollars. **Another counter** is when an individual pays a percentage of the hospital bill, for example, 20%. This is called *co-insurance*.

Adverse selection is the second problem faced by insurance companies. Adverse selection is the tendency for sicker people or people who will become sick to purchase health insurance. For example, if I have a heart problem, diabetes, or leukemia, then I intend to purchase health insurance for without insurance I will most likely go bankrupt. Or if I have a risky occupation such as working with asbestos, then I'm definitely going to purchase health insurance. One consequence of adverse selection is to raise the price of health insurance for all people. But why should the insurance company accept these free loaders? Why not just let them die? Well, as with moral hazarding, there are a number of ways for insurance companies to counter adverse selection.

The first way insurance companies counter adverse selection is to *deny people coverage* that have preexisting conditions; that is, just let them die. Brutal but effective! **The second way** insurance companies counter adverse selection is to *charge higher prices* for existing conditions. **A third counter** insurance companies can employ is to *exclude service* from the policy that relates to the preexisting condition. **A fourth way** is through *compulsion* by the creation of an extremely large pool of people who are forced to buy health insurance. For example, Medicare, because it is a very large group, eliminates adverse selection within that group. This is also the strategy being attempted by ACA.

Private Health Insurance

Before ACA approximately 85% of Americans were covered by health insurance while the remaining 15% were uninsured. Remember that the ACA is aimed at the uninsured 15% and not the insured 85%. In 2012 health insurance covered about 165 million people while the uninsured amounted to between 40 and 60 million.

One hundred and fifty million of those insured got their health insurance through their employer. That is, they had ***employer-sponsored insurance***. Within this category larger firms are more likely to offer health insurance than smaller firms. For example, about 98% of firms with 200 or more employees offer insurance whereas, just 50% of the firms with fewer than 10 workers provide insurance.

Why this discrepancy? Well, there seems to be three reasons for the discrepancy between the larger and smaller firms offering health insurance.

First, the larger firms get better insurance prices because they have a larger pool making the risk more predictable.

Secondly, workers at the larger firms have higher wages so that health insurance is a smaller fraction of their compensation and,

Third, the larger firms have human relations departments making it more efficient and practical to negotiate lower cost health insurance.

The next logical question is: Why do firms offer insurance at all? There seems to be two reasons for this.

First, highly skilled workers want health insurance and in order to hire and retain these workers firms offer health insurance as a "***golden handcuff***". Most employees believe the myth that their employers pay for their health insurance. For example, in 2012, on average, employers paid 74% of insurance premiums of a family and 83% of the premium for individual coverage. The truth, however, is that the employee pays for their health insurance through lower wages because employers simply substitute one form of compensation for another.

Second, employers' contribution to their employees' health insurance is tax exempt. Remember, in 1954 the IRS ruled that the employer's contribution to health insurance were excluded from the workers taxable income. That is, the employer takes advantage of an IRS tax-exclusion.

What I found surprising in doing the research for these series of letters is that this is the single largest tax break in the entire U.S. tax code. For example, in 2013, mortgage interest deduction was worth about $70Bwhile the health tax-exclusion was worth about $250B - that is a B as in Billion. Go figure!

Public Health Insurance

In addition to Private Health Insurance many people have their health insurance through public means, that is, through federal or state insurance plans. For example, 31% of Americans, about 97 million, have their health insurance through a variety of public programs such as Medicare, Medicaid, Tricare, etc. By far the two largest are Medicare and Medicaid. Both were created in 1965.

Medicare, in 2012, covered approximately 51 million Americans at a cost of $552B. **Medicaid**, since it is handled by both federal and state, covered 57 million Americans at a cost of $238B for the US Government and $176B for the states.

Medicare is classified as **social insurance**. People pay about 1.45 percent of their salary (this is FICA) and are eligible for Medicare when they become 65, or are disabled. Medicaid, even though it was passed at the same time as Medicare, is funded by both the federal and state governments but administered by the states.

Medicaid, prior to ACA, was a **means tested, needs test** program. That is, people are eligible for Medicaid if they are poor and are children, blind, physically disabled, elderly, mentally ill, pregnant, or mothers with young children. Many Americans are eligible for Medicaid, about 5 million, but do not enroll because many states, in order to reduce their budget, discourage enrollment through requiring many forms and documentation as well as frequent re-enrollment. (Some of the poorer Americans call Medicaid a **Mean Tested** program.)

Uninsured

About 15% of the population, between 40 and 60 million, are uninsured (to be factual no one knows the exact number of uninsured.). Approximately 2 million are undocumented aliens, however, the vast majority of those uninsured are the working poor. The Republicans, for whatever reason, view them as lazy and/or simply gaming the system. They do not seem to understand or want to understand the impact that sickness has on the efficient operation of the work place. The truth is that 40% of the uninsured have incomes under 100% of the poverty line (about $22K) and 55% of those earning under 100% of the poverty line are not offered insurance from their employers because they are employed by small companies.

Eight million are children and of that eight million, five million qualify for Medicaid but for one reason or another (primarily because the state governments want to save money) are not enrolled. 51% of the uninsured have been uninsured for three years or more.

I have never been able to understand why such a wealthy country as ours could morally justify such a large uninsured population especially its children.

Who Pays the Medical Bills - The Payers

The next logical question is this: When you get sick and have insurance who pays your medical bill? Just as there are two major categories of insurers there are also two major categories of payers - Private and Public.

Private Payers include such organizations as:

(1) **For-Profit Health Organizations.** There are about 1000 for-profit health organizations. The top eleven, in 2012, earned about $301.8B with a profit of $13.7B. The top five for profit are United, Aetna, Wellpoint, Cigna, and Humana, They alone earned $255.2B with a profit of $12.5B. The health care industry is obviously a highly profitable business and is highly interested in making a profit for their shareholders.

(2) **Blue Cross and Blue Shield.** These organizations were historically not-for-profit, state based plans; however, over the last couple of decades many have become for-profit organizations. Those organizations that are still not for-profit, Blue Cross/Blue Shield organizations insure around 40 million Americans with earnings of $179B and profits of $5.5B.

(3) **Health Maintenance Organizations (HMO)**. This includes organizations such as Kaiser and Group Health of Puget Sound. A typical HMO, for legal and liability reasons, is divided into a health subsidiary and an insurance function with both regulated by state officials. For example, the Kaiser Permanente Medical Group provides the health care while the Kaiser Health Plan provides the insurance. Kaiser, the largest HMO, as of 2012, insured around 9.1 million Americans, employed approximately 15,000 physicians, operated 37 hospitals and earned around $50.6B. I don't know what their profits were.

There are two additional Private health organizations worth mentioning – ERISA and COBRA.

ERISA or Employee Health Plans are plans sponsored and funded by either the employers or employees. Typically an employer hires an insurance company to process and pay the medical bills from hospitals and physicians. If, for example, Aetna, is hired to process the claims they provide *administrative service only* (ASO) only even though the employee thinks he may have insurance from Aetna.

Finally there is **COBRA or Consolidated Omnibus Budget Reconciliation Act**. This act provides that employees who have been terminated, work less hours or are retired may purchase the companies health insurance at reduced rates. The employer does not pay any of the premium so this insurance is typically more expensive.

Public Payers include organizations such as Medicare, Medicaid and Tricare. I will only discuss Medicare and Medicaid, however, most of us Oneys also fall under Tricare.

(1). **Medicare.** Of the two, Medicare is by far the largest and, as of 2013, enrolled about 50.8 million Americans. Medicare is divided into a number of separate parts of which the most common are Part A, Part B, Part C, and Part D.

> **Part A,** passed in 1965, pays for hospital care and is paid for by a 1.45% payroll tax (FICA) for both employees and employers. Interestingly, only about 20% of those eligible for Part A actually wind up in the hospital each year.

> **Part B**, also passed in 1965, pays for such things as physicians' visits, physical therapy, X-rays, most laboratory tests, walkers, etc. There are about 47.8 million Americans enrolled. Part B is funded by both a general federal revenue (75%) and income inked premiums (25%). Most Oneys will belong to Medicare Part A and Part B.

> **Part C**, Medicare Advantage, was passed in 1997, and enrolls about 13.6 million Americans. This is a preferred provided plan offered by insurance companies to Medicare beneficiaries. It covers the same benefits as Part A

and Part B but also include things such as prescription drugs, vision care, gym memberships, etc. We Oneys may want to look closely at this option. **Part D**, was implemented on 1 January, 2006, as part of the *Medicare Prescription, Improvement and Modernization Act of 2003*. This act was intended to subsidize the prescription medication cost of Medicare patients. Medicare beneficiaries have the option of applying for drug coverage through a Prescription Drug Plan or Medicare Advantage Plan. As of April 2010, there were 27.6 million Medicare Part D enrollees. I know of no Oney that has Part D coverage since most of us use Tricare for our prescription drugs.

Medicare is administered by the ***Centers for Medicare and Medical Services* (CMS),** an agency within the Department of Health and Human Services. CMS also administers the Medicaid and CHIP (Children's Health Insurance Program) Programs. CMS receives over one billion claims per year but does not actually pay the bills but instead contracts with private contractors, normally insurance companies, to pay the bills. Once a month Oneys should receive either a paper or electronic copy of their past expenditures in Medicare and/or Tricare. Interestingly, Medicare is filled with extra payments that encourage certain activities. For example, hospitals receive extra money (about $10B) to support the training of interns and medical residents. This is called *Graduate Medical Education (ME)*. In addition, Medicare also provides extra money (about $11B) to compensate hospitals for the care of the uninsured. This is called the *Disproportionate Share Hospital (DSH)*.

(2). **Medicaid** is jointly financed and administered by both the state and the federal government. The federal government sets minimum standards of service for Medicaid in addition to establishing eligibility and quality of care. The states have flexibility in determining eligibility standards, services paid for and the payment rates for hospitals and physicians; therefore, actual Medicaid benefits can differ from state to state.

There are approximately 56.5 million Medicaid enrollees for a total expenditure of $414B. Children account for 49 % of Medicaid enrollees but consume only about 20% of the total expenditure whereas the disabled make up 15% of the enrollees but consume approximately 42% of the expenditure. The elderly make up approximately 10% of the enrollees and consume about 23% of the funds.

The elderly and disabled whose income is below 100% of the federal poverty level (about $11,490 for an individual) are eligible for both Medicare and Medicaid (you Oney boys forget it. You are not eligible for Medicaid).These so-called *dual eligibles* are expensive and use about 40% of Medicare dollars and about 36% of Medicaid dollars.

Medicaid has generous benefits but few people seem to get those benefits. Why? This is primarily due to state requirements and low hospital and physician participation. Both physicians and dentists complain about low Medicaid payments and excessive paperwork; therefore, fewer than half the physicians and dentists participate in Medicaid.

Who Provides Health Care – The Providers

In the last section I discussed the **Payers;** that is, those organizations and individuals who actually pay for health care. In this section, I want to discuss those who provide health care, the **Providers**, to those requiring health care concentrating on hospitals, physicians and drug companies.

Make no mistake this is big business. For example, in 2012 the total national health care expenditure alone was $2.87 trillion. The hospitals alone provided 32% ($921 billion), physicians and clinical services about 20% ($555 billion), while 10% ($280 billion) went to drugs. The other 38% went to such things as dental care, nursing home care, home health care, etc.

Hospitals

Hospitals account for the majority of the total health care spending. In 2010 there were approximately 4,985 acute care hospitals with 800,000 beds and 4.6 million employees. 51.4% (2,561 hospitals) had 100 beds or less and were located in rural areas. All hospitals, in 2010, admitted over 35 million patients (I was one of those) and had 127 million emergency room visits (I was also one of those).

Eighteen percent (893) of hospitals were for-profit hospitals and are located primarily in the south. Interestingly, physicians are increasingly opening specialized hospitals. For example, there are approximately 240 physician for-profit hospitals specializing in cardiac or orthopedic practice (I recently visited one of those).

Prior to 1983, hospitals were primarily fee-for-service and were paid for the services they provided. In 1983 Medicare shifted to paying hospitals for a particular diagnosis – *diagnosis- related groups (DRG)* – such as hip replacement, heart attacks, etc. The DRGs were subsequently modified to account for age, health, etc. These modified DRGs were called *medical-severity adjusted diagnostic related group systems (MS-DRG)*. At the latest count there are 335 DRGs and 740 distinct MS-DRGs.

DRGs are called *prospective payments*. That is, rather than pay the hospital whatever cost they charged to treat Medicare patients, the payment, instead, was based on a predetermined set rate for the patient's treatment. The objective of this change was to encourage the hospital to be more efficient and to bear the financial risk for slow recovery.

Ever wonder why patients are pushed out of the hospital as soon as possible. Well, there you have it – DRGs. Needless to say the length of stay in hospitals has significantly declined. The way in which Medicare determines the cost of a DRG is complicated and I will not even attempt a discussion in this missive.

Ever wonder why hospitals seem to have different billing rates. Well, it turns out that hospitals have six different billing rates and each hospital differs in those rates. The payment rates are as follows.

First is the **Charge Master Rate**. This is the list price the hospital charges for such things as lab test, medical procedure, drugs, supplies, etc. Very few patients, except the Oil Sheiks, actually pay this rate.

Second is the **Medicare Rate**. This is the rate Medicare says they will pay for a DRG. This is not a negotiated rate but is set by Medicare and is obviously much less than the Charge Master Rate.

Third is the **Commercial Insurer and Blue Cross/Blue Shield Rate**. This is the rate paid by the commercial insurers and is negotiated with each hospital. The commercial rate is normally a percentage of the Medicare Rate. For example, if a hip replacement cost for Medicare is $16,000 then the commercial rate might be 130% of that. This rate will obviously depend upon the bargaining power of the hospital.

Fourth is the **Usual, Customary and Reasonable Rate (UCR).** This is the rate paid by insurers to out-of-network providers and is supposed to reflect the 'reasonable' cost to providers in a geographical area.

The fifth rate is the **Medicaid Rate**. This is the rate at which Medicaid reimburses hospitals and physicians. It is normally quoted as a percentage of Medicare. For example, it might be quoted as 17 cents on each billed dollar. It is always the lowest of any rate and is obviously disliked by both hospitals and physicians.

The sixth rate is the **Actual Cost**. This is the actual cost to the hospital of providing a service. This includes the cost of the physician, supplies, technology, time, labor, etc. No one really knows this rate. Each hospital administrator cannot tell the actual cost of a day in the hospital because there are simply too many people interacting with the patient. This obviously creates problems when the hospital claims that the Medicare rate is lower than the cost of delivering a service.

Physicians

Physicians account for about 20% of the total health care cost. In 2010 there were approximately 985,375 physicians in the US or about 3.19 physicians for every 1,000 Americans. Presently about 75% are male while about 25% are female, however, that seems to be changing since women currently occupy about 50% of the medical school slots.

There is, however, an imbalance between specialists and general practitioners. There are presently about 643,000 physicians classified as general practitioners working in family medicine, pediatrics, gynecology, etc. Between 1975 and 2010 the number of physicians more than doubled; however, there was only an increase of 10% in family practitioners with most doctors deciding to specialize. This trend is obviously going in the wrong direction.

Physicians specialize because of one reason – money. The average salary of a family practitioner is around $199K, the average salary for a cardiac surgeon is around $522K, while that of an orthopedic surgeon specializing in spinal surgery is around $615K. Over a 35 year practice this could amount to a difference of over $14 million dollars. Well, which do you want to be, a general practitioner or a specialist?

In addition to a difference in specialization there is also a difference in geographical distribution. For example, in the northeast there are 4.63 physicians for every 1000 Americans while in the mountain states the ratio is 2.60 physicians for every 1000 Americans. From my perspective, this is not surprising since higher income personnel just seem to want to live in urban areas that provide greater social and cultural advantages to the family.

Physicians have been notoriously independent and want to either work alone or in smaller groups. In 2008 just under one-half of all physicians worked in a group of five or smaller while only 19% worked in a group of 6-50 physicians. Smaller groups mean that care is fragmented especially for patients with chronic conditions who may be receiving care from several physicians.

The number of small physician groups are declining as hospitals buy their practices. I suspect physicians are selling because of lower payments from both Medicare and Medicaid while hospitals can assume the administrative burden associated with patient care. It is expected that in 2014 a threshold will be crossed in which more physicians will be employed by hospitals than will be self-employed.

Well back to physician pay. The way physicians are paid generally involve three steps.

First, a physician first renders the service he provided into a medical code. That is, the service a physician renders during an office visit, such as a physical exam, is then converted into a *Current Procedural Terminology* (CPT) code which are maintained by the American Medical Association (AMA). For example, I seem to be constantly undergoing physical therapy which is billed under the code, 97110 - Physical Medicine and Rehabilitation. The codes are then aggregated and linked to a specific diagnosis such as strep throat. These diagnostic codes are specified by the *International Classification of Diseases* (ICD) code maintained by the World Health Organization (WHO).

Most doctor offices employ a clinical coder – also known as aedical records technician – who is a health care professional whose main duties are to analyze clinical statements and assign standard codes using the CPT and ECD classification system.

Second is the medical billing. Codes and CPTs are converted into a bill based upon the financial cost of the CPT code. The physician's document is then submitted with the CPT code and ICD diagnosis to the insurer, Medicare and or Medicaid.

Third is the action of the payer who takes the codes and the physician's bill and determines what will really be paid. For example, Medicare uses a ***Relative Value Unit*** (RVU) to determine what will actually be paid. The RVU, again, is too complicated to cover in this missive. Most insured simply take the RVU number specified by Medicare as their number and pay accordingly. For example, a bypass surgery may equate to 58.28 RVUs. In 2012 each RVU number equated to $38.251 per RVU which meant the physician made $1,984 dollars. The RVU, fortunately, is updated every five years to accommodate changes in physician services.

Drug Manufacturers

Drug manufacturers develop, produce, and market drugs and account for about 10% of the total health care spending. If a drug has a therapeutic value and is without serious side effects it is submitted to the FDA as **an *Investigational New Drug*** and goes to clinical testing. The drug then undergoes 3 phases of testing in progressively larger trials and, if successful, it then becomes a ***branded drug***. It takes between 8-10 years to get FDA approval for a drug. The FDA approves only 1 in 10,000 compounds while only 3 in 20 approved drugs ever recover their development cost. This is obviously risky and expensive business and the drug companies maintain it cost about $1 billion dollars to develop and market a drug. Others claim the cost to the drug company for a marketed drug is around $100 million.

Either way, the drug companies want to recover their research and development cost, and the drugs are priced accordingly, so even though there are substantial risks in developing a new drug, the profit margins can be substantial. For example, Phizer, the largest pharmaceutical company, had revenue of $67.9 billion in 2011 and a profit margin of 14.7 %. Gilead, the most profitable drug company, had a profit margin in excess of 33%. All told, about 45% of drug company profits are from the US market.

When a drug loses its patent protection other drug makers can manufacturer the drug making it a "*generic*" drug. Typically, when drugs become generic, the price will drop by 80 to 90% and over the past ten years the use of generic drugs has dramatically increased. Out of 4 billion prescriptions per year the generics have increased from 47% in 2002 to 80% in 2011. The biggest factor in this increase seems to be Medicare, Part D. This was particularly true as pharmaceutical benefit managers began shifting seniors from brand name drugs to their equivalent generics.

Another interesting development is the marketing of drugs to physicians. Traditionally, marketing to a physician was through *detailing* where a salesman actually visited the doctor's office. Beginning in 1997 the FDA began to permit the direct-to-consumer (DTC) advertisement bypassing the physician and hospitals. The US and New Zealand are the only two developed countries now permitting DTC marketing. That is now all you see on TV; however, experts expect DTC marketing to decline. I'm unsure why this is.

The Problems with Our Current Health System

Some people say our current medical system is the best in the world. In fact John Boehner, the House Speaker, and Mitch McConnell, the Senate Republican leader, claim the United States has "the finest health care system in the world." From my perspective that is utter nonsense! Well, this is my missive and I can call it as I see it. Perhaps a better viewpoint is that it is the best system money can buy. From the description of our current medical system there seems to be three major problems that need to be addressed.

There are many sub issues that need to be addressed but I think those can easily be subsumed under the three major issues although, to be truthful, health experts list many more than three. The three major problems, from my perspective, are enumerated below.

Problem One: The Uninsured

There are approximately 15% of all Americans (between 40 and 60 million) uninsured (nobody seems quite sure how many uninsured there really are). These people are not lazy as the Republicans claim, but either work for employers who do not provide health insurance or are in such low paying jobs that they cannot afford health insurance.

Think about this. One in seven Americans do not have health insurance even though we have a GDP that is 23% of the world's total economic output. I have always found that hard to grasp because I believe the ethical character of a nation is defined by its health care system and that we have an ethical and moral obligation to be concerned with the health of all our fellow citizens.

It is not that the uninsured do not receive some health care. Rather, it is that they, by some estimates, receive only about 65% of the health care if they had insurance. Romney once famously stated, "We don't have people who become ill or die in their apartments because they don't have insurance ….." Not so!

Joseph Doyle of the MIT Sloan School of Management did an interesting study on car accidents in Wisconsin and found that the uninsured received about 20% less treatment than those with insurance. In addition, he found a mortality rate of 40% higher for the uninsured than for the insured.

The American Cancer Institute did a study in which they found a survivable rate after five years of those uninsured and with Medicaid was 8% less that those with insurance. No one is sure why the survivable rate for the uninsured and Medicaid is less than those with insurance. Some suspect it is the delay the uninsured and Medicaid patients experience when they go for treatment.

Romney is right in one respect in that the uninsured can go to a hospital emergency room and get treatment and they do so in droves. It turns out, however, that the cost of that treatment is passed along to insured Americans through something called *cross-subsidization*. Some claim this is a hidden tax for it is buried in the insurance premium for health insurance as the cost of providing care for Americans without insurance. For example, the hospital must somehow recover the cost of the uninsured therefore it distributes the cost of their care to those with insurance which in turn raises the cost of insurance premiums. In addition, the hospital receives money from the government from the ***Disproportionate Share Hospital*** (**DSH**) program which also helps cover the uninsured.

Well, there it is. Americans pay for the uninsured through higher insurance premiums and through higher taxes that fund the DSH payments. In 2008 the uninsured took advantage of this by receiving approximately $116 billion in health care.

Problem Two: The Cost of Being Uninsured

In 2012 the US spent over $2.8 trillion dollars on health care which makes it the 5th largest economy in the world. To give some perspective, $2.8 trillion is larger than the entire GDP of France. One independent finding estimated that we spend approximately $800 billion more on health care than we should.

What seems most worrying to economists is the rate of health care growth. For example, over the last 40 years health care cost has grown 2% faster than the economy. Economists express this as GDP+2% and their projections indicate it is simply not sustainable.

Why not? Well, in 1970 six cents of each dollar went to health care. In 2010 it was nearly 18 cents. This means that in the last decade 25% of our economic growth was in health care and not industry. Scared yet? Well, what about some more projections.

It is expected that the growing cost in health care, if left unchecked, will result in:

(1). **More uninsured Americans** with resultant bankruptcies and death. Rising health care cost will inevitable mean that the poorest of Americans will not be able to afford health care. Since 2000 the cost of health care has more than doubled and the number of uninsured, by some estimates, has risen from 36.6 million to approximately 48 million (I suspect this figure really approaches 60 million but the real number is unknown).

(2). **Further cuts to education and other state programs** in order to fund health care. Public colleges and universities have recently been financially squeezed resulting in their raising tuition. This has been caused by the reallocation of state funds from education to health. Remember that governors and state legislators are faced with three options due to rising health care costs: (1) raise taxes to pay for health care which Republican Governors and Republican Legislators are not going to do, (2) cut health care programs which they have already done by restricting access to Medicaid or (3) cut other state programs which they have done, for example, by cutting funds to education.

Welcome to the world of short term politics and governors and legislators more concerned with politics and the short term view rather than what is best for their citizens. Education is the foundation on which a viable economy is built.

Unfortunately, Republicans seem intent on sacrificing our economic future based on their stated principle of not raising taxes or increasing the size of government. From my perspective, principle over practicality has never worked.

(3) **A growing federal deficit and debt**. During the last years of the Clinton administration, the government ran a budget surplus that decreased the national debt and gave the possibility of finally eliminating it entirely. Unfortunately, the Bush administration chose to run higher deficits rather than raise taxes to fund the Afghanistan war, the Iraqi war, the tax cut and unfunded programs. I have always thought lowering taxes while fighting two wars was the height of irresponsible government. But, hey, the Americans got their wars and their tax cut. Let the good times roll!

Economists estimate that if the cost of health care continues to grow it will consume about 50% of the federal budget by 2035 with Medicare making up the majority of this growth. They further estimate that by 2025, if nothing is done, that revenues will fund only the debt interest rate, Medicare, Medicaid and Social Security.

Problem Three: Medical Malpractice

Now for one of the biggest concerns of physicians and hospitals – medical malpractice suits. Their concern, it seems to me, is justified. For example, the risk of a physician being sued in a family practice is about 70% over the lifetime of his/her practice. However, the risk rises to 100% in specialties such as neurosurgery. Medical malpractice insurance is not inexpensive. For example, an obstetrician in Florida pays over $100,000 per year for malpractice insurance.

Well, why medical malpractice insurance? Experts seem to feel there are three major reasons for this type insurance. **First**, to provide prompt and timely compensation to people harmed by mistakes; **second**, to hold hospitals, physician and other providers accountable for their mistakes and; **three**, to provide an incentive for providers to take action to reduce mistakes and improve the quality of care.

Unfortunately, most experts seem to think that our present system does a poor job of accomplishing any of these objectives. For example, in a recent study of over 30,000 medical records it was found that only about 1% showed negligence of the physician or hospital and of the negligence cases only about 3% resulted in a malpractice suit. The average time to settle a suit is around 20 months. In addition, only about 40 cents of every dollar paid in malpractice premiums goes to injured patients. The rest goes to administrative cost, insurance profits, and litigation cost, think trial lawyers. In addition, there are some physicians who think that the risk of a malpractice suit results in higher levels of defensive medicine which increases the cost of health care and, to me, this sounds logical.

Well, the malpractice system does, in my opinion, seem to be flawed and needs to be fixed. There have been a number of suggestions to fix the system but none have caught on I suppose because of the power of trial lawyers. There seems to be three popular proposals to fix the system.

First is the proposal by the University of Michigan to encourage all hospitals employees to report adverse incidents which would be investigated and, if indeed, a malpractice event existed then the patient would be notified and a standard compensation offered.

Second is the "safe harbor" approach in which the physician would be presumed innocent if they implemented medical records to help them follow appropriate guideline treatments. If the guidelines were not followed, then the physician could be sued. Many health workers like this approach because it encourages adherence to a quality of standard care.

Third is specialized malpractice courts. This option may be more problematic because malpractice oversight is the responsibility of the states and not the federal government.

Nevertheless it seems to me a combination of safe harbor and specialized malpractice courts might represent a possible solution.

Summary
Well, this is what the American health care system looked like before the Affordable Care Act (ACA) was enacted. It was complex and expensive, 40-60 million Americans were uninsured, quality was uneven, there was little transparency on price or care quality, and physicians were obsessed with medical malpractice. However, with that said, there are some areas where American medical care, such as medical technology is outstanding, perhaps even the best in the world.

What has always concerned me, however, is the number of uninsured Americans. In my opinion, any Health Care system we have should reflect our moral obligation toward caring for the welfare of our fellow countryman. Unfortunately, from my perspective, our current health care system fails in that regard for it seems to be based upon the market principle to make a profit off other people's misery. Our health care is rationed by wealth; that is, those who can pay are cared for while those who can't get sick and die. There are simply too many uninsured people who either go bankrupt or, worse yet, die from lack of health care.

Both democrats and republicans were aware of the shortcomings of the current health care system and throughout the 1900s there were numerous attempts at Health Care reform but none succeeded prior to Affordable Care Act. Throughout the century there were six major attempts, by both democrats and republicans, to implement a National Health care act.

For example, in 1912, Teddy Roosevelt, a republican, made national health insurance, based primarily on the German Bismark model, a part of his presidential campaign. Unfortunately, he was not elected. Progressives, like Roosevelt, continued to push for a National Health Care system but were successfully opposed by Samuel Gompers, President of the American Federation of Labor. WW1 and everything German seems to have been the final nail in the Bismark model.

In 1935, President Franklin Roosevelt, a democrat, as part of his new deal to combat the Depression, intended to include National Health Care in his congressional acts but ran into difficulty with AMA opposition to compulsory health care and, for political reasons, never brought it to congress.

In 1946 Richard Nixon, a republican, ran for congress on a platform that included a health care initiative and cosponsored the National Health Care Act which was spurned by the democrats.

In 1950 Harry Truman, a democrat, perhaps the president who was the strongest proponent of compulsory health insurance, attacked the 'do nothing' republican congress for their failure to address health care. This was the republicans first deployment of the charge of "socialized medicine" and it proved exceptionally effective.

In 1974, with Nixon now president, a republican, a comprehensive Health Care Act was once again attempted. This one may have passed but, unfortunately, Nixon began to be embroiled in the Watergate controversy while Rep Wilbur Mills, the strongest congressional advocate, became enflamed with Fannie Fox and wound up in the Tidal Basin.

In 1993, President Clinton, democrat, attempted to formulate and pass a comprehensive health care bill entitled the *Health Security Act* but could not pass it due to (1) mismanagement of the bill, (2) it was too closely identified with the Clintons and not with Congress, (3) Rep Dan Rostenkowski, the prime congressional mover of the bill, was embroiled in a scandal, (4) support among the democrats was fragmented, (5) the bill threatened the insurance companies and they launched, perhaps the greatest ad campaign in history, "Harry and Heloise", which effectively undermined the bill, and (6) perhaps most importantly, the Congressional Budget Office ruled the bill "expensive" which provided ammunition for Newt Gingrich.

As you can see, for one reason or another none of these succeeded. democrats and republican changed sides on policy, scandals affecting Rep. Wilbur Mills and Rep. Dan Rostenkowski contributed to ruining two chances of passages, major opposition on the part of the AMA or Drug Manufacturers ruined another and another failed due to a failure to manage congressional egos.

One author listed managing the following principles as necessary to pass health care legislation and to a large extent the ACA management team seems to have been successful. Of course, I suspect luck counted a lot, for any health care enactment always faces long odds, for it is much safer for a politician to vote against a health care act then it is to vote for one.

The principles adhered to in successfully passing the ACA were:

1. The lack of unity on health care pretty much dooms a health care act to defeat. A smaller more focused group standing on principles will defeat a more moderate, practical bill every time.
2. Washington is full of massive egos and unless they are messaged nothing will pass.

3. Speed in passing a health bill is critical because the more it is debated the more opposition to the bill will develop. Pass something quickly even though it may need modifying later.
4. Congress does not like new things because they do not have time to understand them. A health care bill should be built of previous templates which minimize what is unknown.
5. Those against a health care bill will always couch their opposition in terms of antigovernment, or "socialized medicine." This line of attack is tried and true and must somehow be countered.

The ACA seems to have somehow successfully negotiated these principles. Luck, though was on their side because the death of Ted Kennedy with brain cancer became its rallying cry.

References:

As always I wish I could claim some originality in this missive but, again, as always, I cannot. Instead I must stand on the shoulders of others who are far more qualified than me to assess the ACA and the health care system that preceded it.

If you are truly interested in finding more about our health care system to include the ACA then I recommend the following books which is the primary source for this and other missives.

1. *Reinventing American Health Care* by Ezekiel J. Emanuel
2. *The Healing of America: A Global Quest for Better, Cheaper, and Fairer Health Care* By T.R. Reid

Letter 2 - The Healthcare Philosophy

Our current health care system seems to be based upon the market principle to make a profit off other people's misery. That thought process was perhaps applicable when conquering a new land, but I'm not sure that kind of attitude is the most appropriate in a modern society that derives its roots from Athens and Jerusalem, and I'm not sure it should be the context for a new health care system. When living in herds as we do now we enter into a societal contract to do such things as obey laws, not to harm other (unless they intend to harm us), and generally adhere to the Christian creed to behave as we would have others behave toward us.

Underlying this agreed to behavior is the belief that we must behave toward our fellow citizens in an ethically and morally acceptable manner. In my opinion, inherent in this concept is the underlying philosophy that we must be concerned with the health and well-being of our fellow citizens.

If the ethical character of a nation is defined by its health care system then, in my opinion, we have an ethical and moral obligation to be concerned with the health of all our fellow citizens. Therefore, any new health care system we create, such as the Affordable Care Act (ACA), should reflect our moral obligation toward caring for the welfare of our fellow countryman. Unfortunately, I don't think this philosophy will fly due to the ingrained bias of both the republicans and democrats toward the profit motive.

The Current World Health Care Structure

As one looks around the world there are a number of health care models that have been implemented.

  A. **The Bismarck Model** is implemented in Germany, Japan, France, Belgium, and Switzerland. In this model both care providers and payers are private entities.

B. **The Beveridge Model** is implemented by Great Britain, Italy, Spain, Scandinavia, and Cuba and is what republicans call "Socialized Medicine." In this model, health care is a basic public service which is provided and financed by the government through tax payments. Boys, heads up, did you know that TriCare, Medicare and Medicaid, are forms of "Socialized Medicine", that is; a government funded health care system. Well, for those fortunate enough to participate, we already have "socialized medicine".

C. **The National Health Insurance Model** is implemented in Canada, Taiwan, Australia and South Korea. In this model the health providers are private but the payer is a government program that citizens pay into.

D. **The Out-of-Pocket Model** is implemented in most undeveloped countries. Someone characterized this system succinctly as 'the rich live and the poor die'. Life is brutish and short in these countries. This model is implemented in Africa, India, China, and South America.

E. **The American System** has no recognized model but is a combination of all the above:
   a. We are German for those under sixty five.
   b. We are Canadian for those over sixty five.
   c. We are British for veterans, military personnel, and Indians.
   d. We are African for approximately 60 Million Americans who are uninsured.
   e. Separate classes of people have separate classes of care depending upon their wealth and the profit of the care provider (rather brutal but a fact).

I do not expect the ACA to create a massive change in the new health care structure since most Americans seem to like the idea of the private provider and private payer concept. The public competition option will not fly because there is too much resistance by both democrats and republicans. I suspect the best we can expect from the ACA will be some tinkering with the current American systems. I personally prefer the private provider and the single payer model (i.e., Universal Health Care) but that will not happen this time. However, if the ACA, as implemented, survives the republican onslaught, then I suspect it will eventually be modified to such an extent that it will for all practical purposes eventually become Universal Health Care.

Well, back to a philosophy of what I envision as a health care system.

1. **Universal Health Coverage**. As indicated previously, I believe the ethical standards of a nation is reflected in the underpinning of the nation's health care system. By that standard we are not doing too well since ours seems to be based upon profit. If there is not universal health coverage then that nation's health care is somehow rationed and in the US, unfortunately, health care is rationed by wealth. Someone once said we have the best health care money can buy (perhaps a congressman?). I believe health care is a right and should therefore be universal and not just for those who can afford it. We must have a health care system for everyone paid for by everyone. This will not fly in our current political environment; however, I hope the ACA will cover at least a portion of those currently uninsured.

2. **Not for Profit**. As I indicated in a previous missive, our present health care system now consumes approximately 17% of our GDP and in the near future perhaps as much as 40% if we follow the present cost trajectory. There are two major things we must do to control the cost.
   a. **First**, health care must become a nonprofit service. I realize in the near term that this will not fly because of an entrenched insurance bureaucracy with literally billions of dollars of profit and millions of dollars of bonus money at stake. Unfortunately, neither party has the political will to go this far. We must, however, make a start in that direction even if it is only a small step.
   b. **Second**, health care cost must be controlled. This means we must establish a basic floor of universal health care which is provided to everyone. Everyone must be cared for; however, everything cannot be covered. Anyone wanting greater coverage would pay a premium for

this optional coverage. For example, emergency medical service must be covered but not optional medical services such as breast implants, liposuction, Botox, etc.

Is this rationing? Absolutely! Not by wealth, but by necessity. There must be standard prices for standard procedures. The rub is how to establish standard prices in the face of an entrepreneurial economy. My only thought here is that it must be done by medical specialists and not by Washington bureaucrats. In the near term, this also will not fly due to the entrenched lobby of the American Medical Association; but we must start because the current cost trajectory is unsustainable. In this regard, doctors must be the medical gatekeepers, not some mindless, faceless bureaucrats.

3. **No Adverse Selection.** Where is the profit in insuring someone who is sick or potentially will become sick? Health insurance companies report to their stock holders who are interested in getting a return on their investment and sick people, by any standard, are a bad investment. There is simply no profit in them, therefore, why should they be insured? And so they aren't! Brutal but effective. Now this is the ultimate in health rationing and few people complain because it is for profit and no one seems to care – except for those who are sick and dying but, hell, you lose money on those people so let them whine and die. In my opinion, everyone should have health insurance, especially those who are sick.

4. **No Rescission.** If the health insurance company knows you are sick, what is to prevent them from cancelling your insurance? Absolutely nothing, so it is done all the time. Again the sick are a very poor investment, and they lower the bottom line so the insurance company solution is to chuck them overboard.

This has always reminded me of the famous question: How can you tell an Army Comptroller? Answer: He is the one who, after the battle, shoots the wounded! I have always thought it funny as hell because it contains so much truth. Unfortunately, finance folks will do anything to save money and the insurance companies are no different. No one should have their insurance cancelled because they are sick.

5. **Claim Denial**. Currently 30% of a health care claims are denied by insurance companies. Since the doctor is the medical gatekeeper he determines what medical procedure or tests are necessary. However, if the doctor is paid by the number of patients he/she has maybe they will live longer for there is no profit in someone who is dead. It seems to me this will not only lower the cost but also emphasize preventive care. If the doctor feels a procedure is necessary and forwards a claim, that claim should be paid within, say, one week by the insurance company.

6. **Medical Records**. One of the major costs in our current health care system is the cost associated with medical records since each doctor and hospital keeps their own paper records. There has been some attempt by doctors and hospitals to automate those records but not on a national scale. In my opinion, medical records will need to be automated and centralized by region with the various regions interconnected. However, the records themselves need to be decentralized and held by the individual seeking medical care.

   For example, DOD is going to Smart Cards such that each soldier, Sailor, Airmen or Marine carries his records embedded in his ID card. Why not do the same for civilian medical records? The initial outlay for such a system would be great but cost savings would be even greater. France and Taiwan have this system so why not the US?

7. **Medical Education**. When a doctor finishes his schooling he is anywhere between $300-400,000 in debt. If this trend continues, how can we ask doctors to sacrifice their pay with this kind of debt? Let the public pay for a doctor's education. This is not new and at one time was quite common. Guess where? Eastern Kentucky! The best and brightest were given a free ride with the understanding they would come back to the hills to practice.
   a. **Doctor Pay**. Medical insurance now pays doctors a fee-for-service. That is, the doctor performs a service for which the insurance

company is billed. They, in turn, pay the doctor a fee for that service. Unfortunately, this says nothing about the quality of service or the expected medical outcome. The doctor may be tempted to increase his pay by increasing his service which results in a treatment that may be unnecessary for that patient. Some hospitals, e.g., the Mayo Clinic, pay doctors a flat salary. In my opinion, this does make some sense since a doctor is now concerned with his patients and not with his Mercedes Benz. A third way is to pay the doctor a flat fee for each patient. This seems to work in Germany, but I'm not sure it is viable in the U.S. since it would result in longer waiting periods (think Canada) and Americans are notoriously impatient. In the final analysis, I suspect we will eventually see a combination of salary for hospital doctors and a fee per patient for private care physicians - but not just yet.

b. **Death Panels**. Death is a fact of life. At birth we are given a fixed amount of time on this earth and as much as we would like, that time cannot be extended. It is up to each of us how we live our life and it should be up to each of us as to how we end our life and there is no reason why this should not be done in consultation with our physician and/or pastor.

   For some unknown reason, the republicans call this consultation a "death panel" and, in my opinion, this is the height of irresponsibility. A person should be allowed to die with the dignity with which he has lived his life. If a person does not want any life sustaining measures, that should be his choice and not that of the physician or someone who feels guilty. If a person wants to die at home surrounded by the people he loves that should also be his choice. To call those type decisions made in consultation with one's physician and pastor a "death panel" is utter nonsense.

8. **Malpractice**. Malpractice suits make up about 2% to the overall cost of health insurance. This is not insubstantial when considering the trillions spent on health care. Doctors order additional tests as a purely defensive measure thus adding to the overall costs. Some say the real problem with our

health care system is the unwanted and unnecessary tests conducted by doctors to limit the risk of a malpractice suit. Congressional tort reform is unlikely due to the abnormal contribution trial lawyers make to the Democratic Party. The best suggestion I have heard was that of creating medical courts run by experts to rule on malpractice claims with no punitive damages. I have always thought this was an extremely good idea but, unfortunately, it will not happen due to the trial lawyer's hold on the Democratic Party.

Conclusion.

Well, hopefully you get the point from this short rant. I think I have hit all the major items that should be in included in the new Health Care system. A lot of others I have not highlighted such as Public Health Service, insurance portability, etc.

Will these issues be included? I think some will be included but in a scaled down version. Until some catastrophe occurs we will not see a comprehensive health care bill. Congress seems to be good at coming together during a crisis because of some incident that forces their hand and, because there is no major crisis in the medical field (at least as perceived by the insurance companies) I expect no major change. Perhaps the best we can hope for is some incremental improvement that provides an increase in health care at a reduced cost. But don't count on anything comprehensive. The democrats don't have the political will while the republicans simply want to do nothing.

Until the Christian conservatives (the republican base) and the liberal left decide to adhere to their Judeo-Christian heritage and recognize that the nation's health is a moral/ethical issue and not an economical one, then real Health reform has no chance of passage.

References:

As always, I wish I could claim some originality in this missive but, again, I cannot. Instead I must stand on the shoulders of others who are far more qualified than me to assess the ACA and the health care system that preceded it.

1. *Reinventing American Health Care* by Ezekiel J. Emanuel
2. *The Healing of America: A Global Quest for Better, Cheaper, and Fairer Health Care* By T.R. Reid

Letter 3 - Purpose and Goals of the ACA

Before I cover my take on the purpose and goals of the ACA I would like to once again to return to the rationale for the ACA but from a slightly different perspective. That is, an attempt to answer the question: **Why do we need health reform**?

There seems to be **five fundamental reasons** health reform is critically needed in the U.S..

<u>First</u> is the high uninsured rate among Americans: In July 2012, the CBO estimated that over 55 million Americans under the age of 65 are currently uninsured; representing 1 out of 5 Americans in that age group (a total estimate of uninsured Americans is around 60 million). Without the ACA, the uninsured rate would continue to rise, meaning poorer health for Americans and a worse quality of life. For businesses, this would mean less productivity.

<u>Second</u> is the unsustainable spending on health care: Health care spending represented 17.9 percent of our Gross Domestic Product (GDP) in 2010, and is expected to reach 20 percent by 2020. This is simply unsustainable, therefore, something must be done. ACA is expected to at least slow this growth rate.

<u>Third</u> is the lack of emphasis on preventive health care: today, seven in ten deaths in the U.S. are related to preventable diseases such as obesity, diabetes, high blood pressure, heart disease, and cancer. Seventy five percent of our health care dollars are spent treating such diseases. However, only three cents of each health care dollar spent in the U.S. go toward prevention. ACA provides a greater concentration on prevention.

<u>Fourth</u> is poor health outcomes: The U.S. spends far more on medical care than any other industrialized nation, but ranks 24th among 30 Organizations for Economic Co-operation and Development (modern, first world countries) countries in terms of life expectancy.

<u>Fifth</u> is health disparities amongst Americans: While inequities related to income and access to coverage exist across demographic lines, population-based

disparities are impossible to deny. As reported by Families USA, "African-American women have the highest death rates from heart disease, breast and lung cancer, stroke, and pregnancy among women of all racial and ethnic backgrounds" and "Hispanics had poorer quality of care than non-Hispanic whites for about 40 percent of quality measures, including not receiving screening for cancer or cardiovascular risk factors."

The bottom line for businesses is that poor health means poor productivity and, according to current demographics, African-Americans and Hispanics are our present and future workers.

Some More Background

I have watched with interest as the Tea Party shutdown the government over their opposition to the Affordable Care Act (ACA). From my perspective this was the height of political theater and is really not in the best interest of the nation or the best interest of the Tea Party. After all the ACA is the law of the land and is already funded.

One of their fellow conservative Republicans called them "**lemmings with suicide vests**". I always thought this was a pretty good picture of their behavior. The Tea Party claims their stand is based on principles. From my perspective, principles should be used to govern and not to shut down the government.

Several years back I wrote an analysis of the ACA (see *Mutterings of A Madman 1: Letters to My Family on War and Politics*) in which I indicated the ACA was a step in the right direction, but still contained defects that needed to be addressed. I still think that is the case. The problem with the ACA is that it is so large and so complicated that few if any people really understand it.

Well, with that philosophical background, what exactly is the ACA?

The ACA is a series law composed of **ten titles with hundreds of provisions** that make it exceptionally difficult to understand, and certainly that is true for me. In addition, Obama has not done a very good job of educating the American citizens on the law while the Republicans, under McConnell, have obfuscated the ACA by providing misleading information. For example, the idea that the act contains provisions for "Death Panels". There are apparently some people who still believe that.

Bear with me as I try to educate myself, and you, in an attempt to better understand the ACA in this series of letters. This particular letter is intended to put the ACA in context.

The Goals of the ACA

There are two primary goals of the ACA. The **First Goal** of the ACA is to provide health care for over 60 million Americans that are currently uninsured while the **Second Goal** of the ACA is to make already existing health insurance better.

The Model for the Act

The model for the Act was the 2006 Massachusetts act proposed by then Gov. Mitt Romney. Why Romney now disclaims the act I don't know. If he has any accomplishment he can be proud of, it should be this one because it helped so many people.

The Impact

The ACA is expected to impact both those people already insured and those with no insurance.

Those Already Insured: Over 160 million Americans (about half of all Americans) already have insurance. For those Americans, the ACA has no impact unless their current insurance needs improving. The following are examples of what I mean by improving already existing insurance.

1. Previous options such as prescription drugs, childbirth, and mental health must now be paid by the insurance companies.
2. Insurance companies are not allowed to charge for such things as routine checkups and cancer screening.
3. ACA now limits yearly out of pocket fees.
4. ACA prevents the insurance company from dropping you when you get sick.
6. Your paycheck must now reflect how much your boss pays for health insurance.

Those Uninsured: There are currently between 40 and 60 million Americans uninsured (nobody seems quite sure how many uninsured there really are but it is thought to be somewhere in this range). ACA is intended to accommodate those without insurance though two primary means: Medicaid expansion and health insurance.

(1). **Medicaid Expansion:** Over one-third of Americans are on Medicare (senior citizens) or Medicaid (poor and disabled). Nothing will change with Medicare except it may be easier to get prescription drugs. Medicaid, however, will expand to include nearly all families making less than $31K. This is expected to encompass seventeen million of the estimated sixty million uninsured. Medicaid will be transformed from a safety-net program for the most vulnerable to a broad-based program. The expansion of Medicaid is ideological divisive especially at the state level with most Democratic states implementing Medicaid expansion, and most Republican states not implementing Medicaid expansion based upon either the governor's ideology or their perception of the cost. That is, Democratic states are expected to implement Medicaid expansion, Republican states are not, despite the fact that the federal government will pay 100% of the initial cost for three years gradually decreasing to 90% of the cost.

(2). **Insurance:** It is estimated that approximately 22 million of those with no private insurance and don't qualify for either Medicare or Medicaid can acquire insurance through State or Federal Insurance Exchanges (I will talk more about State and Federal Exchanges in a future letter). The uninsured can buy different levels of coverage – Bronze, Silver and Platinum – depending upon how much money the applicant makes. The government is expected to kick in anywhere from nothing to a lot.

One interesting more interesting aspect of the ACA is that insurance companies have to cover every legal resident in the US that wants coverage. However, they can charge smokers up to 40% more, can vary premiums by age and can choose not to offer policies in some geographical areas.

(3). **The Remaining:** There is still expected to be 20 million Americans without insurance and access to medical care. Well, these people will just have to suffer and die but, hey, the ACA, in an attempt to satisfy republican conservatives, is based on free market concepts.

Public Perception.

The public's perception of ACA is influenced by a number of things. Foremost of these are the following issues:

1. **The number of people signing up for ACA.** The healthy will be the young, who are expected to subsidize the older who are the sickest, and those who will now sign up because they are sick and cannot be denied insurance. The young must sign up for the insurance under ACA to be viable. This is the individual mandate. If they do not sign up in numbers then I don't see how this act can be viable. I don't expect the viability of ACA to be known for 2-3 years after its start.

2. **The people in rural areas.** It is expected that medical care in urban areas will be available but limited in rural or mountain areas. This expectation is based upon the insurance companies who participate in offering insurance. They obviously will offer insurance in those areas that will be most profitable ,and urban areas have always proven to be more profitable than rural areas.
3. **Price stability.** The issue here becomes one of profitability in the first year. For example, if too few healthy people sign up to offset the cost of the sick then insurance premiums are expected to rise in the second year.
4. **Small Employers.** Nothing is expected to occur for those employees insured through large employers; for example, those over fifty employees. But what about those employers with ten or less employees? It is expected that those employers will drop their coverage and encourage their employees to acquire coverage from either the state or federal exchange.
5. **Paying a Penalty.** The subscribers to the ACA will undoubtedly get more for their money but they may also be paying more, and if the cost of insurance is too high, then they may decide to drop insurance altogether and pay a penalty.
6. **Medicaid Expansion.** Many Republican states are expected to decide not to expand the Medicaid program even though the federal government will pick up the majority of the expense. This is expected to leave many of the poorest in Republican states uninsured. Again, Democratic states will expand Medicaid for their poorest citizens while Republican states will not. I suspect many Republican Governors, after several years of ACA experience, will ultimately decide their poorer citizens should also be covered by Medicaid.

That concludes a brief description of the purpose and goals of the Affordable Care Act. In my next letter I will discuss the State Insurance Exchanges.

References:

As always, I wish I could claim some originality in this missive, but, again, as always, I cannot. Instead I must stand on the shoulders of others who are far more qualified than me to assess the ACA and the health care system that preceded it.

1. *Reinventing American Health Care* by Ezekiel J. Emanuel

2. *The Healing of America: A Global Quest for Better, Cheaper, and Fairer Health Care* By T.R. Reid

Letter 4 – The State Insurance Exchanges

The ACA's health insurance exchanges are meant to be a virtual marketplace where individuals and families can comparison shop for private health insurance coverage. Remember, these exchanges are intended to accommodate those people currently without insurance, between roughly 40 and 60 million people. There will also be exchanges for small businesses but more on that in a future missive. The exchanges are to be operable starting October 1, 2013, and states have three models regarding their design:

Model 1: States can establish their own insurance exchange,

Model 2: States can establish an insurance exchange in partnership with the federal government, or

Model 3: States can let the federal government establish the State Insurance Exchange for them.

Exchange Subsidies

The exchanges will be most useful for those who don't have access to employer-based coverage, and who don't qualify for public programs like Medicaid. Individuals and families with incomes between 100 percent and 400 percent of the federal poverty level ($23,050-$92,200 for a family of four in 2012) will receive income-based subsidies to help them afford coverage. The amount to subsidize their health insurance cost will be anywhere from 2 to 9.5 percent of their gross pay.

One interesting provision is that if you're age 26 or below, and don't have insurance through an employer, your parents' insurance can cover you.

By 2022, the Congressional Budget Office estimates that 25 million Americans will have coverage through the exchanges. I personally consider this figure optimistic considering the resistance of many Republican states to the exchanges.

Levels of Coverage

In the Insurance Exchange there will be four levels of insurance coverage: **Bronze, Silver, Gold** and **Platinum**. These levels correspond to the amount of health costs insurance will cover for the average applicant: 60 percent for Bronze, 70 percent for Silver, 80 percent for Gold, 90 percent for Platinum coverage. There's also a bare-bones "**Catastrophic**" option available to applicants under age 30. The insurance policy purchased in 2013 will kick in on January 1, 2014.

However, if you make less than the poverty level, and live in a state that refused to expand Medicaid, you're pretty much out of luck. Because of a shortcoming in the law, if you want insurance coverage you must pay full price on the exchanges.

Still, if you blow off Obamacare and don't get insured by April, 2014, your grand total fine is only about $100 (though it will increase over the years). And there's another loophole: If the policy costs more than 10 percent of your annual income or you don't pay any federal taxes, you won't have to pay a penalty anyway.

Obamacare is not intended as an entitlement program, however, it does have an entitlement component — the exchange subsidies — which will involve about 2 percent of Americans during the first year. About 20 million Americans are expected to eventually get subsidized insurance — a check that goes not to the individual but to insurance companies.

Exchange Status

The law envisioned that most states would set up and run their own online exchanges, with federally-run exchanges as a backstop. However, only 16 states and the District of Columbia established state exchanges (Model 1); seven more states are partnering with the federal government (Model 2) to operate their exchanges.

In the other 27 states, people without insurance will use federally managed exchanges to shop for coverage (Model 3). Those 27 states, many of which have

Republican Governors who actively opposed the health care law, contain about 20 million uninsured people. There is at least one state, Florida, that has not only refused to set up a State Insurance Exchange but has also barred federally funded "navigators" from using its offices for outreach efforts.

The State Insurance Exchanges opened on 1 October, 2013, with mixed results primarily from two major issues.

First, are the technical issues such as a lack of adequate bandwidth, page linkage, etc. These are common technical issues affecting all new systems. It will generally take about a month or two to fix these type issues. However, there appears to be several State Exchanges (eg., Maryland, Oregon, Massachusetts and Vermont) that will never be fixed due to either crippling design issues or bad contract management. Those exchanges will fail and their function most likely be assumed by the Federal Exchanges.

The **Second** issue is more management headspace than anything else. That is, the user system assumption grossly underestimated the interest surge factor for the October 1, opening particularly with regard to reporters, random shoppers, drive by users, etc. This issue will be resolved when issue one is resolved, which will be in the November timeframe. Even then, there will continue to be anecdotal issues that are raised by individuals. (Note: As an aside, assumptions are always the weakest link in any project.)

In my next missive on the ACA I'll look at its impact on small businesses.

References:

As always, I wish I could claim some originality in this missive but, again, as always, I cannot. Instead I must stand on the shoulders of others who are far more qualified than me to assess the ACA and the health care system that preceded it.

1. *Reinventing American Health Care* by Ezekiel J. Emanuel
2. *The Healing of America: A Global Quest for Better, Cheaper, and Fairer Health Care* By T.R. Reid

Letter 5 - Small Businesses and the ACA

Health insurance has always been a form of gambling. That is, what are the odds that you will get sick and need to pay for health care? If the odds are high due to old age, for example, then you might need assistance in paying your bills and this is where your bet on health insurance comes in.

There are two competing value systems underlying the health insurance business and the disagreement between these two competing value systems play into the current disagreement between Democrats and Republicans dealing with the ACA.

The first health insurance value system is called the *solidarity principle*. This is the view that health insurance is to protect all of us from the impact of high medical expenses. In this system, we look out for each other, and the payments we make today for someone else will benefit us when we need it tomorrow. In the 1920s, this was the first type of health insurance to be offered in the United States. As an example of the solidarity principle, the Blue Cross/Blue Shield health system was organized to take on all comers and charge everyone the same premium.

The second competing health insurance value system is called *actuarial fairness*. That is, we only share risks and premiums with others like "us". For example, if I don't smoke, then for health insurance, I don't want to be lumped with people that do smoke. I want to be lumped with people that do not smoke. From an ethical perspective, this is neither right nor wrong but simply a different value and world view. In the 1940s, for profit commercial health insurance entered the state markets and honed *actuarial fairness* into *actuarial accounting*. For example, older applicants were charged more than younger ones ,and more premium was charged for preexisting conditions (or the insurance company simply refused to write a policy). The health insurance accounting books were organized to favor newer, younger, and healthier blocks of applicants, because that is where the profits are located. Well, we all know there is no profit in insuring the old and the sick so let them whine and die!

The ACA is seeking to move the US health system to the *solidarity principle* value system which helps explain why those that favor the *actuarial fairness* system dislike the new law. That is, the ACA laws will gradually change the health insurance business from private, profit-making enterprises into near-public utilities. This, of course, is not the only reason for the current dislike of ACA but more on that in a later missive.

Small Businesses

In addition to the State Exchange for individual insurance, the ACA also has a Small Business Health Options Program. This is called the **SHOP** Exchange.

While the ACA's main focus is extending coverage to millions of Americans without health insurance coverage, it is also meant to help small businesses by pooling their health requirements since they don't have the leverage of larger companies with their greater employees to demand low premiums. Because of this, they often end up paying approximately 18 percent more for health coverage.

The ACA SHOP exchange was intended to operate like this: A small business would decide it wanted to provide insurance to its employees, but didn't have the time or money to deal with the hassle of finding an insurance plan and picking the best option. Instead, it would contribute a set amount to each employee's health premiums, send that money over to the health exchange, and let employees pick their own coverage. The smaller business would be lumped together creating a greater employee pool, thereby lowering the premium

However, under a newly-proposed rule — the rule that's attracted a lot of attention — small business employers on the federal exchange (Model 3) will pick just one plan for all of their workers rather than letting each worker pick his own plan. The employer will have to decide on Aetna, Kaiser, or whatever other insurance option — and that's a lot like what they already do right now, but instead of sending their money to an exchange, they send it directly to an insurance company. A lot of employers don't like this change because they thought they would be able to offer their employees a range of health plans, and, now, in some states, they won't have that option, at least at the outset.

This rule, however, only applies to the 33 state exchanges where the federal government is setting up the marketplace (Model 3). In 17 other states, they still have the option to offer the full array of insurance choices to their employees. This option, however, will not disappear completely for states with federal exchanges. It has, instead, simply been delayed for a year due to technical glitches.

The one big advantage to employers to buy on the SHOP exchange is pooling. One of the reasons small businesses would want to buy on the exchange is that they'd be joining a pool of thousands of other people in small businesses. That would give them the kind of leverage to drive down health premiums much like large companies do.

Discussion

It's been uttered by every opponent of ACA health care reform: Obamacare will kill small businesses. All one has to do is listen to Cruz, Lee, Paul or McConnell to hear that oft repeated refrain. Why is that?

Under ACA small businesses are faced with something called an ***employer mandate***. That is, all firms that employ 50 or more full-time workers — or the equivalent in part-time workers — must provide health-care coverage to all of their full-time employees. If they do not, starting in 2014, the government will assess a fine based on the number of employees the businesses have. That is, businesses with 50-plus workers will face $40,000 in penalties and $2,000 for each additional full-time employee. This is nothing to laugh about, and will somehow need to be accommodated by modifications to the ACA.

Because the employer mandate exempts firms with fewer than 50 workers, there's a huge incentive for firms to stop hiring at 49; therefore, those opposing the employer mandate fear that companies on the cusp of hiring their 50th full-time employee might hold back, while other businesses might try to cut their employees' hours. They view this as job killing.

Is this a valid concern? Well, this can be argued both ways. For example, it turns out that only 3 percent of small businesses — those with fewer than 500 employees — have more than 50 workers, so 97 percent of small employers are exempt from the law's mandates. Meanwhile, virtually all large companies, those businesses with over 500 workers, already offer health insurance to their employees.

In addition, there are signs that more than 99% of those in work-sponsored plans have insurance that meet most Obamacare coverage standards. Aside from things such as reporting requirements, it is expected that the employer mandate will directly obligate only about 1 percent of American businesses to do anything different.

That is, current data shows that only a tiny sliver of the nation's small businesses face the new rules, and even fewer face any changes. For example, of the country's 6.5 million workplaces, only 1% must actually start providing insurance next year. That is, about 71,000 businesses will be affected. Again this is nothing to laugh about, but is far different than the projections of the doomsayers.

There are still other concerns. Some in opposition to the plan argue that uncertainty about how much healthcare premiums will rise under the law could discourage hiring, at least until the cost picture is clearer to businesses.

On the other hand, people supporting ACA argue that people won't be as locked into their jobs, since they won't have to stick with certain employers to ensure they have healthcare coverage, and that will make it easier for people to move into jobs they're better at, thereby promoting entrepreneurship.

They further argue that with more reliable care, workers might better manage the symptoms of one-time or chronic illnesses, which could cut down on the number of sick days they take thereby increasing business efficiency.

I expect the arguments related to the SHOP exchanges to become more volatile during the next year, and to continue unabated for the next several years as modifications are made to the ACA.

In my next missive I'll cover funding the ACA.

References:

As always, I wish I could claim some originality in this missive but, again, as always, I cannot. Instead I must stand on the shoulders of others who are far more qualified than me to assess the ACA and the health care system that preceded it.

1. *Reinventing American Health Care* by Ezekiel J. Emanuel
2. *The Healing of America: A Global Quest for Better, Cheaper, and Fairer Health Care* By T.R. Reid

Letter 6 - Funding and the ACA

The Congressional Budget Office estimates the ACA will reduce the budget deficit by $210 billion during the years 2012-2021. This is based on a gross cost of $1,390 billion with an anticipated offset of $1,601 billion.

The ACA is funded in part by the individual mandate, cutting payments to hospitals, creating new taxes for rich people, an increase in the tax on medical device makers and health insurers, etc.

Cost of ACA

As I indicated, the ACA is estimated to cost approximately $1,390 billion for the years 2012-2021. Below is a noninclusive, category list of the costs associated with the ACA.

Medicaid Expansion: The ACA gives money to states to expand Medicaid eligibility to Americans under the age of 65, who are below 133% of the federal poverty limit, but states can decline without losing existing funding. The Act gives states 100% Federal funding for the first 3 years for newly eligible individuals, beginning January 1, 2014, and ending December 31, 2016. On January 1, 2017, the funding will be decreased to 95% with the next 2 years each decreasing by 1% until the year 2020 at which time it will be decreased to 90% and stabilized at that level.

Tax Credits: Tax credits will be available for individuals and families with incomes up to 400 percent of the federal poverty level ($43,420 for an individual or $88,200 for a family of four) that are not eligible for Medicaid, employer sponsored insurance, or other acceptable coverage. Other types of acceptable coverage would be Medicare, military insurance, grandfathered plans, and CHIP (Children's Health Insurance Plan). This means that these tax credits are for individuals and families who obtain health insurance from the state run Health

Insurance Exchanges. These are state-run bodies and not to be confused as insurers that will regulate the private insurance companies to comply with the consumer protection set forth in the ACA.

The ACA law states that "Individuals with incomes below 400 percent of the Federal Poverty Level (FPL) who purchase coverage in the Exchange are not required to spend more than a set percentage of their income on health insurance. If they cannot find coverage at a price that falls below this threshold, they are then eligible for a premium credit to ensure they do not spend more than a certain percentage of their income on health insurance coverage."

The tax credit is calculated on a sliding scale based upon an individual or a family's income, from 2%-9.5% of their income. The amount of tax credit is reduced as individual or family income increases, phasing out at 400 percent of the federal poverty level.

Cost-Sharing Subsidies: Cost sharing subsidies are intended to protect lower income individuals with health insurance coverage from high out of pocket costs at the point of service. The cost-sharing subsidy applies to individuals and families who enroll in a qualified health plan in the Silver level of coverage in the individual market offered through an exchange, and whose household income is between 100 - 400 percent of the poverty level for a family. A different plan than Silver may be purchased but no cost-sharing subsidies will be provided.

Persons who are offered coverage through their employer also may be eligible for the subsidies provided through the exchange, if their employer's plan premium would exceed 9.5 percent of the employee's income.

These subsidies are meant to limit out-of-pocket costs before the insurance companies pay for all medical expenses, and helps reduce out-of-pocket costs significantly for low to middle class. If they are 200% below the Federal Poverty Level, their out of pocket costs will be reduced by two-thirds. They'll be decreased by half for persons below 300% and one-third for persons below 400% FPL.

Both premium credits and cost-sharing subsidies are refundable tax credits paid in advance directly to the health insurer. Any costs above and beyond what the credits and subsidies do not cover are the responsibility of the individual or family.

New High-Risk Insurance Pool: $5 billion will be designated to create a federal program which provides stopgap coverage to the medically uninsurable, due to a pre-existing condition, until the Health Care Reform is completely in place and Insurance Exchanges are created.

Federal Agencies' Administrative Costs: Beyond the expenditures listed above, another significant overhead cost will be the excess work required at the various federal agencies; for example, the IRS will now be responsible for processing this new individual mandate fee/tax. Also, the new workforces and insurance exchanges which will be formed will also incur costs.

Paying for ACA

Well, if the ACA is anticipated to cost $1,390 billion, then how will this cost be offset? It is anticipated that an increase in tax provisions and other income will amount to approximately $1,601 billion, which will result in a deficit reduction of approximately $210 billion during the 2012-2021.

Well, where does the offset money come from? There are numerous NEW or INCREASED taxes and fees to fund all that is required by this law. I suppose this is one reason why a lot of people do not like this law because they are simply opposed to taxes. The major discussed and disliked tax provisions are shown below:

There is a new 3.8% tax on unearned income for high-income taxpayers earning $200,000 for individual and $250,000 for joint filers. There is also a new annual fee on health insurance providers, and a new tax on health insurance policies costing more than $10,200 for an individual or $27,500 for a family.

There is a New Annual Fee on manufacturers and importers of branded drugs and, the most controversial tax is a 2.3% new tax on manufacturers and importers of certain medical devices. This is a thoroughly disliked tax, and in all probability will be repealed.

In addition, there is a 10% new tax imposed on each individual for whom "indoor tanning services" are performed and a 3.8% new tax on investment income.

Cost of Repealing ACA

The Republicans want to repeal the ACA. Al the last count this has been attempted by the Republicans forty-two times. Well what happens if the ACA Law is repealed? The CBO estimates that repealing the ACA would increase federal budget deficits by $109 billion over the 2013–2022 period. Repealing the coverage provisions would save $1,171 billion over that period, but repealing the rest of the act would increase direct spending and reduce revenues by a total of $1,280 billion.

In my next ACA missive I'll look at the states and the ACA.

References:

As always, I wish I could claim some originality in this missive but, again, as always, I cannot. Instead I must stand on the shoulders of others who are far more qualified than me to assess the ACA and the health care system that preceded it.

1. *Reinventing American Health Care* by Ezekiel J. Emanuel
2. *The Healing of America: A Global Quest for Better, Cheaper, and Fairer Health Care* By T.R. Reid

Letter 7 - The States and the ACA

The ACA, as conceptualized, was a three legged stool. The first leg was a mandate for people to buy insurance if affordable. The second leg was a prohibition against insurers from barring any buyers because of a pre-existing condition(s). The third leg was a huge expansion of Medicaid to provide free health care for the old and the poor.

Remember that Medicaid is a health coverage program for low income and families enacted in 1965 as a social safety net. It is jointly administered and funded by the federal government and the states. The federal government sets basic guidelines while the states have broad authority to modify Medicaid as they see fit, as long as they adhere to the federal guidelines.

The Medicaid expansion created consternation among many Republican states because it changed the eligibility guidelines, thereby increasing the number of insured eligible for Medicaid. For example, it created a new eligibility group: all adults not already eligible, which includes adults without dependent children (primarily old people), expanded the eligibility income to 133% of the Federal Poverty Level (FPL) for everyone except the elderly and disabled, and included several other changes, which expanded the eligible Medicaid roles.

(Note: 133% of FPL would include individuals making up to $14,856 and a family of four making up to $30,675. I personally don't see how it is possible for people to exist at this level of income.)

It should be noted that states, because of the recent recession, were having financial problems and one way to save money was by keeping eligible people off the insurance roles; therefore, they went to court against Obamacare even though the federal government will pay 100% of the state Medicaid expansion for the first three years and from thereon cover at least 90% of the cost of Medicaid.

In 2012, Supreme Court upheld two legs of the stool; however, it made Medicaid expansion optional for the states effectively cutting off the third leg of the stool. As a result you have 23 states, primarily Democratic, opt-in while you have 18 states, primarily Republican, opt-out. Those hit hardest by opting out were the southern states where 68 percent of African-Americans and two-thirds of all single mothers were excluded from the Medicaid rolls.

However, we now have many states with Republican Governors (the ones I know of are Arizona, Florida, Michigan and Ohio) who are now attempting to convince their Republican legislature to opt-into Medicaid expansion. One, Arizona, has been successful.

Although the Republican led state legislatures will continue to oppose Obamacare, I see no reason why the trend to expand state Medicaid, with modifications, will not continue. Many state legislatures, however, still have reservations about the additional cost burden imposed on the states after the three year period of 100% federal funding.

In my next missive I'll take a quick look at the short and long term issues with the ACA.

References:

As always, I wish I could claim some originality in this missive but, again, as always, I cannot. Instead I must stand on the shoulders of others who are far more qualified than me to assess the ACA and the health care system that preceded it.

1. *Reinventing American Health Care* by Ezekiel J. Emanuel
2. *The Healing of America: A Global Quest for Better, Cheaper, and Fairer Health Care* By T.R. Reid

Letter 8 - Short/Long Term ACA Issues

From my perspective, it is obvious we need to change the trajectory of health care in America and the ACA is Obama's attempt to do that. Unfortunately, it is plagued with both short and long term issues. Here is my take on those issues.

States have the choice of opting-in or opting-out of ACA. As a result you have 23 states, primarily Democratic, opt-in while you have 18 states, primarily Republican, opt-out. Those hit hardest by opting out were the southern states where 68 percent of African-Americans and two-thirds of all single mothers were excluded from the Medicaid rolls.

However, only 16 states and the District of Columbia intend to set up state exchanges (Model 1); seven more states are partnering with the federal government (Model 2) to operate their exchanges.

In the other 27 states, people without insurance will use federally managed exchanges to shop for coverage (Model 3). Those 27 states — many of which have actively opposed the health care law — contain about 20 million uninsured people.

The Insurance Exchanges opened on 1 October, 2013, with mixed results for State and Federal exchanges. The State Exchanges, for the most part, seem to be operating effectively. For example, KYnect, here in Kentucky, has received nothing but high praise from its subscribers. However, the same cannot be said for the Federal Exchange covering the 27 states that opted-out.

This, in my opinion, is primarily due to ten major issues. Bear in mind, this is sheer speculation on my part because the project has not released a report.

The overarching problem subsuming a number of issues was **poor management and poor personnel selection**. Typically on this type project there is a Project Manager who has overall responsibility and authority for project execution/implementation. Again, bear in mind that the ACA is an act of congress and they never consider execution as part of their mandate, yet they are the first to investigate when something goes wrong.

In the spring and summer of 2010, there was a debate in the White House about the necessity to hire an outside Project Manager who was experienced at this type implementation. The ACA economic team were the primary advocates of this approach. Unfortunately, the internal political partisanship mandated against this approach because at this time the Republicans were attacking the White House for having too many czars. Unfortunately, Obama caved and bowed to these complaints. Of course, his management style meant that outside consultants were rarely if ever used to manage important initiatives.

The other thing working against bringing in a Project Manager was that the independent economic experts were leaving government. Jeff Liebman, Bob Kocher, Peter Orazag, Larry Summer, and Rahm Emanuel were all leaving and all were advocates of hiring an ACA Project Manager with experience.

Nancy Ann Deparle, head of the White House health reform effort, was chosen to head the implementation of the Federal Web Site. She was a policy wonk with no implementation experience as were the remainder of the implementation staff. The resulting train wreck was inevitable.

In truth, Deparle offered John Kingsdale, who created the Romney Massachusetts website, the job of CEO (Project Manager) but he refused the position. Before accepting the position, Kingsdale had performed an analysis of the position structure and quickly realized the job was all responsibility with no authority. He wisely refused the position.

As an aside the first rule of management is that authority must be commensurate with responsibility. Kingsdale was right to refuse the position for without authority you cannot properly implement a project. Normally you hire a manager with experience to implement the project then back him/her with an Executive Board that supports his/her decisions across government. At the beginning of the ACA implementation project, the decision making authority was delegated downward to a board with little or no authority across government. Instead, the created board concentrated on impending regulation and not implementation. Well, as could be seen everything thing that could go wrong, in fact, did go wrong.

Short Term Issues

The mismanagement of the project resulted in a number of short term issues that, combined with the long term issues, created a disastrous Website implementation that delighted the Republicans and left a bad taste in the mouth of most Americans.

The shore term issues resulting from mismanagement, in no particular order, are as follows.

The **first** issue are the technical issues such as a lack of adequate bandwidth, page linkage, etc. Response time for the most part, seems to be greater than 3 seconds and users are typically unhappy with anything greater than 3 seconds. These are common technical issues affecting all new systems. It generally takes, with proper management, about a month or two to fix technical type issues.

The **second** issue is more headspace than anything else. That is, the user system assumption, which grossly underestimated the interest surge factor for the October 1 opening, particularly with regard to the desire of reporters, random shoppers, drive by users, random browsers, etc., to access the WEB site. An assumption was made to build the system to handle 60,000 simultaneous users. On the first day 350,000 users attempted to access the system. Can anyone spell OVERLOAD? These issues will be resolved when issue one is resolved which I suspect will be in the November/December 2013 timeframe. As an aside, assumptions are always the weakest part of any project. Just look at the first three letters in ASSumption.

The **third issue** is requirements change, sometimes called requirements creep. Numerous last minute software changes were levied upon the software engineers. This, in turn, means schedule changes and a reallocation of resources all leading to project turmoil. Can anyone spell REQUIREMENTS CREEP? This is always a recipe for disaster.

The **fourth issue** is a lack of Independent Verification and Validation (IV&V) expertise. That is, there was no one from a comparable industry with related experience who provided insight into the project. Normally, projects of this size have a major element that is independent of the "doing" function that looks over their shoulders and provides independent recommendations.

The **fifth issue** is project complexity. Because at least 27 states opted out and, therefore, invoked a Federal Exchange vice a smaller and less complicated state exchange that meant the Federal exchange would be built to accommodate at least 34 states instead of one. This, in turn, meant that the software became more complex and the response time more critical. More complexity means more coding, which in turn, means more schedule time which, unfortunately, was not allowed due to implementation constraints.

The **sixth** issue is inadequate testing. For example, most systems undergo a **Beta (Pilot)** test in which typical users access the system. This takes place before the system goes online. Another type test is volume testing in which the system is stressed. Apparently a type of **volume test** was performed which everyone deemed inadequate. 1 October was written in stone; therefore, they went ahead with the system start. It must be remembered, however, that a system is tested for normal operating conditions and not for unusual conditions. No system can ever be completely tested and rendered bug free; therefore, most operational systems will have software or hardware issues when they are implemented. The errors experienced by this system, however, were abnormally high due to a lack of testing.

The **seventh** issue is not technical in nature but deals with the users. This is a high deductible system requiring a greater knowledge on the part of the user. Users are simply not accustomed to thinking about their needs, so I suspect that is 2-3 years away. As an aside, users typically never know what they want until they see it.

The **eighth** issue is the sheer complexity of the system and its proper management. To my knowledge there were over 55 contractors developing pieces of the total system which needed to fit flawlessly together. Proper management of that many moving pieces, and integrating the individual hardware and software pieces into an operational system is a daunting task under any circumstance. As an aside, systems generally fail at the interface of their individual pieces or at the outer bounds of their performance envelopes. In this system, both factors seem to be in play. A **Systems Integrator** should have been brought aboard to assure the proper integration of all software and hardware components.

The **ninth** issue was the system contractor. CGI, a Montreal based company, was awarded the contract to build the ACA web site. CGI federal, the developer of the website was filled with executives from a company, AMS, that mishandled at least 20 other government IT projects, including a flawed effort to automate retirement benefits for millions of federal workers.

The **tenth** issue is the project management methodology. Whoever was in charge, I never could find out who it was, chose to utilize a "waterfall method" implementation methodology rather than employ a "cyclical (iterative) method." A waterfall method organizes the project constraints (time, money, people) into individual steps (requirements, design, analysis, etc.) that must be completed and approved in sequence. This is a known high risk methodology that has been abandoned by most competent managers in favor of a cyclical methodology in which each step becomes an iterative cycle (design, program, test, modify and repeat) thereby reducing the risk by giving the user something to see early in the cycle instead of waiting to the very end to show the user the end product. Remember what I said previously; the user typically does not know what he wants until he sees it.

The **eleventh** issue is the short term, political viewpoint on the part of the Obama administration policy makers in implementing ACA. For example, one of the documents a project manager normally publishes at the start of the implementation process is a "Concept of Operations" statement. The policy makers cum implementers worried that the Republicans would seize on this and double their attacks on the project, so they did not publish it. The same went for a draft "request for proposal" dealing with the website. They refused to publish that document also. In addition, the policy makers cum implementers refused to issue or delayed the issuance of federal regulations pertaining to the operation of the federal health insurance market in order to minimize any political controversy and a resulting impact on the 2012 election. It is always easy to sacrifice effective project implementation to these short term political gains, unfortunately, these short term gains contributed to the disastrous rollout of the ACA Website.

I expect most of the managerial and technical issues will be resolved by about mid-December, 2013, but that is by no means certain. An experienced project manager is finally being hired and the project staff is being increased to attempt to fix the technical glitches, however, the more staff, the more complex and lengthy the communication process becomes thus affecting the overall project schedule.

In the meantime, the emotional political volume is ramped up which also diverts the attention of the project staff. In addition, the Republican Committees want to hold hearings and have the project staff appear before them to explain the glitches, thereby, reducing their time to work on the problems. Really great political theater but poor project management, but, hey, let the uninsured die. After all, according to Republicans, it is their responsibility to properly manage their own lives and not the responsibility of the federal government.

With that sarcastic remark aside, users can buy health coverage on the marketplaces from Oct. 1, 2013, to March 31, 2014, so I suspect, even with these outside interruptions and diversions, the glitches should be fixed in time for user enrollment. Again, I suspect, by about mid-December, 2013.

Finally, **a caveat** on my expectations. If it is discovered that the system has a major design flaw, then all bets are off.

Long Term Issues

There are five real problems, however, with the long term survivability of the ACA.

The **First** issue is the poor sustainable ACA design because its finances depend upon forcing large numbers of young and healthy persons to buy insurance. Past Massachusetts experience has indicated that the young and healthy are the last to enroll, if they ever do. Without the young enrollment to pay for the poor and elderly, premiums will rise making the ACA look more like for profit health care.

The **Second** issue is that governmental insurance regulation will lead some employers to restructure their plans, force employees into public insurance exchanges, and make greater use of part-time employees. These potential employer actions will have a tendency to destabilize the current health care system which now covers most Americans. Remember, the ACA was primarily directed toward the estimated 40-60 million without health insurance and was not expected to interfere with those already insured. Employer actions to reduce their bottom line is expected to impact the current health care system.

The **Third** issue is that malpractice suits make up about 2% of the overall cost of health insurance. As mentioned previously, this is not insubstantial when considering the trillions of dollars spent on health care. I think it was a mistake not to include Tort reform in this bill. This problem needs to be fixed, hopefully, at the next bill change cycle.

The **Fourth** issue is the political dysfunction caused by the congressional split in the House of Representatives. The split between Democrats and Republicans and between the Republican extremes is making the House of Republicans and, therefore, the country almost ungovernable. That is, the Tea Party extremists in the House are holding everyone hostage to their demands to either defund or repeal ACA. There seems to be **two primary causes** for this extremism.

> The **first cause** is a self-sorting on the part of the population. This seems to be occurring in two different ways. **First**, people are geographically moving to areas with like-minded individuals and, **secondly**, they unconsciously associate themselves with like-minded people by listening to TV, radio stations or commentators they agree with. This is called the **echo chamber** effect.
>
> The **second cause** is that state legislatures, both Democrat and Republican, have gerrymandered districts to create safe seats. Unfortunately, this has had an unintended side effect. Those candidates running in the primaries in those safe districts must appeal to the extremists in that district to get elected. That means that in the general election only extremists are ultimately elected, resulting in a lack of House moderates. This has resulted in the election of Tea Party extremists who would rather cause a world-wide recession than compromise on ACA.

As an aside, the other side effect caused by gerrymandering has resulted in the extremist strategy to break up the Republican Party. That is, the Republican extremists are gradually arriving at the idea of gaining control of the Republican Party by breaking it up and moving it to the Libertarian wing of the party. It will be interesting to see how the moderates in the Republican Party counter this strategy.

The **Fifth** issue is the poisonous political environment fostered by the Republicans. Perhaps no era has been more poisonous since the Civil War, particularly as it pertains to the ACA. This resulted in **three major initiatives** to block the implementation of the ACA.

First, the Republicans are determined to delegitimize and undermine everything related to the ACA. Their motto from day one has been "repeal and replace." Unfortunately, they do not seem to have anything with which to replace ACA. From the Republican perspective, especially that of the conservative wing, their belief is that the ACA represents an alarming increase in the size of the federal government and an imposition of federal authority in a place where individuals should be responsible for their own health and insurance.

As an aside, I think the idea of "repeal" applies by Republicans also to the presidency of Obama. From day one McConnell has stated right up front that he intends to do everything he can to make Obama fail (even if that means the nation fails). The words in parenthesis are my words not McConnell's but I believe that is exactly what he means, and I think his attitude goes far beyond the fact that Obama is a Democrat. I suspect the heart of the matter for McConnell is that Obama is black.

Second, Republicans constantly lament any increase in spending on federal programs preferring to federally finance programs by entrusting them to state administration.

What surprised me about the republican state reaction to the ACA and the increase in Medicare, is the blind observance to ideology over practicality, as the states governed by republicans rejected the opportunity to create state exchange to provide their citizens medical care. Their rationale was that it would cost too much even though the federal government would fund 90% of the cost. In my opinion, this was simply a blind ideologically driven decision that ill served the people of their state.

To be truthful I did not expect this and I suspect a lot other people did not as well because this is what the Republicans normally want, and, that is, to allow the states to manage their own systems. Yet this was turned down by the republican leaders leading me to believe the decision was not only made for ideological reasons but also in an effort to delegitimize the ACA.

Third, and I found this fascinating, was that even though the ACA contained some funds for implementation, the Republican congress appropriated insufficient funds for all affected government agencies to effectively support the implementation of ACA. I personally thought this an extremely effective move on the part of the Republicans to attempt to block the implementation of ACA. Unfortunately, it led to insufficient funds on the part of many government agencies to properly perform their function of serving the American people.

Summary

This act is a good first step but does not go far enough in (1) controlling the burgeoning health care cost and (2) covering all Americans. As far I'm concerned, this act merely tinkers with the edges and will need several more iterations before it will solve (if ever) the escalating cost of health care which is the result of two major factors. The first is the wasteful and inefficient fee-for-service pay system based on procedures and not outcome and, second, our innovative technological approach to medicine which is excellent but expensive.

Well, it's better than nothing. An economist commented that the bill does not get us what we need, health care solvency, but at least it gets us on the path to slowing the rate of increase. I think that sounds about right.

In my next missive on Health Care I will discuss the opposition to the ACA.

References:

As always, I wish I could claim some originality in this missive but, again, as always, I cannot. Instead I must stand on the shoulders of others who are far more qualified than me to assess the ACA and the health care system that preceded it.

1. *Reinventing American Health Care* by Ezekiel J. Emanuel
2. *The Healing of America: A Global Quest for Better, Cheaper, and Fairer Health Care* By T.R. Reid

Letter 9 - Opposition to the ACA

About 82% of Americans are quite happy with their health care and the ACA will have little or no impact on them. The problem the ACA is attempting to fix is the other 18% which are those without insurance. There were between 40 and 60 million Americans (no one really knows how many) who had no health insurance, and as a result, many people, in attempting to pay their health bills, endured such things as losing their homes or going bankrupt. Even with enactment of ACA there will still be about 20 million Americans that will remain uninsured so the ACA is by no means universal health coverage as some claim.

Well, if the ACA is supposed to relieve the suffering and illness of so many Americans, then why are so many people opposed to it. The answer lies in their philosophy and ideology. There seem to be three major groups opposed to the ACA.

The **first group** opposed to the ACA are those American who believe in a **Single Payer** system. That is, socialized medicine where the government pays all the medical bills similar to the health care system now operating in Great Britain. They are opposed to a patchwork of private insurers and want a one-payer system. To put it bluntly, this is wishful thinking because such a system is politically impossible. There are simply too many lobbyist and politicians opposed to it.

The **second group** opposed to the ACA are those who believe the ACA will **cost too much** and will **reduce the quality** of the doctor's care. They believe the existing system has a few problems but on the whole is working just fine. They feel that the ACA, with its insurance exchanges, will make their own existing insurance more costly, less generous, and liable to failure.

The **third group** is the **Tea Party** and **extreme conservatives**. First, let me admit I was wrong about the Tea Party. In a letter I wrote in about '08 or '09 (see *Mutterings of a Madman 1: Letters to my family on War and Politics*), I indicated something to the effect that they were simply angry conservatives. I was wrong for they have proven to be conservatives with different stripes. They are basically **reactionary conservatives** that seem to operate from a paranoid perspective. They are basically against change, against Obama, and against the ACA no matter the cost. For example, in a recent survey 71% of the sampled Tea Party indicated that they "believe Obama will destroy the country." The description they give of themselves relates to concerns about the growth of government, the rise in taxes and the management of the economy. However, the underlying empirical data by one political scientist, under these umbrellas, showed the Tea Party extremists were racist and all were certainly anti-Obama. I think the political scientist is going too far in painting all Tea Party members with this brush and suspect he is speaking from a statistical standpoint.

However, one thing is certainly obvious about the Tea Party – they will not compromise. For the Tea Party members to compromise is to capitulate, and they will not. To capitulate means abandoning their ideology of little or no government. That is, anyone who disagrees with them or wants to compromise is not just a political opponent but is without a guiding ideology.

If you think this is an exaggeration, then simply look at the House of Representative and the 28 members comprising the Tea Party. They are all in for defunding/repealing the ACA, and have no intention of compromising, even if that means a default on our national debt and a resulting massive national and worldwide recession. They are currently Boehner's Palace Guards (although I suspect that is slowly changing as Boehner realizes how extreme their positions really are and how unmanageable they have become.). The Tea Party has been behind the attempted repeal/defunding of Obamacare over 42 times, and there is no reason to believe they will back off just because of a potential world-wide recession.

I suspect that is why a conservative republican called them "**lemmings with suicide vests**." One of the things I have noticed recently, though, is that the Republican establishment has finally awakened to the danger the Tea Party poses to them and is finally putting more moderate conservatives up for election hoping to draw the party back from the extremist positions of the Tea Party.

Some Problems

Many opponents of ACA have raised two real problems associated with the long term survivability of the ACA which I feel are valid. I will briefly mention these problems once more. They are:

First, it has a poor sustainable design because its finances depend upon forcing large numbers of young and healthy persons to buy insurance.

Second, governmental insurance regulation will lead some employers to restructure their plans, force employees into public insurance exchanges and make greater use of part-time employees. These potential employer actions will have a tendency to destabilize the current health care system.

These are just two of the sustainability issues dealing with ACA. Since the ACA is the law they will need to be fixed, and these issues, along with many others, cannot be fixed by shallow analysis, political breath-holding, or pledges of repeal.

In my next and last missive I'll look at the Supreme Court's decision regarding the ACA.

References:

As always, I wish I could claim some originality in this missive but, again, as always, I cannot. Instead I must stand on the shoulders of others who are far more qualified than me to assess the ACA and the health care system that preceded it.

1. *Reinventing American Health Care* by Ezekiel J. Emanuel
2. *The Healing of America: A Global Quest for Better, Cheaper, and Fairer Health Care* By T.R. Reid

Letter 10 - The Supreme Court Decides

On March 21, 2010 Obama signed the Affordable Care Act (ACA) into law. In the same month, practically the same hour, Florida, and twenty other Republican states, filed a lawsuit challenging the constitutionality of the law. This was surprising to many because they focused their lawsuit on the individual mandate, which was not a liberal cause, but was adopted from the Heritage Foundation, a conservative Republican think tank, thereby giving the impression that this was simply another Republican anti-Obama tactic.

By November, 2011, there were four federal circuit court rulings with differing interpretation of the constitutionality of the law. The 9th Circuit Court (covering the west coast, Alaska and the Pacific Islands) and the 11th Circuit Court (covers Alabama, Florida and Georgia) ruled the law unconstitutional. The 4th Circuit Court (covers Maryland, North Carolina, South Carolina, Virginia and West Virginia) ruled the lawsuit must be dismissed under a federal law governing tax collection. However, the 6th Circuit Court (covers Kentucky, Michigan, Ohio, and Tennessee) and the DC Circuit Court upheld the constitutionality of the law.

Since there was disagreement among the various Circuit Courts on the law's constitutionality, the Supreme Court decided to accept the case in order to resolve the conflict among the Circuit Courts and to establish a uniform law of the land.

There were two major issues brought before the Supreme Court.

The First Issue

The first issue brought before the Supreme Court was the constitutionality of the **individual mandate;** that is, the requirement that individuals have a minimum essential insurance coverage or face a financial penalty.

The ACA stated that Individuals who did not have health insurance coverage by January 1, 2014, must pay a penalty unless:

1. They are exempt of religion reasons.

2. They are Native Americans
3. They are incarcerated or fit some other exempt category

The IRS will collect this penalty through an individual's tax return. This penalty, by year, would be:

1. In 2014 the penalty would be $95 or 1% of an individual income whichever is greater capped at $285 dollars.
2. In 2015 the penalty would be $325 or 2% of individual income whichever is greater capped at $975 dollars.
3. In 2016 the penalty would be $695 or 2.5% of individual income whichever is greater capped at $2,085 and rising thereafter with the cost of living.

The Unconstitutional Argument

The Republican states had a very simple argument. They said that, yes, the constitution gave Congress the power to regulate commerce; however, by forcing people to pay a penalty congress, was forcing people to enter into commerce. That is, Congress could regulate activity but they could **not regulate inactivity**. If the court accepts the fact that Congress can require people to buy health insurance, then why couldn't it do the same for other areas of commerce.

The Constitutionality Arguments

Those people stressing the constitutionality of the ACA had 3 arguments.

Argument 1 was that Congress had the power to regulate commerce and this power was amplified by the Necessary and Proper clause. Congress enacted this law to address the health care marketplace involving 18% of the GDP. Health insurance will fail because of **adverse selection** in which only the sick buy insurance. In this case the insurance premiums for all people will rise to unacceptable levels unless there is an individual mandate to balance the sick and the healthy and the mandate is the only way insurance companies can offer Americans affordable coverage regardless of their health status. Congress was not regulating inactivity but simply regulating when people paid for the health coverage.

Argument 2 again relied upon the Necessary and Proper clause of the constitution. The government argued that this clause gave congress the power to do whatever is necessary to ensure its power to regulate commerce. Therefore, the constitution sanctioned the mandate because Congress thought it was necessary to impose the mandate in order to ensure a well-functioning insurance market.

Argument 3 postulated that the individual mandate was a tax, and since Congress had the power to tax the individual mandate it is constitutional because it functions just like any other tax. Many people thought this argument ironic because initially the Republicans insisted the mandate was a tax while the Democrats insisted it was not. Now the situations were reversed, with the Republicans insisting it was not a tax while the Democrats insisting it was. Go figure!

The Second Issue

The second issue brought before the Supreme Court was **the constitutionality of the Medicaid expansion,** which asked that the states expand their Medicaid and for those states that did not expand Medicaid, the law required the federal government to withhold **ALL** Federal Medicaid monies not just those to be used for expansion.

The Unconstitutional Argument

The states argued that the federal government cannot order the states to adopt certain policies. It can only 'bribe' states by conditioning the receipt of federal funds on compliance with federal rules. The Supreme Court had ruled in *South Dakota vs Dole* that sometimes these inducements might cross the line and become coercive. The states maintained that withholding **ALL** Medicaid funds was not inducement, but rather compulsion and coercion.

The Constitutionality Arguments

There were four arguments employed against the coercive argument.

The **first argument** was that when Congress enacted Medicaid in 1965, it reserved the right to amend the Medicaid requirements, and in the future it could and would change the program.

The **second argument** was that Medicaid was a minimal burden on the states, because the federal government is bearing 100% of the Medicaid expansion cost for the first three years, and that the government's proportion would slowly decline until the government assumes 90% of the cost burden.

The **third argument** was that the Medicaid expansion was scheduled to begin 4 years after the enactment of the ACA which gave the states plenty of time to make alternative arrangements.

The **fourth argument** was that the law did not require the federal government to withdraw ALL Medicaid funds. That is the ultimate penalty. Instead, it can elect to withdraw lesser amounts.

The Supreme Court Decision

Chief Justice John Roberts wrote the majority decisions for both issues.

The Individual Mandate Issue

The court ruled 5 to 4 (this majority included Roberts, Scalia, Thomas, Alito and Kennedy) that congress's power to regulate commerce **DID NOT** support the individual mandate.

Roberts argued that Congress did not have the power to regulate inactivity. He stated that the power to regulate commerce presupposed the existence of commercial activity to be regulated. He further stated that the commerce clause does not justify the individual mandate, because the mandate compels individuals to become active in commerce by purchasing a product.

The majority, however, did rule 5 to 4 (this majority included Roberts, Sotomayor, Breyer, Ginsberg, and Kagan) that the individual mandate was a lawful exercise of congressional taxing power. Roberts argued that the individual mandate is a tax and, therefore, justified by Congress's taxing power. He said this view is bolstered by the fact that the payment is made to the Treasury when tax payers file their income tax return. The conservative minority, however, held that because Congress had not specifically labeled the mandate a tax, it could not be considered a tax. Roberts held, on the other hand, that just because the mandate was not labeled a tax was immaterial for the question of constitutionality. That is, the constitutionality of the question was not controlled by Congress's choice of a label.

The Medicaid Expansion Issue

The court ruled 7 to 2 that the threat to remove all federal Medicaid funding was coercive. Roberts again wrote for the majority in declaring that removing all Medicaid payments to the state went too far; that is, the ACA changed Medicaid into a new program. The majority felt the states must not be coerced into accepting the ACA deal; the states must be able to reject the deal if they do not like the policy they are being asked to adopt.

Summary

Well, after the 28 June, 2012 Supreme Court ruling the ACA was clearly the law of the land. It had been passed by Congress, signed by the President, and upheld as constitutional by the Supreme Court. The act could now be implemented but with problems and challenges.

To get people insured, the ACA sat on **three provisions** that included a mandate for people to buy insurance, if affordable, a prohibition on insurers from barring any buyers regardless of health status, and a huge expansion of free health care for the poor through Medicaid.

The Supreme Court decision kept these provisions in place albeit with certain modifications. The health care system could extend coverage to about 30 million Americans and eliminate some of the most unpopular insurance practices such as no adverse selection and no rescission.

The Supreme Court's decision kept in place the law's linchpin, the individual mandate, which requires Americans to obtain health insurance or face a penalty. The ruling did limit one significant portion of the law, which sought to expand Medicaid to cover millions more poor and disabled people. The program is a joint federal/state effort, and the Supreme Court said the law's requirement is that states rapidly extend coverage to new beneficiaries, or lose all existing federal payments was unduly coercive.

The gutting of the ACA, the outcome hoped for by the conservatives, was narrowly avoided. Once the ACA starts working and delivering insurance, it will become practically impossible to repeal as more and more people get covered. So conservative opponents have attempted to kill it before it gets started. Thus far, the U.S. House of Representatives has voted to repeal Obamacare more than 42 times since passage, but it has been blocked by the Senate.

Despite conservative threats and the drama surrounding threatened government shut-down and the debt ceiling limit, the ACA law is almost certainly here to stay but it does need improving.

<u>References:</u>

As always, I wish I could claim some originality in this missive but, again, as always, I cannot. Instead I must stand on the shoulders of others who are far more qualified than me to assess the ACA and the health care system that preceded it.

1. *Reinventing American Health Care* by Ezekiel J. Emanuel
2. *The Healing of America: A Global Quest for Better, Cheaper, and Fairer Health Care* By T.R. Reid

Part 3

Demographics in America

Part 3 – Demographics in America

Context for the Demographic Letters

Well, as you know by now, I believe that context said or written is everything, for how else can you understand the statement. The current mid-year election is a good example for individual candidates to take statements out of context in order to build a negative attack ad against their opponent. This is nothing new; however, for it has been going on since the founding of the republic and it does make for interesting politics. Not surprisingly, Americans are exceptionally gullible, therefore, because of partisan politics, most people tend to believe the worst.

Over the next four letters I have attempted to highlight some of the more interesting demographic trends in the US and the world, but be aware that demographics must have context as statistics can also be taken out of context in order to prove just about anything. Remember, there are lies, damn lies, and then there are statistics.

Some of the statistics presented in the following letters will prove educational such as the fact that America is becoming more "brown" or perhaps alarming for Republicans is that nonwhites (Black, Hispanics and Asians) are expected to become a majority by 2043. This, of course, is expected to have dramatic implications for future elections since most Hispanic, Blacks and Asians vote Democratic.

Some will prove interesting such as the greying of America, and its projected impact on the social safety net. For example, every day 10,000 baby boomers turn 65 and this retiree flood is swamping the federal budget. It is estimated that by 2022, absent any changes, that Social Security, Medicare and the non-child share of Medicaid will exceed 50% of the federal budget, up from 11% in 1960 and 30% in 1990. To make room for the elderly, defense, education, and many other programs, domestic programs are being relentlessly squeezed.

Scared yet? Well read on about immigration, prison population, old age, the digital darkside, etc. Don't be afraid. Read on!

J.T. Oney

Letter 1 - Demographics in America

As you know I am a moderate in my beliefs and an independent in my political orientation. As a result I have a foot in both the Republican and Democratic camp but attempt to avoid the excesses of each. For example, I am a social liberal but a fiscal conservative.

In my previous letters over the last few years I have attempted to summarize the political differences between the political parties by sometimes quoting from others. One author said, tongue in cheek, that the difference between a Republican and a Democrat is that *"a Democrat will take your money while a Republican will get you killed."* I have always thought there was a bit of truth in that, because Democrats seem to concentrate on social issues while Republicans seem to concentrate on security issues.

There has always been a philosophical gap between the Republican and Democratic parties but, unfortunately, there seems to be a growing partisan gap that has accelerated during the Bush and Obama years. I suspect the divide accelerated during the Bush years because of his adventures in the middle-east and during the Obama years because he is black.

For whatever reason, according to a recent Pew Research Center report, the partisan political divide has far outpaced the divide from any of the other contentious issues such as religion, race, gender or education. This divide seems to be the result of both parties becoming smaller and more ideologically similar. Republicans seem dominated by self-described conservatives, while a smaller but growing number of Democrats are self-described liberals. Among Republicans, conservatives, buoyed by the Tea Party, outnumber moderates by roughly two-to-one. And there seems to be as many liberal as moderate Democrats.

Unfortunately, moderates in both parties seem to be a dying breed, Moderates, from my perspective, have been the only ones able or willing to govern, because to govern one needs to compromise, and extremists, from both the right and left, seem unwilling to compromise. Instead, they seem to confuse ideology with governing principles.

There is another factor that seems to be increasing the divide and that is a self-sorting of Americans. That is, there is a tendency among Americans to sort themselves into political parties based upon ideology. This sorting of America seems to be caused by three things:

First, people sort themselves into economic, cultural, political generational like neighborhoods;

Second, state gerrymandering based upon politics has resulted in safe-seat districts and;

Third, the rise of the amen chorus in the news media and the social media as exemplified by FOX and MSNBC news.

Among the media there seems to be the Red truth and the Blue truth which is primarily caused by the echo effect (the so called amen chorus) of the news media. That is, people listen and watch news programs they agree with. In addition, stations share news with like-minded stations resulting in news insularity. For example, in the presidential election of 2012 the conservative news media traded their facts back and forth in an echo chamber, and, as a result, predicted that Romney would win in a landslide, and seemed to have difficulty adjusting to the fact that Obama won.

In addition, news and commentary now seem interchangeable. A recent Pew Research survey looked at MSNBC and FOX news and compared the commentary to news content ratio. The news to commentary content ratio was, wait for it, FOX, 55% and MSNBC, 85%.

Patrick Moynihan once said, paraphrased, *"Everyone is entitled to their own opinion but not their own facts."* That no longer seems to hold with either the Democrats or the Republicans. Senator Ted Cruz, a Texas Republican, immediately comes to mind. Senator John McCain, an Arizona Republican, called him a "Wacho bird." I found that a fairly accurate description.

As indicated, there are several major divides between the parties, but the most prominent seems to be over the scope and role of government particularly in the area of economics. Democrats, for the most part, believe that government can and should play a constructive role, while Republicans generally believe in minimal or no government interference. This difference is followed by lesser divides with regard to the social safety net (think Obamacare, food stamps, etc.), immigration (think 11 million illegals), labor unions (think the recent defeat of unions at the Tennessee VW plant), and the environment (think global warming as a false science). These lesser divides can, however, easily be subsumed under the umbrella of the divide over the perceived role of government.

One worrisome trend for the Republicans, however, is the fact that they have grown more homogenous (White, Anglo Saxon, and Protestant) whereas the Democrats have grown more diverse (White, Black, Hispanic and Asian). I say unfortunate, because the three fastest growing US populations are the Hispanic, Blacks and Asians while the fastest diminishing population are the Whites. This trend should seriously concern the Republicans.

Different Generations

Not only is there a growing difference between Democrats and Republicans, but there also seems to be a major divide between adult generations on just about everything, which seems to play out in different political agendas. For research purposes, the adult generation is divided into the Millennial Generation, the Gen X Generation, the Baby Boomer Generation, the Silent Generation and the Greatest Generation. Most research has been done on the first four since the Greatest Generation, born before 1928, is gradually dying out and now has little impact in the political arena.

According to Paul Taylor, the primary author of *The Next America:*

The **Millennials**, born after 1980, are taking longer to grow up and are living longer with their parents. They are a strong supporter of a larger, more activist government and have voted more democratic than the older generations. They are a racially and ethnically diverse generation and are at ease with racial, ethnic and sexual diversity. They are the least religiously connected of all the generations.

The **Gen Xers,** born between 1965 and 1980, are navigating middle age with mounting anxiety about their economic future. They seem to represent the dividing line on many issues between young and old. They favored Obama in 2008 but were divided in 2012. They also take a more liberal view of social issues than other older generations. Jobs are the number one issue among this generation and they seem to be concerned about their financial future with 46% saying they are concerned they will not have enough income and financial assets to last through retirement. Finally, they are the product of the divorce revolution and the single parent family.

The **Baby Boomers,** born between 1946 and 1964, are approaching retirement not nearly as secure as they had hoped. They seem divided on their politics and will vote either Republican or Democratic. For example, in 2008, Obama was preferred more by older Boomers than younger Boomers; however, a majority now seem to prefer a smaller government that provides fewer services. Many Boomers express reservations about the changing face of America, that is, the fact that America is becoming browner not whiter. They oppose cutting entitlements to reduce the deficit while simultaneously also supporting reducing the Social Security and Medicare benefits of higher income seniors. On the other hand, they oppose raising the eligibility age for Social Security and Medicare benefits.

The **Silents,** those born between 1928 and 1945 (All Oneys belong to the Silent Generation), are the most financially secure of the four adult generations but also the most unsettled by the pace of social change (think gay marriage).They have become more Republican in recent years as opposed to the Greatest Generation (our father and mother) which were primarily Democrats. They are the most politically energized of all age groups and are both angry and frustrated with government. They strongly disapprove of Obama for whom they did not vote. Their discontent does not seem to be based on economics but upon race. They are the whitest of all generations and are least accepting of the changing face of America (think Obama with a brown face). They view with displeasure interracial marriage and immigrants and their top voting issue is, yes, you guessed it – keep your hands off Social Security and Medicare.

Statistics

The current divisive trends are, of course, statistically based and are derived through questions about what people are interested in. Mark Twain once attributed the following quote to Disraeli, *"there are lies, damn lies and there are statistics,"* and for anyone who has utilized or looked at statistics they quickly realize that with statistics you can prove just about anything. One researcher stated the problem like this: *If you ask an American whether he favors more assistance to the poor, 70% will say yes but if you ask him whether they favor spending on welfare then 70% say no.* Well, which is it? Probably both for the answer you get depends upon the question you ask.

However, despite its ability to lie based upon the question you ask, statistics can be useful for looking at long term trends and then attempting to interpret those trends in light of our present situation. With that in mind, several weeks back, I ran across a book entitled "***The Next America***" by Paul Taylor, a researcher at the Pew Research Center and a Pew Research Study entitled, "*Trends in American Values: 1987-2012.*"

I found the book and research study exceptionally interesting because it posits three major trends (among others) in America and their relationship to defining our current political dysfunction. That is, the political divide among our citizens resulting in our current political dysfunction can be traced to the philosophical differences on how we handle these three major trends in America and the role of government in each trend.

These major trends are immigration, family breakdown, and the aging population. These trends, however, subsume a number of major political issues under their umbrella.

First, immigration.

There is a term, **Generational Replacement**, which is used by demographers to describe population change. For example, in 2014 approximately 4 million Americans will be born, 1 million will arrive as immigrants and 2.5 million will die. With this churn in population also comes the issue of longevity. For example, the average life expectancy in the US was 47 years in 1900, 62 years in 1935, 79 years in 2014 and is projected to be about 84.5 in 2050. I suspect with the addition of bionic implants, etc., that by 3000 our life expectancy should approach 120 years. I hope not, but suspect that will be the outside limit of human longevity.

The problem most countries face is the fact that with longevity comes lower birth rate. It is just a fact of life that, as humans live longer they have less children, because the children live longer. This has some interesting consequences.

Japan, for example, has the highest longevity and as a result their market for adult diapers is greater than the market for baby diapers (Well, I thought it was an interesting statistic!). The problem facing most nations is the implication that the less youth they have the less workers they have. I suppose that is one reason why Japan puts so much emphasis on robots.

Fortunately, because of our immigration problems, the US is not faced with a declining population problem. By 2050, immigrants and their U.S. born children are projected to represent 37 percent of the population, slightly higher than in 1900, when the country last experienced a wave of mass immigration. Between now and 2050, however, it is expected that immigrants and their children will generate roughly 75% of the population growth and account for 90% of the growth in the US labor force. Now, I did find THAT interesting.

One of the interesting phenomenon immigrants and their children have created is the "**Browning**" of America. That is, the skin color of Americans is gradually changing from white to brown and as a result whites are becoming a minority. We are no longer going to be all Black, all Hispanic, all White, all Asians, etc., and, therefore, I'm not sure those sort of labels are going to apply in the future.

Well, why not?

Well, 25% of all Hispanics and Asians are marrying someone of a different race and so are 1 in 6 blacks and 1 in 11 whites. As these couples have children how will we label them? According to color? I suspect that due to interracial marriage that the color of the average American will eventually be, yep, you guessed it – brown. In labeling people we are certainly going to have to be more nuanced than we currently are, yet, we are certainly not going to be color blind because we are simply not wired that way. There will always be the issue of "us and them!" That is simply a survival instinct ingrained into our very genes.

As an aside us Oneys don't need to worry about our racial purity since our gene pool was polluted a long time ago by Blackhawk – just look at the browning of Dad, Bill, Rita and Larry. Hey, to be truthful, I wish I was a little browner particularly when it comes to getting out in the sun. Certainly, if Deke was a little browner, he would not have to worry about the precancerous bumps on his head and ears.

The "**Browning**" of America does, however, have some political implications. Hispanics and Asians currently make up 22% of our population and in 2012, 71% of Hispanics and 73% of Asians voted for Obama. In 2060, they will make up about 40% of the US population. They are hard-working, family-oriented, entrepreneurial, and freedom loving, all characteristics that should make them good Republicans. Unfortunately, the current anti-immigrant rhetoric of the Republican Party has driven them into the Democratic camp where they favor active government and are socially liberal which makes them good Democrats.

Immigrants, since the founding of America, have always created a cultural backlash and that seems to be the case today. From my standpoint, the question is whether newcomers will be constructively assimilated or whether, as most Republicans seem to believe, they "take our jobs, drain our resources, threaten our language . . . and import crime."

Whatever one believes about immigrants, America's population profile is changing. In 1960, 85 percent of Americans were white and 10 percent were black. In 2014, 63 percent are white, 13 percent black, 17 percent Hispanic and 5 percent Asian. In 2050, those shares are projected to be 47 percent white, 13 percent black, 28 percent Hispanic and 8 percent Asian. The census bureau estimates that by 2043 **nonwhites** will become the majority of the US population. This, obviously, has massive implications across the social and political spectrum.

Well, back to my letter. Obama was elected in 2012 not by whites but by Blacks, Hispanics and Asians. It is estimated by some pollsters that if only whites had voted then Romney would have been elected by 18 million votes. (Now you know why Republicans want to implement VoterID laws.) As it was he received only 17% of the nonwhite votes. As a result, Jeb Bush lamented that the Republicans were perceived as a party of "anti-immigration, anti-woman, anti-gay, anti-science,...". Apparently anti-everything since they have become known as the party of "NO."

Obviously the Republicans need to address the immigrant issue but for some reason cannot seem to come to grips with it but instead have engaged in an intra-party civil war between the Republican establishment and the Tea Party on who will control the future of the party. This is obviously good for the Democrats but bad for the country. I used the term civil war but I'm no longer sure that is the proper term. The battle seems to be becoming more of a free-for-all and is reminding me more and more of the Democratic Party. *Question: How do you tell thirty Democrats from thirty Republicans; Answer: Thirty Democrats will have thirty opinions while thirty Republicans will have one opinion.* The answer now seems to be that thirty Republicans will also have thirty opinions especially when it comes to immigration. At last, the parties now seem to have something in common.

One of the things I worry about is the obstinate refusal of both parties, state and federal, to adequately support education for if our population is gradually dominated by Blacks, Hispanics and Asians then they must be properly educated if the American experiment is to remain viable. I have always imagined education as being a three legged stool with the three legs being teachers, parents and the social environment in which the students live. If one leg is broken or fails then the education of our children is affected which then effects the survivability of country. Unfortunately, both Democrats and Republicans don't seem to want to do anything about repairing any of the three legs of the education stool.

As an aside, from my perspective, parents, not teachers, have the prime responsibility for educating their children. Unfortunately, parents seem to view education as a teacher responsibility and have abandoned their responsibility to teachers.

Second, Family Breakdown.

There currently seems to be less people marrying and more people divorcing leading to a breakdown of family structure. For example, amongst the Millennials, 18-29, just 20% are married compared to 59% in 1960.

In one form or another, marriage has been a foundational social institution upon which the world's cultures have been built yet it now seems to be on the decline. This is especially true in the Scandinavian countries where cohabitation has replaced marriage.

The declining marriage rates seems to be a class based phenomenon. That is, in 1960 the marriage rate of college graduates was 74% while those with just a high school diploma was 72%, a difference of only 2%. In 2011 the marriage rate for college graduates was 63% while for those with high school diploma was 46%. A difference now of 17%. It may now be that economics has begun to play a major role in marriage.

I find the decline in marriage rates interesting because of what it says about marriage in general. For example, marriage has been generally viewed as an efficient way to allocate and combine labor because it promotes values and behavior associated with economic success. If marriage seems to make people more economically secure then why aren't people marrying?

Well, most analysts point to the impact of the economic structure. One reason, they cite, is the movement of women into the workforce which undid the male template as the family breadwinner. This is compounded by the development of the knowledge based economy, which has diminished the job prospects for those less educated, which means the less educated become less desirable marriage partners, and from an educational standpoint, the female has far outstripped her male counterpart. In the modern market place, fewer women want a husband for financial security, and fewer men can provide it, which means less marriages.

As an aside when I was growing up in the 40s teachers paid particular attention to the male student. Now teachers seem to pay more attention to the female student. I'm not sure why that is; perhaps female students simply cause less problems for educational institutions.

Modern society seems to base marriage on love; however, for centuries marriage had little to do with love, but thrived as a way to propagate the species, establish a place in the social order, acquire wealthy and powerful in-laws, organize productivity, provide child labor, and distribute resources from parents to children. It was only in the age of Enlightenment (starting in about the mid 1500s) that love and mutual fulfilment started to be associated with marriage. Today, love seems to play the dominate role in marriage. I'm not convinced that marriage based solely on love provides a more stable base than does a marriage based on economic self-interest. America now seems to be in a great experiment to see how that will play out.

However it appears, marriage seems to have become a lifestyle choice rather than a love or economic choice, and, as a result, 27% of all households are now headed by a single person. As marriage has declined, there has inevitably been a rise in births outside marriage. For example, in 1960, 5% of childbirths were to unmarried mothers whereas in 2011, 41% of all births in the US were to unmarried mothers. Strangely, this is not due to teenage pregnancies. Today teenagers give birth to only 10% of all babies and 18% of babies born out of wedlock while the rest is attributed to women in their 20s and 30s. I was unable to find any research to indicate why that is.

The Single Parent Family

I need to elaborate further on family breakdown, especially black families, but first some background. In 1965, Patrick Moynihan, who at that time was Assistant Secretary of Labor, produced a report entitled, ***The Negro Family: The Case for National Action,*** that has been politically and racially divisive for decades. Moynihan's thesis was that the progress toward racial equality would be held back because so many black children were being raised by single parents. He argued persuasively that the black family was a by-product, not just of the environment, but of a matriarchal family culture tracing its roots to slavery. Moynihan attributed the increase in single black parents largely to the precarious economic position of black men, many of whom were no longer able to play their traditional role as their family's primary breadwinner. Moynihan argued that growing up in homes without a male breadwinner reduced black children's chances of climbing out of poverty, and that the spread of such families would make it hard for blacks to take advantage of the legal and institutional changes flowing from Johnson's civil rights legislation.

The Democrats ran with the report and ramped up the Aid for Dependent Children (AFDC) program while the Republicans bemoaned the rise of the "**welfare queen**." This conflict has been raging ever since. Moynihan was concerned by the fact that in 1964 the out-of-wedlock births among black women was 25%.

Should he have been worried?

Moynihan was demonized but clearly prescient in thinking that America's black families were changing in a fundamental way. In 1965, when Moynihan's report was released, roughly 25 percent of black children and 5 percent of white children lived in families headed by an unmarried mother. By the 1980s these percentages reached about 50 percent among blacks and 15 percent among whites. After 1980, the rate of increase in single families began to decrease. In the 1990s fifty-four percent of black children were being raised by an unmarried mother but had decreased to about 50 percent in 2003. Among white single parents the rate rose slowly through 1990s but now stands at about 36%

This year Sara McLanahan, Princeton University, and Christopher Jencks, Harvard Kennedy School, produced a document entitled, *Was Moynihan Right.* This study shows the out-of-wedlock births among black women is now 72%, among Latinos the rate is 54%, while among whites the rate is 36%. Even with the increase of out-of-wedlock births the racial makeup of single-mother families has not changed significantly. For example, in 1970, 31 percent of single-mother families were black, 68 percent were white, and 1 percent were "other race." In 2013, the figures were 30 percent black, 62 percent white, and 8 percent "other."

Strangely, nowadays no one seems shocked by these statistics or at least wants to admit their shock. I suppose because of the furor raised by the Moynihan report.

There is consistent evidence that a child of an unmarried mother reduces a child's chances of employment, increases the chances that a child will divorce as an adult, and that a daughter will also have a birth out-of-wedlock. In addition, children with unmarried mothers will normally have a biological father who is in prison, beats his partner, cannot find or keep a steady job, and/or makes his living by selling drugs.

Unmarried mothers have seldom done well in school, many lack even a high school diploma, and few have completed college. If these mothers can find work, their earnings are usually lower than working married mothers. Their hours are often long, erratic, or both. Unmarried mothers are also more likely than married mothers to have physical and mental health problems, and probably less likely to have habits or skills that help children escape from poverty.

Obviously none of these characteristics can be expected to produce a successful child.

Divorce Rates

The other reason for single parent families is the divorce rate. Divorce rates have been declining in the US from its peak in the 1970s and 1980s. Part of what accounts for this decline is that less people are marrying, hence less divorces. One exception to the declining divorce rate is the rising divorce rate among the elderly. The, so called, *"gray divorce."* In the 1960s, the divorce rate among those 50 and older (the Baby Boomers) was 2.8% while in 2011 the rate of divorce for those 50 and older is now 15.4%. One author noted that there are now more Americans in this age group divorced, 15.4%, than widowed, 13.5%.

Most women of this age group are the ones that initiate the divorce since they seem to not want to *"wait it out."* This seems to imply that the Baby Boomers divorce rate may also be a reflection of the advance in their overall quality of life and women's changing roles, opportunities and expectations.

Despite the economic advantage of marriage, unmarried women, in 2011, accounted for 41% of U.S. births, up from 5% in 1960. This trend crosses all major population groups. As mentioned previously, the rate is 29 percent for whites, 53 percent among Hispanics and 72 percent among African Americans. Although 60 percent of single mothers have live-in boyfriends, half of these relationships end within five years. In summary, the stigma of single parenthood is gone.

The Brown Bag Story

At a recent dinner with Nora and her mother we got into an interesting discussion about Rep. Paul Ryan and his Brown Bag story. Rep. Ryan was attempting to make the point that there was no need for schools to have free lunches for that simply **"provided a full stomach but an empty soul."** Ryan was telling a story he had heard from Eloise Anderson, who served in Gov. Scott Walker's cabinet (the Governor of Wisconsin). He was attempting to make the point that children did not want free school lunches and that what they wanted was a brown bag lunch fixed by their parents to take to school. As an aside, this story subsequently earned Ryan four Pinocchios and the ridicule of Jon Stewart (the Comedy Hour) since the boy in the story actually advocated for a free lunch.

Nora, as many of you know, teaches 7th grade English at Poe Middle School in Fairfax County, one of the most affluent counties in the country. Unfortunately, Poe also sits in the middle of a disadvantaged area, and 65% of Poe students receive free or reduced meals. She commented that Rep. Ryan should visit her school, among many schools, for a first-hand look at the reality of child hunger that exists even in the middle of wealth and what a "Brown Bag Lunch" or any food really means to children. She indicated at her school the children, as part of the free or reduced lunch program, are fed a free breakfast, lunch, and dinner and that these are often the only meals they get—and they don't refuse them to make a political statement.

The school has a cafeteria, but since the program does not pay for dinner, that meal is provided gratis by local churches and other support organizations. Apparently different churches alternate on a weekly basis to feed the children. In addition, she said, brown bags of food are provided to the children on Friday so that they and their families will have something to eat over the weekend.

The reason I mention this story is that the majority of these children are from poor, single parent families or immigrant.

Gay and Lesbian Marriage

I think I would be remiss if I did not address Gay and Lesbian Marriage. When looking at the research of marriage, one of the things I found interesting was that just as there has been a general decline in marriage among the general population, there has been a corresponding increase in marriage among gays and lesbians. They seem to view marriage as crucial in their quest for civil rights and social acceptance. For decades the argument by conservatives against gay marriage was that it would weaken the link between marriage, child birth, and child rearing. Unfortunately, since more straights are not marrying this is becoming a more difficult case for the conservatives to make.

At the same time as the decline in marriage has been occurring there has been a dramatic change in the public perception of same-sex marriage. Many researchers think this is the largest swing in public opinion that they can ever recall. In the 2004 election, the GOP strategists went out of their way to put the issue of gays and gay marriage on state ballots, and it was widely thought to have increased turnout among socially conservative voters in several key states since, at that time, 36% strongly opposed gay marriage while just 11% strongly favored it. In a 2012 survey, 22% say they strongly support allowing gays and lesbians to marry legally while an identical 22% strongly oppose gay marriage. A more recent survey indicated a more dramatic split in age groups in that 70% of Millennials favor the legalization of same-sex marriages while only 31% of the Silents were for it.

This view does not seem to relate to how people feel about marriage, but how people in general feel about gays. Familiarity seems to lead to acceptance since 87% now say that know someone who is gay or lesbian in contrast to 61% in 1993. This may have been helped by the recent **"coming out of the closet"** by an NFL and NBA player. This, however, does not seem to indicate an acceptance of homosexual behavior since in a 2013 survey 45% of Americans indicated it was a sin.

In addition, even though gays view same-sex marriages as the crown jewel in the quest for acceptance, they are still not rushing to the altar. A recent survey of LGBTs (Lesbians, Gays, Bisexuals and Transgenders) indicate that 60% say they are married or would like to get married while for the general public that figure is 76%.

As an aside, defining marriage between same sex partners as a family form has caused me some difficulty. However, as I look around, I am struck by the different family forms that seem to run the gamut from two parents, to single parents, to same sex, to multigenerational, to biracial, to God knows what all. Strangely, Americans, on the whole, seem to be rather nonjudgmental about family forms. For example, 90% say a single parent with a child is a family while 60% say same sex couples are also a family.

I must admit to some uneasiness in my attempt to come to grip with same-sex marriage and am still struggling to accept the new forms of marriage.

The Prison Population

Although the United States comprises just five percent of the world's population, we incarcerate almost 25% of the world's prisoners. The normal rate of incarceration for countries comparable to the United States is around 100 prisoners per 100,000 residents. The U.S. rate is 500 prisoners per 100,000 residents, or, as of 2014, about 2.3 million prisoners in 1,719 state prisons, 102 federal prisons, 2,259 juvenile correctional facilities, 3,283 local jails, and 79 Indian country jails as well as in military prisons, immigration detention facilities, civil commitment centers, and prisons in the U.S. territories. Not included in these figures are

3,981,090 people on probation and 851,662 people on parole. This amounts to over six million Americans.

In addition, there is a tremendous amount of *jail churn* since 688,000 people are released from prisons each year while almost 12 million people cycle through *local jails* each year.

Men make up 90 percent of the prison and local jail population and the majority of those are in their 20s and early 30s. According to a recent survey the average state prisoner has a 10th grade education, and about 70 percent have not completed high school. Incarceration rates are significantly higher for blacks and latinos than for whites. In 2010, black men were incarcerated at a rate of 4,347 per 100,000 residents; Latinos were incarcerated at 1,775 per 100,000, and white men were incarcerated at 678 per 100,000.

Becky Pettit, a University of Washington Sociologist, writes that blacks, ages 18-34, are at least six times more likely to be incarcerated than young white men. She found that 37 % of young black males without a high school diploma were more likely to be in prison or jail on any given day than the 26% working. She went on to say that *"over the past 35 years the penal population has increased five-fold. There are 2.3 million Americans now behind bars and 1 in 31 American adults is now under some form of correctional supervision. Nowhere is incarceration more prevalent than in the African American community. My research shows that one in nine black men was incarcerated on any given day in 2008 and that 37 percent of young, black, male dropouts were behind bars."*

` I have always thought these statistics were a sad commentary of the state of our country, particularly when the blacks currently make up about 13% of our population, we have a black president and a growing black middle class. Unfortunately, it seems America has lost an entire generation of black adults.

The only example that black men seem to serve to their children living in a single parent family is that a prison term is a rite of passage to black adulthood.

Third, Aging.

Every day 10,000 baby boomers turn 65 and this retiree flood is swamping the federal budget. It is estimated that by 2022, absent any changes, that Social Security, Medicare and the non-child share of Medicaid will exceed 50% of the federal budget, up from 11% in 1960 and 30% in 1990. To make room for the elderly, defense, education, and many other domestic programs are being relentlessly squeezed.

While spending priorities have become oriented toward the top of the age pyramid, the economic need of the children and the poor has migrated to the bottom of the age pyramid. Right now, for example, the government spends $7 per capita for senior programs versus $1 per capita for children's programs.

In 1967, 33% of households headed by adults 65 or over lived in poverty, while only 12% of the households age 35 or under lived in poverty. As of 2014, the percentage has flipped. Now just 11% of households 65 and over live in poverty while 22% of those household 35 or under live in poverty. This reduction in elderly poverty is directly attributable to Social Security and Medicare and, as one author put it, "a great triumph of social policy." In the process of supporting the elderly, we seem to have forgotten about our children.

The aging issue is not just a problem in the US but is also a world-wide problem particularly in Europe and East Asia. It is estimated that by 2050 six European countries will have a median age of 50 or older. China's once wondrous economy, due to its one-child policy, will be particularly affected since it is expected *"to get older before it gets richer."* By 2050 over 438 million Chinese will be 60 or older, with the nation having an inverted family tree pyramid of four grandparents, 2 children and 1 grandchild. In 1975 there were 12 Chinese children for every 2 seniors; in 2035 it is estimated there will be 1 Chinese child for every 2 seniors. Who will now support the elderly? Chinese public one-child policy has had unforeseen consequences for both their elderly and their young!

China is not the only industrial nation experiencing the problem of aging. Currently Japan has the oldest population in the world. Right now the median age in Japan is 45 and by 2050 is expected to be 53. By 2060, 37% of Japan's population will be 65 or older.

Aging societies have trouble maintaining their economic vitality because the elderly simply do not have the energy, imagination, entrepreneurship, or drive of their youth. The real problem with Japan is not longevity, but fewer births. Today Japan's population is 127 million, by 2100 it is projected to be 84 million and could, as some scientist project, be as low as 47 million. Japan's fertility rate is 1.4 per woman whereas 2.1 births per woman is required just to maintain the population level.

No one seems to know why this occurred. Some attribute this decline to losing faith in themselves and their collective future; some attribute it to individuals turning their life to self-fulfillment, while others attribute it simply to a falling sex drive. I suspect there is no one thing, and I'm not even sure this trend can be abated due to the xenophobic and insular nature of Japanese society.

Countries as diverse as Italy, Spain, Japan, and Russia are experiencing the same aging problem but not due to a misguided public policy such as a one-child policy but due to a mix of globalization, urbanization, education and changing culture. Russia seems to be experiencing the most precipitous decline in fertility and is offering "baby bonuses" of $8,300 for the third child. Singapore seems more desperate in that they are offering the equivalent of a $135,000 bonus for the first seven years of a child's life.

Even the Muslim countries are experiencing the same phenomenon. More than 20 Muslim countries have experienced a fertility decline of 50% since the 1970s. For example, a typical Iranian woman, as of 1970, had 7 children. Now the typical Iranian woman has 1.9 children well below the sustainable rate of 2.1.

As an aside, I suspect that our increased world population and crowding has brought about this low birth rate. This may be a naturally occurring phenomenon among species caused by crowding. I have no proof of this, but nevertheless suspect it is true.

The graying of the population has helped polarize our politics, put stresses on our safety net, and presented unprecedented challenges to our politicians, who seem unable or unwilling to tackle these problems, particularly as they apply to Social Security and Medicare. These two programs are the most popular with about 90% of the population who believe they have been good for America.

That support, however, is unequal across generations. For example, 56% of the Millennials and 66% of the Gen Xers say Social Security should be completely overhauled, while 62% of the Silents say it works just fine. The difference in approval between generations is reflective of how each generation views the future funding of the Social Security program. That is, the Silents have theirs; however, the Millennials and the Gen Xers do not expect the safety net to be there for them when they retire. In essence, each generation seems to favor their own self-interest. This is why governing by surveys simply does not work.

Well, how do we fix the funding for Social Security such that it is supported by all generations? One idea is to **raise the age of eligibility**. The Silents favor gradually raising the age eligibility criteria for Social Security and Medicare, whereas the younger generation does not. That is just about what one would expect since it does not benefit the younger generation.

Another idea is **means-testing**. That is, reducing the benefits for well off seniors. From a means-testing perspective, 53% of Americans favor reducing Social Security benefits for seniors with higher incomes while 55% of Americans favor reducing Medicare benefits for seniors in the higher income brackets. For most Americans this makes some sense with regard to senior citizens with higher income but not for lower income senior citizens. For others, it is just "**Mean-Testing**" designed to pit one generation against another.

Decreasing benefits for all senior citizens can be a problem because 56% of retired people indicate that Social Security is their only source of income. However, among those who are not retired, 65% say that Social Security will not be their only source of income. Generations differ on this in that 57% of Millennials and 70% of Gen Xers expect financial shortfalls in Social Security and Medicare will lead to reduced benefits. Obviously, people's expectation of Social Security and Medicare has a major impact on policy changes to the safety net.

Well, if the safety net is not going to be available to the younger generation who will take care of them in their old age? Among the people surveyed there seems to be only two workable options: the government or individuals. Here the public seems to be fairly evenly split; 43% say the government should be responsible for ensuring a minimal standard of living while 40% say it is the responsibility of their families. The divide seems to be greater across income levels, since 33% of household with incomes of $75,000 or over say government should provide a minimal level of care, while 53% of households earning $30,000 or less favor the government providing a minimal level of support.

No matter the level of income most seemed to feel that the government should be the ultimate backstop.

When looked at from a political party standpoint, 69% of Democrats, 52% of Republicans, and 56% of Independents say that the government does not do enough for the elderly. I personally found this interesting because the government's spending priorities already seem to favor the elderly. I especially found it interesting because most Republicans are against big government, yet 52% of them said the government is not doing enough for the elderly.

Now Some History

Taylor tells the story of Ida May Fuller, SSN 00-000-001, who on Jan 31, 1940, on her 65th birthday, received the first check from Social Security for $22.54. The checks kept coming and by the time she died at 100 she had collected $22,899 from Social Security. Not much by today's standard but indicative of the problem facing Social Security. That is, the Silents and Boomers will get more out than they paid in while the Gen Xers and Millennials, absent any changes, will get less in benefits than what they paid in.

At its core, this is a problem of generational inequity. That is, the young are paying to fund the social security net that supports the old yet they have no prospect of collecting when they are old.

Certainly, a fact that FDR never envisioned when he created Social Security. In the early 1930s millions of people were homeless, tens of millions had lost their life savings, unemployment was at 25%, and the elderly were poverty stricken. To alleviate this condition Franklin Delano Roosevelt created the New Deal, and one program, designed to alleviate the poverty of the elderly, was the Social Security Act, which was signed into law in 1935.

Americans have always valued self-reliance and looked on welfare as charity, but the depression changed all that. For the Social Security system to operate and be accepted by the American people, Roosevelt knew the law must be **contributory** in nature. That is, workers would pay taxes that the government would hold, invest, and eventually pay out when you got old. However, Roosevelt's cabinet and congress (both Liberals and Conservatives), over his objection, negotiated a generation **transfer** program in which todays workers are taxed to pay for the benefits of the old.

In truth, the system is a hybrid because the payments are based not only upon what is paid in but also in part on a formula which serves a range of social purposes. Interestingly, the taxes were made **regressive** (the lower income brackets are taxed most heavily) while the benefits are **progressive** (the lower brackets get the most return). The social security net is really interesting because it is weighted in favor of one-earner married couples, those who live to an old age while simultaneously serving as a life insurance policy and as a disability insurance policy. If one looks at the current Social Security beneficiaries 41 million are retirees, 10 million are disabled while 7 million are either early retirees or survivors of deceased workers.

Social Security is basically a scheme to redistribute the wealth from the rich to the poor, from the young to the old and from everyone to those with a long life. From this perspective, it is easy to see why conservatives from Reagan, to Bush, to Paul Ryan have proposed privatization programs to replace Social Security. Milton Friedman, the father of trickle-down economics, has been especially critical since he prefers distributing wealth to the rich, which then supposedly trickles down to the poor. Bush Sr always called the trickle-down theory of economics **Voodoo Economics** and so it has proved to be. The conservatives have rightly identified problems with the safety net, but the privatization solution will never fly.

The problem with Social Security is basically this: When Social Security was first enacted there were 42 workers for every retiree. Unfortunately, this ratio has declined over the years to where it is now 3 workers for 1 retiree and is expected to drop to 2 to 1 by 2035.

Remember, I previously indicated that in 2010 the oldest Boomers, 10,000 per day, will turn 65 and apply for Social Security the same time as the system begins to fall below annual payouts. According to the Social Security Trustees, the Medicare trust fund (this is your FICA tax) will be empty by 2026 and the main Social Security trust fund will be empty by 2033.

The main driver in this is Medicare. In the 1950s and 1960s health care costs were affecting millions of Americans and driving them into poverty (Well, it still is) causing Lyndon Johnson, as part of his Great Society program, to attach the Medicare program to the Social Security system. The program was designed to help pay for the Medical Care (Medicare) of everyone 65 and older. It was funded by a tax (FICA) of 1.45% on each employee. Well, since we now have less workers, we have less money in the Medicare Trust fund which means the Medicare Trust fund in 2026 will be unable to cover promised medical benefits.

From my perspective this is due to three factors: a decreased tax base, people living longer and the rising cost of medical care. I would also point to the fee-for-service based medical payment system as a major driving cost. Right now we spend approximately 17.6% of our GDP on medical care. This is roughly twice the median share spent by other countries. The Affordable Care Act was intended to stabilize the rising medical cost, but unfortunately has encountered a faulty implementation and a major Republican roadblock. If you are interested in the Affordable Care Act, I encourage you to look at Part 2 of this book.

Analysis

America's future rests heavily on how these current trends play out. Democracy works best when the political system can mediate between the often inconsistent demands of public opinion and larger national needs. This, for whatever reason, the current crop of America's leaders, Reid, McConnell, Bohner, Pelosi and Obama, can't or won't do. Faced with immutable trends, they have not adapted to change. Instead, they pander to partisans with soothing, though outdated, stereotypes where ideology poses as policy and principles.

The graying of America is certainly one of the problems we face. I am now in my mid-70s and can look farther back than I can forward. Hell, the truth is, I now know more people dead than alive!

My youth and growth to manhood was in the 40s: A time of intact families, polite politics and, fortunately, a consensus building media. I now live in a time of broken families, dysfunctional politics, and a polarizing media that revels in "gotcha' moments and attack politics. Getting old can be a bitch but it does have its upside. (I will return to the aging problem in a future letter.)

One major character in demographics is the Baby Boomers. There are 76 million Boomers and only the Millennials, at about 80 million, outnumber them. The Boomers are a result of the Greatest Generation returning home from WW2 and settling into domestic life. The Boomers have always been a mixed bag, with some fighting the war in Vietnam while others burned their draft card and went to Canada. They defined themselves as counterculture when they partied at Max Yasgur's farm in Woodstock, NY. When the oldest Boomer entered the work force the nation's debt was in the millions; it crossed the 1 trillion mark in 1981 and now stands at about 17 trillion.

It was the Boomers political passivity that allowed the problem to get out of hand and now their frustration at the size of the federal debt has helped fuel the growth of the Tea Party and the rise of small government conservatism. They did not pay the tab for the goods and service they asked for from the government and now their debt is being passed on to their children and grandchildren especially the Millennials. The challenge associated with the Boomers is gradually being magnified by their age. The oldest Boomer turned 65 in 2011. When the youngest Boomer turns 65 in 2030 there will be about 80 million retirees, double the figure in 2000 all competing for Social Security and Medicare benefits. This is in addition to the "**old-old**", those 85 and older, who will more than triple between now and 2050 to about 19 million.

Fewer workers supporting the old is not a good formula for economic growth or a rise in the standard of living. Unfortunately, as the Boomers have grown older they have become more conservative, making them unlikely candidates to restrain the growth in the social safety net.

That leaves the Liberals, who won't come to terms with aging, believing that spending on the elderly and near-elderly constitutes the essence of progressivism. They seem to ignore the affluence of many elderly, with some liberals even supporting raising these benefits. The paradoxical result is that the pro-government party has become an instrument of anti-government policies, because accommodating all the elderly's benefits means quietly condoning deep cuts in most other programs, particularly those of the poor and young and, by its very nature, this brand of liberalism discriminates against the young and the poor especially in education.

The new demographics of aging mean that we have made promises to the Silents and the Boomers that we now cannot pay for. When the safety net was put in place we had more workers than retirees, fewer people living to old age and health care costs that had not gotten out of control. The young are now paying taxes to support the older generation that they themselves cannot expect to receive when they get old. That mean we will either have to shrink the safety net for the oldsters, raise taxes, or both.

This has the potential to set off a generational war although it does not have to if we and our politicians have the will to address the issue which they don't seem to have the courage to do. The Democrats will eventually need to address the coming age of austerity. Rebalancing the entitlement programs such as Social Security and Medicare to the demographic realities will be a massive challenge to the Democrats, and I'm not sure they have the courage to handle it.

Conservatives have a parallel hang-up. They can't adapt to the permanence of Big Government or the presence of so many immigrants, including an estimated 11 million who are here illegally. Even if some ineffective government programs are cut, federal spending will easily exceed one-fifth of national income, which is more than today's taxes will cover. Higher taxes, contrary to GOP dogma, will be needed. Similarly, illegal immigrants won't conveniently vanish. I believe that a path to citizenship will inevitably need to be provided, even though that will create a furor among the conservatives. This is a massive challenge for conservatives and, unfortunately, because they have confused ideology with governing principles, they also do not have the courage to handle this problem.

One interesting phenomenon, which is not a result of the trends but seems to parallel, them is the hollowing out of the middle class which has been accompanied by a rise in inequality between the richest Americans and everybody else. According to researchers, if one looks at wealth rather than income, the gap in inequality is starkly aligned by race and age. It is estimated that as of 2011, the typical White household has 14 times the wealth of the typical Black household, which I suspect can be partially attributed to the breakdown in Black families and the residual effect of racism. The typical older household has 26 times more wealth then the typical younger household, which I suspect can be attributed to public policy that favors the elderly.

Technology does, however, seem to play a role in the hollowing out of the middle class in that whole classes of workers have been wiped out due to the influence of computers, robots, and technologies associated with the Internet. Over time, however, technology seems to create more jobs than it destroys although these jobs demand more advanced skills, training, and education than the middle level jobs they replace. The technology (digital) revolution has resulted in a digital divide that has left the middle class in worse shape than it found it, while shrinking government services and looming tax increases compound the damage. (I may also take a look at the impact of the digital world in a future letter.) Education, I suspect, is the answer to this problem. Unfortunately, state and federal legislatures are short changing educational institutions due to the lack of funds caused by an imbalance between taxation and misaligned spending priorities.

Another surprising survey finding is that there is little evidence that the rich is resented; however, Americans do seem to resent the policies and institutions, both political and economic, that they believe are rigged in favor of the rich. This is one trend that will need to be watched closely and something done about it; however, I'm not sure the Republicans are capable of addressing this since their ideology is centered on the trickle-down theory of economics in which the wealth is distributed to the rich in hopes that it will trickle down to the poor. George Bush senior called it **'voodoo economics'** and so it has proved even though Republicans grasp it more firmly than ever.

Government can't do much about the decline in marriage, but there will need to come a day when the entitlement programs for seniors are trimmed, and families will have to reclaim some of the caregiving they have relinquished to the state. I really don't know how this will play out because of the changing structure of the American family. The family is in constant churn due to nonmarriage, divorce and short lived cohabitation. Compounding these problems is the fact that 4 in 10 children are born out of wedlock, and in the US, when compared to other nations, a child has less chance of being raised by both biological parents. This may shape the future middle class because growing up in a single-parent home puts children at a disadvantage. Paul Taylor summarized the Social Science research finding that children in two-parent homes — despite millions of exceptions — are *"healthier, do better academically, [and] get into less trouble as adolescents."*

What's needed is a bargain in which Democrats trim retiree benefits (Social Security and Medicare) and, in exchange, Republicans deal forthrightly on immigration and taxes. This seems unlikely, because it would require both parties to accept the world as it is, not as they wish it to be. Ideology always seems to trump good politics which is based upon practicality. What politician wants to be practical when they can be an ideologue and shout how they stand for principles, while all the while we are surrounded by political dysfunction.

Appraising America's democratic prospects in the mid-1940s, historian Denis Brogan wrote that "the pessimists have always been wrong." Maybe, but from my perspective they're starting to look more like Nostradamus. However, I am an optimist and believe that if we can get our spending priorities and generational inequities in order, we can keep our economy second to none especially in comparison to China, Germany, Japan, and Russia whose populations will be even older.

One researcher presented this picture of the US: We are growing older, more unequal, more diverse, more mixed race, less married, less fertile, less religious, less mobile and less confident. Our politicians, media, and population have become more polarized and partisan. Our middle class is shrinking, the medium income has flat-lined, our social classes are more divided, the wealth gap has widened, and our neighborhoods sorted by parties. Marriage is in decline, the single person households are growing, 4 in 10 newborns have an unwed mother, and, finally, younger adults are taking longer to grow up, the middle-aged longer to grow old and the elderly longer to die.

Well, this is about all the news from Lake Woebegone and perhaps all the news you can stand.

Just remember these are only statistics. Right?

References:

I wish I could claim some originality in the research used in this letter but like so many other past letters I cannot. Instead I must stand on the shoulders of others in order to attempt to determine where we as Americans are going.

If you want to know more about the current demographic trends in America here are some of my sources.

1. *Mass Incarceration: The Whole Pie, A Prison Policy Initiative* by Peter Wagner and Leah Sakala, March 12, 2014
2. *Incarceration is Not an Equal Opportunity Punishment, A Prison Policy Initiative* by Peter Wagner Updated August 28, 2012
3. *The Next America* by Paul Taylor, Public Affairs, 2014
4. **Trends in American Values**, The Pew Research Center, 2012
5. http//www.prisonpolicy.org/reports/pie.html
6. *The Rise of the Single Fathers*, Pew research Center, July 2. 2013
7. *The Brown Bag Story*, The Washington Post, March 6, 2014
8. *Was Moynihan Right*, Sara McLanahan and Cristopher Jenck

9. Various Newspapers, Magazine Articles, the Internet, etc.

Letter 2 - The Digital Native

It is amazing how technology changes over time and how it, in turn, changes people, politics, policy, the economy, and the social landscape. I first became aware of this when my children where young and became interested in my first computer. I could not afford to purchase a computer so I decided to build one. I purchased the parts from Heathkit and spent the next couple of months soldering the resistors, capacitors, etc., to the circuit boards. This was in the 70s so you can imagine what a home brewed PC looked like. As I recall it had a small green screen, an integrated keyboard, a 5 inch floppy disk and 64 KB of memory and employed a one-of-a- kind operating system controlled by a series of keyboard commands.

As the children got older, and I became more experienced, in 1981 I purchased one of the first IBM PCs that came on the market. It cost about $2k and had a small green screen, two floppy disk drives, a keyboard, 128 KB of memory and a DOS operating system IBM had purchased from Bill Gates. Tom Watson Jr, President of IBM, decided not to get involved in the PC operating system but to leave that to Bill Gates. Watson made very few mistakes but this was obviously one of them.

As I began to work with the computer and its Basic language, the children were just starting basic math so I decided to write a multiplication quiz program for them and, not surprisingly, they found it exciting and would spend several hours at a time sitting at the keyboard. Their knowledge of computers grew over the years because that was all they knew and did not find it strange, so computers gradually became just another tool to use in their everyday life. For them the computer simply disappeared because it was so ubiquitous. It had become like the telephone - if you needed it you picked it up, used it, and put it back down until such time as you needed it again. They were the forerunners of the digital native and they, eventually, became digital natives themselves. Unfortunately, even though I taught Information Technology and Security, I could never cross the threshold to becoming a digital native, I suppose because of my age.

Well, what is a digital native? It is someone whose familiarity with and use of digital technology allows them to become the essential mediator of social and information acquisition. The term digital native seems to apply primarily to Millennials but does seem to encompass some GenXs. Digital technology is not something they adapted to but something they grew up with. It was part of their everyday life and played a fundamental role in shaping their friendships, the way they earn a living, the way they allocate time, and perhaps, most importantly, it shapes their view of the world.

Their familiarity with digital technology is so complete they are now part of the WEB.

Some Back ground

What is the WEB? The WEB is made of three parts: the Internet (a large I), the communication protocol, and the World Wide Web (WWW).

The internet is really nothing more than a series of interconnected transmission lines and servers that, in turn, are connected to backend data farms which holds the data everyone accesses with their computers. In order to connect the parts of the internet, the servers, data farms, and computers must somehow talk or communicate with one another.

That is the purpose of a communication protocol called Telecommunication Control Protocol/Internet Protocol (TCP/IP) that is composed of many specialized sub protocols. The Internet was created by DOD as a survivable Command and Control system in response to the cold war.

The third part of the WEB, WWW, sits on top of the Internet and allows the underlying communication protocol, TCP/IP, to actually locate, acquire and present information to the computer screen. WWWs fundamental attribute is the Universal Resource Locator (URL). You see the URL displayed as something like http://www.amazon.com where http is the TCP/IP sub protocol to be employed, www is the World Wide Web resource, Amazon is the resource, while .com indicates the domain in which Amazon resides. This is simply a way of organizing the Internet and its information such that it is transparent to the user. The WWW was created by Tim Berniers Lee while at the CERN laboratory in Switzerland and is one of the great creations of the digital era.

If you did not follow the above, don't worry about it. I teach this stuff (this is really a technical term) and sometimes I don't understand it either and am always amazed that it operates at all.

Thanks to Facebook, Twitter, Linkedin, Google, etc., people now exist as a digital image on the web and because of this digital image no one should have any expectation of privacy in the digital age especially if they belong to a social network.

I first became aware of this in the early part of the 21st century (I love this kind of talk because it means I have lived in two centuries) during a personal discussion with a police friend who was a student in one of my security classes. He had been sent to investigate a complaint at a local high school. A picture of a naked male student had been circulating around the personal computers and cell phones of the High School students, and the parents and staff were decidedly unhappy. His investigation revealed that several students. (friends of the victim) decided to play a joke on him and had contacted the victim pretending to be one of the prettiest girls in the school. The virtual friendship between the boy and the virtual girl blossomed although they never seemed to have struck up a conversation in person. Finally, their friendship had developed to a point where the boys, pretending to be the virtual girl, proposed an exchange of naked photos. Well, you see where this is going. The boys immediately posted his photo on line and the furor erupted.

The cop, I thought, handled it wisely. He determined what had happened then left it with the parents and principal to sort out. I always thought that was a very common sense approach.

This story has always reminded me of a cartoon I used in one of my classes. The cartoon shows two dogs at a PC. One of the dogs has a paw on the keyboard and turns to the other dog and said, **"You never know what dogs you will find on the Internet."** I always liked that cartoon and thought it really funny because it captured the essence of the Internet. That is, the Internet fosters anonymity, and because of that, it has a tendency to take on the nature of the wild west - anything goes.

For example, Facebook, Twitter, etc., provide a play by play description of many everyday lives. Because of this, people expose things on the Internet that they would never expose in real life. The Internet, for many people, is a virtual existence which they think has a certain anonymity about it. Nothing is further from the truth!

The Intelligence community, police, and future employers use the Internet and social media as an information fishing hole in their attempt to learn about people. It is amazing at the number of databases available on the Internet that contains your personal information and that, when aggregated, reveals your digital image – warts and all. Future employers are especially adept at finding information that the prospective employee has posted on the internet, perhaps several years in the past. Many prospective employees have gone into an interview only to be confronted and embarrassed by postings which they thought were anonymous.

Young people seem to post the most intimate of details on the Internet and then, as they mature, realize their mistake and delete that entry and expect it to forever disappear. Remember what I said about there being no privacy in the digital age. Well, unfortunately, information once posted on the internet is forever and is searchable. So all you Oneys beware for there be Dragons on the Internet that can unexpectedly bite you.

Teachers

As a college professor I felt one of my responsibilities was to make sure my students could properly express themselves, both verbally and in writing, so I required both oral presentations and essays. In order to assure the essays were in the student's own words, I would occasionally copy several passages, engage a plagiarism search engine, such as **PlagTracker**, and attempt to find if the student had copied it from another source which they had a tendency to do - at least initially. Students nowadays turn to the Internet, because of the abundance of information, to do much of the legwork for research papers. For example, there are now free on-line **Cliffsnotes** and **SparkNotes** available for students on the Internet.

It is always fascinating to see how teachers look at the information and tools available on the Internet particularly as it affects students and themselves. It is noteworthy that in a recent Pew research survey 77% of the teachers surveyed indicated that the impact of digital technologies had been positive. Certainly, in my case I found this to be true.

In order to enhance my lectures I used two major types of technologies. First, I had a smart board on which I displayed my lectures then, standing at the lectern or board, I could overlay my written comments on top of the displayed lecture. In addition, when I returned to the classroom after losing my leg, I used a chair with wheels to navigate the class room. Since I could no longer stand at the board or walk around the room (in order to keep the students awake!) I used an Ipad electronically connected to the classroom PC which in turn was connected to an overhead viewer to display my lectures on the Smart board. I could then draw on the Ipad screen which would overlay my lecture slides displayed on the board. Really amazing technology.

The same survey found that 99% of the Advance Placement teachers agreed that the Internet provided an exceptionally broad range of information available to the students through various search engines. That allowed the students to find the information quickly and easily. One researcher identified the sources most likely to be used by students were the following:

Google (94%
Wikipedia and other online encyclopedias (75%)
YouTube or other social internet sites (52%)
Their peers (42%)
SparkNotes, CliffsNotes, etc. (41%)
News sites, etc. (25%)
Print or Electronic text books (18%)
Online databases, etc. (17%)
School Research Librarian (16%)
Books other than textbooks (12%)
Student oriented search engines such as Sweet Search, Ivy's Domain, etc. (10%)

Unfortunately, researchers also found that quick access to information in this fashion seemed to condition the students toward a fast-paced, short-term exercise aimed at just completing and satisfying the assignment and away from the slow process of manual research and discovery that leads to intellectual curiosity.

Researchers also think the Millennial (the digital native) will be a quick acting multitasker who will treat the Internet as their '**external brain**.' I found the term, external brain, an interesting phrase because of the extensive amount of online information available to everyone. One of the issues with the extensive availability of information is determining the quality of the information. That is, what is true and what is false. I read somewhere that 40-50 % of the information available through the Internet is false. I suppose that is why there are now so many independent fact checkers awarding Pinnocchios to that which is false. Even after determining what is true, it becomes a real chore to wade through the massive information in an attempt to analyze and make sense of it.

Some experts, however, think the Millennial's external brain would allow them to learn more than previous generations. On the other hand, some researchers responded that the external brain might lead to a thirst for instant gratification, loss of patience, and a lack of deep-thinking ability.

Social Networks

When my daughters were young I thought it might be a good idea if they had a cell phone, you know, just in case of emergency. I figured a cell phone was simply a security tool that could be utilized to call for roadside assistance, call the police, or better yet, occasionally call me or their mother.

Their cellphones have now morphed into smartphones that are used as an extension of their PC, laptop, or Ipad to text, search the internet, go shopping, place voice calls, email, etc.

People now, teenagers especially, seem to treat texting as their primary form of communication. It is now amazing how many text messages will sometimes flow back and forth between the girls and me on a daily basis. For most people it has certainly surpassed voice calling, face-to-face-contact, e-mail and Instant messaging. They think texting is private and covert and they can do it even when they are in a crowd and, unfortunately, do it while walking down the street or driving and paying no attention to the traffic around them.

You Oneys listen. There are simply too many teenagers (and adults) who text (or talk on their phone) while walking, bicycling or driving. Doing that is simply a recipe for disaster. There is something called "***situational awareness***" that all Oneys should practice. That means as you walk you keep your head up and on a swivel constantly evaluating your surroundings for any potential danger. Approach your car carefully, for the best time to launch an attack is when you enter or exit a car. You drive while being constantly alert to the vehicles around you and shifting your eyes, but not your head, from mirror to mirror. You are constantly aware of at least five cars in front of you and five cars behind you. You do not let anyone drive alongside you, especially motorcycles. You park your car in lighted areas and, if necessary, are escorted to and from your car in unlighted or dangerous areas. You approach your car from the rear checking for movement or anyone in the back seat. These are examples of situational awareness and should be practiced by all Oneys.

Most people think texting is an efficient means of communication because you can send your messages anytime and check your messages on your own schedule. It prevents annoying telephone calls, and prevents you from annoying someone else and is a quick exchange of thoughts that takes only seconds.

A recent Pew research survey indicated a great disparity between generations on the use of texting. 97% of Millennials engage in texting while only 39% of Silents text. The percentage is even lower for the Greatest Generation (16%).

From early 2000 the use of social networks has absolutely exploded. Friendster was launched in 2002, MySpace in 2003 while Facebook went public in 2006. The Millennials were the first to adopt this new method of communicating but their parents and grandparents started to become avid users also. The older generation apparently wanted to see what the fuss was about and soon learned that social networks was a way of staying in touch with the activities of their extended families. As of 2013, 89% of ages 18-25 used social network sites, 78% of ages 30-49 used social network sites while only 4% of those 65 or over use social Network sites (that is us!).

As an aside, I am not even one of that 4%. Because of the way I was raised and trained I feel exceptionally uneasy about dropping my shield of privacy and exposing myself in public. Rather an odd way of expressing it but I'm sure you get the point. I learned a long time ago that exposing anything associated with your actual identity allows others to take advantage of any perceived weakness and anything you expose of yourself to strangers is a weakness. Yes, I readily admit I am paranoid and am into such things as situational awareness and protecting my privacy.

The general population is distributed according to a normal curve. The upper few percent are the Saints (certainly not many of those), the middle are the Lambs (the great majority), while the lower few percent are the Predators (the dangerous few) who prey on the old, the weak, and those foolish enough to expose their weaknesses.

The Internet Predators are great at putting together your digital profile from the things you display on the Social Networks, and then developing a scam targeted specifically at you, employing familiar things that you may trust.

My recommendation is not to expose too much of yourself on the Social Networks. If you must go on a Social Network then hide yourself through a false identity and expose nothing of your real personal identity.

Well, back to the Digital Native. The millennials were the first to adopt social networks but now seem to be the first to become cool to its use. For example, in 2013, 94% of ages 12-17 reported using Facebook but many expressed unhappiness with too much sharing of life's minutia, too much drama, too many adults (especially parents and grandparents) on Facebook, and too much stress at the need to constantly tend their online reputation.

Social Operating System

There are some researchers who feel that a new **Social Operating System** is emerging due to the widespread use of broadband, extensive mobile connectivity and the rise of social networks. The defining features of the new system seem to be more personal freedom, an online neighborhood, and less privacy.

More Personal Freedom

In social networks the focus is on the individual and not the family, work unit, neighborhood, or the social group. Many millennials seem to meet their social and emotional needs by tapping into their online network rather than their close associates. In this online social network, the millennials seem to rely on specialized relationships to meet their social needs. This may include medical needs, economic advice, school needs, job search, emotional support, book recommendations, etc. This social operating system gives people a new way to solve problems since it offers more personal freedom due to specialized resources and more capacity to act on their own. This new freedom does, however, demand that individuals expend more energy in developing new strategies and skills for solving problems. That is, this individual freedom comes at the price of expending more time and energy. One researcher expresses it as "**networked individualism is both more socially liberating and socially taxing.**" That is, technology brings extra work.

I found this finding rather interesting because we normally think of technology as liberating us from work, and I suspect that is true especially for manual labor (think robots). It turns out, however, that if we are to reap the benefits of technology we must engage more intensively in 'knowledge' labor. From my perspective that implies that in order to truly reap the benefits of technology the Millennials must be better educated.

The New Online Neighborhood

A recent pew research finding indicated that 80% of most millennials and 66% of most American adults create personal content on social networking sites to which they belong. That is, they have become publishers or broadcasters of their personal information. Due to powerful search engines such as Google, Yahoo or Bing people can easily locate and connect with others of like interest, lifestyles, political beliefs, spiritual practices, hobbies, etc. They, in essence, create a virtual online neighborhood of like interests.

People still value their physical local neighborhood but it seems that local neighborhoods only make up about 10% of their significant ties. They still value their neighbors and coworkers, but most of their contacts are with people who are distant from them in many cases in a foreign land. This differs significantly from the contacts of their parents and grandparents. Digital technology has transferred the point of contact from the neighborhood and coworkers to the Internet where they have created a '**social internet**' of their own to satisfy their needs. That is, individuals now have their own Internet suited to their personal needs.

I found this finding fascinating because it fits into an already existing pattern of **self-sorting** that is taking place in America based upon income, personal interest, political beliefs, etc. The phenomenon of self-sorting is now being extended to the Internet.

It seems we all are beginning to live in an **echo chamber** where we associate with like-minded individuals. I find that a little depressing because what can you learn from people who think like you.

You Oneys, let me encourage you to be adventurous and associate with someone you disagree with. I have always felt that is the only way you can learn something new. Try to listen to them with an open mind instead of formulating a rebuttal. Unfortunately, listening seems to be a lost art because we live in a visual age. That is, an age of television and multimedia where the visual media is the message. I suppose I was fortunate in that I grew up primarily in the radio age where good listening habits could be developed. Unfortunately, I am also one of those that always seem to struggle to practice good listening habits. Well, I am an Oney.

Less Privacy

One of the problems with creating an individual social internet is the need to connect to others, and the need to connect to others means you must share information about yourself if you expect others of similar interest to share information about themselves with you. How else can you identify, connect to, and create a virtual social network? This level and need of personal transparency produces a loss of privacy and the unwanted commercialization of your personal information. Eric Schmidt, former Google CEO, was quoted as saying; "**We know where you are. We know where you have been. We can more or less know what you are thinking about.**" To be truthful, the digital native should have no expectation of privacy in the age of technology. Beware! Big Brother is watching!

Media Consumption

One of the striking things about millennials is the change in the pattern of media consumptions from their predecessors. A PEW survey in 2009 indicated that millennials in the ages 8-18 were exposed to 10 hours and 45 minutes of all kinds of media per day. In addition, they spent 29% of their time per day multitasking several kinds of information. The Kaiser foundation called them **Generation M**, that is, generation media. Linda Stone, a techno analyst, called this a state of "**continuous partial attention**" which I found extraordinarily descriptive. Most people who are digitally connected seem to be in a constant state of FOMO – fear of missing out. For my generation it seems to be a fear of missing a call. Digital connectivity has become addictive. Notice the next time you are with a Millennial how they are constantly fidgeting with their cell phones while only paying '**partial attention**' to what is going on around them.

As an aside when John H. and I have breakfast or lunch together he immediately produces his cell phone and places it on the table. I immediately produce my cell phone and also place it on the table and comment on FOMO while always wondering which cell will ring first. After all, being connected is a sign of importance. I generally laugh at this because at my age I now know more people dead than alive so my chance of receiving a call is getting slimmer each passing year.

News consumption pattern among the digital natives is interesting as well, especially among the different generations. For example, the Millennials seem to graze for the news throughout the day by constantly dipping in and out of the social media stream. My generation, the Silents, still read the morning paper with their coffee and watch PBS. Millennials are most likely to admit that they get their news through the Internet, cell phone, friends, Ipad, and freely admit that comedy shows are always a good source of news. I must admit that people of my generation also get their news from entertainers such as Limbaugh and OReilly (well, as entertainers they do earn about $31 Million each!) and from that perspective we have much in common with the Millennials.

Decision Making

Social Networks are one of the main tools employed by the Digital Native to make decisions. In order to do so they literally have to drink from an information fire hose by, throughout the day, constantly dipping in and out of their social networks.

About 30% of Millennials say they have gotten more involved in politics because of their discussion on social network spaces.

This is another area I have found fascinating because of its influence on 2008 and 2012 presidential elections. Obama was not only the first black presidential candidate but also the first social media presidential candidate to effectively use social media as a major campaign strategy. Pew research shows that 66% of social media users actively engage in political activism online. That estimate is the equivalent of 39% of all American adults – now that is influence especially if a presidential candidate can capture a majority of those numbers which Obama apparently did. In 2008, McCain's campaign was social-media-deaf as Obama's was social-media-savvy. Social media is about relationships, and in the 2012 campaign Obama spent $47M on a social media digital campaign while Romney spent only $4.7M on a social media campaign. I suspect the Republicans have learned their lesson and we will find equal spending on social media in the 2016 presidential election.

The reason this media is so powerful in forming opinions is that word-of-mouth advertising is the most powerful form of persuasion. The social networks take the political message away from mass media and place it in the hands of individuals who are associated with friends on the social networks. Who are you going to trust – your friends or mass media? Your friends, of course, regardless of how dumb the information sounds!

Digital Literacy

The Millennial digital native seems to thrive in the network environment and digital technology because they have mastered many different types of networking or information literacy. One researcher has identified six different types of literacy that make Millennials so effective.

The first is ***graphic literacy*** in which life is viewed through the screen of a PC, cell phone or IPad. They experience life through their communication channel, media displayed and data received from their social networks. They are very adept at interpreting this material and feel comfortable acting as their own broadcaster by publishing personal information, comments, opinions, etc.

The second is **_navigation literacy_**. That is, they have a sense of how the Internet is organized and how to maneuver through multiple information channels and different means of presentation. They have a feel for how information has changed format and presentation through various network links and channels.

The third is **_context and connection literacy_** that allows them to assimilate the many different types of information that flows into their lives and to make sense of it despite its ever-increasing pace. They can take small bits of disaggregated information and then reintegrate them so it makes perfect sense for them.

The fourth type is **_focus literacy_** in which they have the ability to multitask through partial concentration then suddenly, when necessary, to fully concentrate on a particular subject. That is, they know when to be connected and when to disengage.

The fifth is **_multitasking literacy_** in which they have the ability to do several things at once. Well, almost at once. They can monitor multiple information streams from friends, relatives, and work, while simultaneously handling the necessary response or outputs. Let's see a Silent do that!

The sixth and last is **_skepticism literacy_**. That is Millennials seem to have a built in BS meter that allows them to quickly evaluate the information they receive online and to weed out the information that is outdated, biased, incomplete or agenda-driven.

As an aside, when I first started teaching at the college level, I quickly learned that most students will ask questions to which they already know the answer just to adjust their BS meter to my lectures. That seemed to be a rite of passage for each class.

The Future

It is true that no one knows exactly what the digital future holds for humans, especially our children, but since we are human, it is necessary that we speculate on that future since that is one of the things that distinguishes us from the lower animals. A number of futurists have done just that and I find their insights interesting.

From their perspective there seems to be two threads leading to the future of the Millennials and their relationship to digital technology.

The **first thread** is that information and digital technology will be useful in enhancing our children's intelligence by allowing them to learn more; cycle quickly through personal and work related tasks; and become more adept at finding answers. In summary, the changes brought about by digital technology will enhance their learning ability and cognition.

The **second thread** is that digital technology will result in our children retaining less information; becoming distracted away from deep engagement with people; result in a lack of deep thinking ability and a lack of face-to-face social skills. In summary, digital technology will result in a negative outcome for our children's learning ability and cognition.

Well, there you have it, the two conflicting future views of the Millennials. I suspect the future will probably be a little of both views when balanced against the desirable future life skills of our children.

Well, what are these life skills? Most social scientists seem to agree upon six major desired life skills for our children:

First, they need problem solving through cooperative work; that is, the ability to work with others as part of a team.

Second is the ability to search effectively for online information, discern the quality of that information, effectively analyze that information, and then effectively communicate that information to others in many different communication channels and formats.

Third is the ability to synthesize information from various sources. Since they will have access to many different sources of information, the ability to bring together these many different types of information will be important.

Fourth, they need to be strategically future minded. That is, the ability to project themselves into the future then set goals to attain that future. For me this means that our children must view their lives as a project, set objectives, set goals to accomplish those objectives, and manage them accordingly.

Fifth is the ability to concentrate. I suspect this may be the most important of their projected life skills since they will be constantly bombarded by an ever increasing volume of information and an ever increasing pace of technology.

The **sixth,** and final life skill, is the ability to distinguish channel noise from the real message. That is, they need to develop a very sensitive BS meter.

Simon Kuznets, an economist by training, developed an insight into the impact of technology on the Millennials that eventually became known as the **Kuznets curve** and, paraphrased, it goes like this: "The first-generation technology usually causes a net negative social effect; the second-generation technology a net neutral effect; the third-generation technology finally results in a net positive effect but only after the technology is smart enough, the interface is right and it begins to reinforce positive behavior."

Unfortunately, I don't think we will see the third-generation of technology until around 2020 and, if the Kuznets curve is correct, which I suspect it is, then we can expect a net negative effect of technology on the Digital Native, the Millennial, until that time.

References:

As always, I wish I could claim some originality in this research and writing but, unfortunately, like so many other missives I cannot instead I must stand on the shoulders of others.

1. *The Next America* by Paul Taylor and the PEW Research Center
2. *Teens and Mobile Phones* By Amanda Lenhart, Rich Ling, Scott Campbell and Kristen Purcell
3. *Taken Out of Context*: American Teen Sociality in Networked Publics by Danah Michele Boyd
4. *How Obama Won the Social Media Battle in the 2012 Presidential Campaign* by Dr. Pamela Rutledge
5. *How Teens Do Research in the Digital World* By Kristen Purcell, Lee Rainie, Alan Heaps, Judy Buchanan, Linda Friedrich, Amanda Jacklin, Clara Chen and Kathryn Zickuhr

Letter 3 - Old Age

All Oneys are getting old and before too long we are going to be ***very, very*** old. We are born, we grow old and we die. That is just an inescapable fact of life. I wish it weren't, but unfortunately, it is and as I have started to become ***very, very*** old, I have begun to think more about that eventuality and realize the boundary between old age and death narrows with each passing year not only for me but for those I love most in this world.

Throughout history man has been fascinated with old age and death and now is no different. Thomas Hobbs, a seventeenth century philosopher, called life, "nasty, brutish and short" and at that time it certainly was since, in the seventeenth century, the life expectancy was between 35 and 40 years. Well, that longevity was not bad if one were a citizen in the Roman Empire. For them a life expectancy of 25 was normal. Even in 1900 America, the life expectancy was around 47 years. Not much of a change in 1900 years.

However, there is good news. In modern America life expectancy is increasing by about one year every six years. A baby born today can expect to live around 78.5 years up from about 75.4 years only two decades ago. At present some 39 million Americans, 13% of the U.S. population, are 65 and older. This century-long increase of people 65 and older is the product of dramatic advances in medical science and public health as well as steep declines in fertility rates. In the latter part of this century this increase in life expectancy had leveled off but it has begun to rise again when the first wave of the nation's 76 million baby boomers turned 65 in 2011. By 2050, according to Pew Research projections, about one-in-five Americans, 20%, will be over age 65, and about 5% will be 85 and older. Well, I hope I'm that fortunate.

In a recent survey most people aspired to live until they were 89, whereas a recent AARP survey put the desired lifespan at age 92. Well, why not 100? By the middle of this century there is expected to be around half million people in the US who will be 100 years or older.

In truth, these are only statistics and as we all know there are "lies, damn lies and there are statistics." However, what is interesting for me, at least, is why we grow old and, truthfully, scientist really have no idea why, we just do. Don't get me wrong, they know about many of the underlying mechanisms that lead the body to gradually break down but still do not understand the underlying cause of aging. According to one popular theory, based upon evolution, humans are strong and vigorous during the child bearing and rearing years but afterwards are programed at the cellular level to slowly decline. This is called *apoptosis* which I found to be an interesting name. But then scientists are noted for hiding simple concepts behind forbidding names. Nevertheless, I suppose that is one explanation.

When Does Old Age Begin

Several surveys have been done on when the general public believes old age begins with the results being just about what one would expect. For example, those aged 18-29 said old age begins at 60: those in the 50-60 age range said old age begins at around 70 while those over 65 said old age begins at about 74.

There also seems to be an interesting discrepancy between how old people perceive old age. For example, the older people are the younger they say they feel. The difference between how old people feel and their actual age widens as people get older. I can certainly attest to that. For example, I am now in my mid-70s but feel in my mid-50s. I suppose that is why I am so surprised each morning when I look in the mirror and am amazed how old age, a wrinkled face, and a sagging body seem to go together.

Impact of Growing Old

Many ethicists claim, and I suspect they are right, that the primary impact of our own mortality is to increase our desire to make the most of each day. I believe there is some truth to that belief, certainly for me it is apparently true for as my days dwindle you may have noticed that my writing output has increased. I think another example of this desire is the bucket list some people make as they grow older. They want to accomplish those things on their list before they kick-the-bucket which I have always found to be a wonderful expression. One of the things on my list was to complete at least ten books. Perhaps in a few years I may be able to mark that item off my list.

Stanley Hauerhaus, a theologian at Duke University, says that without death, then love, as we know it, would cease to exist simply because the finite nature of life prompts people to wholly commit themselves to others. He summarizes his view by saying that (paraphrased), "**Death makes love possible.**" I have always thought this is another wonderful expression. That certainly seems reasonable. On the other hand, there are other theologians who also view immortality as a blessing since it would not be (paraphrased) "necessary to love this one or that one but to love everyone." I'm not convinced of that logic since humans are hardwired by evolution to be tribal.

Regardless of how we perceive the relationship between immortality and love, immortality would certainly require a rethinking of our entire social fabric and philosophy.

For example, brief multiple marriages could become common place and if multiple marriages become the norm, as some futurists predict, and each marriage produces children, then half-siblings will become more common. In addition, if couples continue the current trend of having children beginning in their 20s and 30s, then eight or even 10 generations of siblings might be alive simultaneously. Furthermore, if life extension also increases a woman's period of fertility, siblings could be born 40 or 50 years apart. Such a large age difference would radically change the way siblings or parents and their children interact with one other. It would not be uncommon for the children to be 100 years younger than their parents or for the siblings to be 60 years apart.

What about the work environment? Well, futurists believe that living longer will inevitably mean more time spent working. Careers will necessarily become longer, and the retirement age extended not only so individuals can support themselves, but to avoid overtaxing a nation's social security system. In addition, with skilled workers remaining in the workforce longer, economic productivity would go up and if people got bored with their jobs, they could switch careers. On the other hand, competition for jobs would become fiercer as older re-trainees beginning new careers vie with young workers for a limited number of entry-level positions.

One researcher thinks workplace mobility would create an especially worrisome problem. Bioethicist Daniel Callahan, a cofounder of the Hastings Center in New York, says that, "If you have people staying in their jobs for 100 years, that is going to make it really tough for young people to move in and get ahead." Callahan also worries that corporations and universities could become dominated by a few individuals if executives, managers, and tenured professors refuse to give up their posts. Without a constant infusion of youthful talent and ideas, he believes these institutions could stagnate.

Chris Hackler, head of the Division of Medical Humanities at the University of Arkansas, points out that the same problem could apply to politics. That is, many elected officials have term limits that prevent them from amassing too much power but what about federal judges, who are appointed for life? Hackler writes that "Justices sitting on the bench for a hundred years would have a powerful influence on the shape of social institutions."

As an aside, I'm not sure we need wait a hundred years for that since the Roberts Court seems to be an active conservative court, which I find interesting and I may decide to explore this concept further in a future letter.

Many ethicists believe that even doubling our life span will not solve but merely exacerbate our social problems. Others, however, believe a greater life span will resolve many of our social ills and allow for greater societal experimentation due to an ability to recognize and recover from mistakes.

Factors in Old Age

There seems to be general agreement among the population that there are certain markers that indicate old age. For example, most people seem to agree that failing health, inability to live independently, inability to drive, and difficulty with stairs are good indicators of old age. Well, since I have experienced all of these markers, I certainly agree that these are indeed indicative of old age.

On the other hand, a recent survey indicated that such factors as forgetfulness, retirement, sexual inactivity, bladder control problems, gray hair, and grandchildren are NOT indicators of old age. You noticed I stressed the NOT on this list because I'm not sure I agree with this perception since I'm old and seem to suffer from a number of these ailments. Well, I believe I did say I was getting *very, very* old.

There was also an interesting survey by Pew research of older people that highlighted the following factors, in order of decreasing importance, as **challenges** to growing old. These factors were: memory loss, inability to drive, a serious illness, not sexually active, feeling sad or depressed, not feeling needed, loneliness, and trouble paying bills. As an aside, I always wondered why not paying bills was so low on older people's concern but, as I became older, that soon became obvious.

On the other hand there were a number of **benefits** to growing old. Those factors identified as benefits to growing old were the following: more time for hobbies/interest, more time with family, volunteer work, more travel, more financial security, less stress, not working, more respect, and a second, third or fourth career.

The majority of older people highlight the number one benefit to growing older was spending more time with their family.

Retirement and Old Age

Most of us look forward to retirement and a life of leisure, however, Social scientists seem to feel that retirement is now a word without a clear meaning. For example, 83% of adults ages 65 and older describe themselves as retired, however, the word retirement has come to mean different things to different people. 76% of those 65 and older fit the classic stereotype of the retiree because they have completely left the working world. However, 8% say they are retired but are working part time (I fit in this category); 2% say they are retired but working full time while 3% say they are retired but looking for work. The remaining 11% of the older than 65 population describe themselves as still in the labor force although not all of them have jobs.

Whatever the fuzziness around the definition of retirement, one trend is crystal clear from government data: the participation rate of those 65 or older in the labor force began to trend back upward about 10 years ago after falling steadily for decades. Well, why are older folks working longer?

Working longer seems to boil down to money since, according to social scientists, there seems to be two incentives for working longer; first, is a change in Social Security legislation and, second, is the gradual transition from a defined-benefit to defined-contribution pension plans.

First, the age at which one can collect Social Security benefits will rise to 67 in 2027 based upon legislation passed in 1983, and this rise in retirement age means a reduction in benefits. For example, when the full retirement age increases to 67, those who apply at age 65 will receive a benefit equal to roughly 87 percent of the full benefit they would have received at 67. It does not sound like much, but for older people every dollar counts; therefore, older people need to work longer to make up the difference.

As an aside, I believe the age at which one can collect Social Security benefits will need to gradually rise in order to achieve a balance in our social safety net. (See my previous letter dealing with Demographics and Aging.)

Secondly, for the retiree there is a major difference in benefits between a defined benefit plan and a defined contribution plan.

A *defined benefit plan* is more costly for employers; therefore, most employers have dramatically scaled back or completely eliminated these plans in recent years. Retirees get a fixed payout from their defined benefit plan. That payout can be either a lump sum or a monthly check. The size of their payout has nothing to do with how well their employer did managing the money. Instead, the workers payout is simply a function of a basic formula that factors in how long you worked and how much you earned. That is, the workers *benefit is defined* by a set formula.

In a *defined contribution* plan, for example, a 401(k) plan, the employee is responsible for investing money from their paycheck into the plan normally with a matching contribution from their employer. In addition, the employee is in charge of choosing how they want their money invested among the offered mutual funds. However, there is no guaranteed payout when they retire since what they end up with depends on how well their investments perform.

Most retirees like to participate in both a defined benefit plan and a defined contribution plan, because a defined benefit plan on its own, if available, likely won't be generous enough to let them live comfortably in retirement.

Living Arrangements.

90% of those ages 65 and older live in their own home or apartment, and the vast majority are either very satisfied (67%) or somewhat satisfied (21%) with their living arrangements. However, many living patterns change as adults advance into *very* old age. For example, just 30% of adults ages 65-74 say they live alone, compared with 66% of adults ages 85 and above. Also, just 2% of adults ages 65-74, and 4% of adults ages 75-84, say they live in an assisted living facility, compared with 15% of those ages 85 and above.

Religion and Old Age.

Religion is an important part of the lives of many Americans, and this is never more true than for older Americans. For example, those 65 and older are more likely to pray, attend worship services, and believe in God than those under 65. As people marry, become settled in their communities, and begin to raise families, they are more likely to affiliate with a particular religion and participate in worship and other religious practices.

Researchers have found that religious commitment generally increases with age; therefore, religion is a far bigger part of the lives of older adults than younger adults. For example, 70% of those that are 75 and older say religion is very important to them, compared with 62% of those 65-74. Also 61% of those ages 50-64 say religion is very important to them while only 54% of those in the age range of 30-39 say religion is very important in their lives. Only 44% of those under 30 say religion is important to them. As you can see, the interest in religion decreases with age.

Young Americans, therefore, are more likely than previous generations to have no religious affiliation. This has resulted in a particularly wide gap between young and old in terms of their religiosity. For example, 25% of those under age 30 describe themselves as atheist, agnostic or nonreligious. This compares with 18% of those ages 30-49, 13% of those ages 50-64 and only 7% of those 65 and older.

The importance of religion also seems to vary by gender and race. For example, 63% of women but only 48% of men say religion is very important in their lives while 80% of blacks are much more likely than whites, 50%, to say religion is very important to them. The gender gap is even more pronounced among older Americans. 76% of women 65 and older, say religion is very important in their lives while only 53% of men 65 and older say religion is very important to them.

I'm not sure the rising religiosity in old age is a case of true belief or a dawning realization that the boundary between aging and death is narrowing and in the words of the old regular Baptist preacher the elderly now realize it is "time to get right with the Lord."

Surveys do, as expected, seem to indicate that older adults dealing with the problems and challenges of old age are among those most likely to say their religious faith has become more important to them. For example, illness and depression are among the more acute challenges some older people face, and 43% of those who are dealing with a serious illness say religion has become more important to them as they have aged while only 32% of those who are not dealing with a serious illness say the same. Similarly, 43% of those who say they often feel sad or depressed say religion has become more important to them as they have gotten older, compared with just 31% of those who are not sad or depressed.

Worries about Being a Burden

One major worry among the elderly is the concern about being a burden to their children. For example, nearly 38% of parents ages 65 and older say they worry that they might become a burden to their children. 44% of women while 31% of men harbor this worry while Hispanic parents are more likely than black parents to worry about this.

However, parental income seems to be associated with fear of becoming a burden. For example, 45% of the parents with a family income of $30,000 or less are worried about becoming a burden, compared to 24% who have a family income of $50,000 to $74,999. Interestingly, at the upper end of the income scale worries seem to return. For example, some 37% of those with a family income of $75,000 worry about being a burden to their children. Not surprisingly, unmarried parents are more likely to worry about being a burden to their children than are parents who are married.

I found these findings interesting but not surprising. At one time older parents were part of an extended family, all living under a single roof. The multigenerational family might be composed of grandparents, parents, children and grandchildren all contributing in one way or another to the welfare of the family. The grandparents primarily served as babysitters to the younger generation and, in doing so, passed along the family traditions and culture. Current single family households simply do not have available to them the tradition of the multigenerational household and, I suspect, this may also be causing a lot of the worry.

Caring for Parents

Through the centuries, poets and philosophers have observed that parents and children often reverse roles as parents grow older. Not so, says the Pew Research survey. Only 12% of parents ages 65 and older say they generally rely on their children more than their children rely on them. An additional 14% say their children rely more on them. The majority, 58%, says neither relies on the other, and 13% say they rely on one another equally.

On the other hand, the children of elderly parents view the situation a little differently. For example, about 20% of the children of older parents say that their parent(s) need help to handle their affairs; the rest say that their parents can handle things on their own. This proportion varies by the age of the parents. About 30% of adults with parents ages 75 or older say their parents need help, compared with less than 10% of adults whose parents are under 75.

Researchers indicated that most of the care for parents who need help comes from family members. Nearly 30% of the adult children of elderly parents say they provide most of the help, and an additional 44% say that other family members provide the help. In addition, 11% say paid help is the major source of care for their parents, and 14% say there is some other arrangement.

Sons and daughters report different patterns of behavior when it comes to caring for parents. Some 18% of men say that they provide most of the help to their parents, but women are twice as likely (36%) to say that they are the main caregivers. Also, men are more likely than women to say that "paid help" is the main care arrangement for their parents in need.

Aging and Public Policy

American public opinion on aging differs dramatically from the views of the nation's foreign economic and political partners. For example, Americans are less likely than most of the global public to view the growing number of older people as a major problem. First, they are more confident than Europeans and Asians that they will have an adequate standard of living in their old age and, second, the U.S. is one of very few countries where a large plurality of the public believes individuals are primarily responsible for their own well-being in old age.

This confidence is certainly not because the U.S. has a young population. In fact, we have a relatively old population. The baby boomers are aging, and about 20% of the U.S. residents are expected to be 65 and older by mid-century and that will be greater than the share of seniors in the population of Florida today – even if the Oneys are included. It is even projected that the share of people 65 and older in the U.S. will exceed the share of children younger than 15 by 2050.

Even with that said, the U.S. is aging less rapidly than most other countries. The median age in the U.S. is projected to increase from 37 in 2010 to 41 in 2050. The U.S. population, driven by immigration, is expected to increase by 89 million by mid-century even as the populations of Japan, China, South Korea, Germany, Russia, Italy, and Spain are either at a standstill or decreasing. For these reasons, the American public has reason to be more confident about aging than most people living in foreign countries.

However, the aging of populations does raise concerns at many government levels around the world to include the US. They are primarily concerned with economic slowdown as the population in the working ages 15-64 begin to decrease. This smaller working-age population will need to support a growing number of older dependents which will undoubtedly create financial stress on their social insurance systems and ultimately dim the economic outlook for the elderly. For example, the public pension expenditures in several European countries are expected to consume about 15% of GDP by 2050. On the other hand, the Pension expenditures in the U.S. are projected to increase by less, from 6.8% of GDP in 2010 to 8.5% in 2050.

This greater expenditure, in turn, will also fuel demands for changes in public investments, such as the reallocation of resources from the needs of children to the needs of seniors. The graying population is expected to strain household finances, cause people to extend their working lives, rearrange family structures and play havoc with Social Security and Medicare.

For example, according to the Social Security Trustees, the Medicare trust fund will be empty by 2026 and the main Social Security trust fund will be empty by 2033. The main driver in this economic problem is Medicare which was designed to help pay for the Medical Care (Medicare) of everyone 65 and older. It was funded by a tax (FICA) of 1.45% on each employee. Well, since we now have less workers, we have less money in the Medicare Trust fund, which means the Medicare Trust fund in 2026 will be unable to cover promised medical benefits.

Attempts at Immortality

Shakespeare wrote that the last of the "**seven ages of man**" is a second childhood. He phrased it thusly, "Last scene of all, That ends this strange eventful history, Is second childishness and mere oblivion, Sans teeth, sans eyes, sans taste, sans everything." Well, Shakespeare did have a way with words.

From Shakespeare's description of the "seventh age" of man it is easy to see why people are interested in living longer and, in order to accomplish this, there have been a number of attempts to see if that were possible.

A first attempt is through things ranging from human growth hormones (HGH) to testosterone which are intended to slow down the aging process. Because the body's HGH levels naturally decrease with age, some so-called anti-aging experts have speculated and claimed that HGH products could reverse age-related bodily deterioration. The use of HGH for anti-aging is not FDA-approved and the medical community shuns the use of this technique because, one, there is simply no scientific evidence that hormones increase a person's life span and, two, HGH has harmful side effects such as nerve, muscle, or joint pain; swelling due to fluid in the body's tissues (edema); carpal tunnel syndrome; numbness and tingling of the skin and high cholesterol levels.

A second attempt is through a combination of medical therapies. The Strategies For Engineered Negligible Senescence (SENS) in Mountain View, California says that aging will only be slowed or conquered though various treatments such as stem cell and gene therapy applied at the cell level to halt the damage caused by aging. I would like to think that is possible but I'm really not sure.

A third possibility to conquer aging is through engineering and computer science. Ray Kurzweil, a proponent of this approach, says it will soon be possible to replace existing biological organs/systems with small, powerful machines. Kurzweil predicts that through more powerful machines and greater use of nanotechnology that we should be able to put microscopic machines in the body. He points to cochlear implants, cornea replacement, and artificial hands and limbs. He goes so far as to claim that humans will eventually become immortal by fully merging with machines. He further claims that wetware (blood, bone and skin) will no longer be necessary. You must remember that he is a futurist.

As an aside there is a new movie out called *Transcendence* with Johnny Depp which explores this concept. In addition, Ray Kurzweil's thoughts in this area has been made into a documentary called *Transcendent Man*. You may find both interesting.

I personally think Kurzweil carries this thought experiment a little too far; however, it certainly makes sense that a combination of the last two approaches holds the potential to increase man's longevity. At least I hope so; unfortunately, I foresee nothing significant until mid-century. Certainly too late for us Oneys.

I find the attempts at longevity interesting and will continue to follow them particularly those described by Kurzweil since I believe they hold the most promise. However, I must admit that I am pessimistic about the benefits of immortality, especially since human nature changes very slowly, if at all, and it has been my experience that humans, by nature, are very cruel.

References:

As always, I wish I could claim some originality in the research used in this letter but like so many other past letters I cannot. Instead I must stand on the shoulders of others in order to attempt to determine where we as Americans are going. If you want to know more about the current aging trends in America here are some of my sources.

1. *The Next America* by Paul Taylor and the PEW Research Center

2. *Growing Old in America: Expectations vs. Reality* by the PEW Research Center
3. *Attitudes about Aging: A Global Perspective* by the PEW research Center
4. *Number of Older Americans in the Workforce is on the Rise* by Bruce Drake
5. *Toward Immortality: The Social Burden of Longer* Lives by Ker Than
    .

Letter 4 - The Digital Darkside

A recent Pew research survey indicated that fully 95% of American teens (ages 12-17) are online, a percentage that has been consistent since 2006. Yet, the nature of teens' internet use has changed dramatically during that time from stationary connections tied to desktops in the home to always on mobile cell phone connections that move with them throughout the day. In many ways, teens have always represented the leading edge of mobile connectivity and the patterns of their technology use often signal future changes in the adult population. Teens are just as likely to have a cell phone as they are to have a desktop or laptop computer. Increasingly, these phones are affording teens always on mobile access to the internet and, in many cases, serving as their primary means of connectivity.

Smartphone ownership among teens has grown substantially since 2011; 37% of American youth ages 12-17 now have a smartphone, up from 23% in 2011. Tablets are also taking hold and 25% of teens say they now have a tablet. With both cell phones and tablets, teens can now stay connected throughout the day and night. After all they are the **digital natives**.

Cell phones are now a part of teen's everyday life. At one time it might have been provided by the parents for emergency conditions but now they are ubiquitous and all teens seem to have them. A Pew research survey in 2004 indicated 18% of teens agers (ages 12-17) owned a cell phone. Another survey in 2009 indicated 58% of 12 year-olds own a cell phone. A more recent survey in 2013 indicated 78% of teens now have a cell phone. Cell phone ownership seems to increase dramatically with age as indicated by these surveys. It is estimated that 83% of teens age 17 now own a cell phone. I don't know what the latest survey for 2014 indicates, but I would think close to 100% of those teens 17 years old now have a cell phone.

As the level of cell adoption by teens has been growing, the capacity and capability of these cell phones has also dramatically increased. For example, of the

78% of teens owning a cell phone, approximately 47% of those are smartphones which translates into 37% of all teens have smartphones, which is up from just 23% in 2011. The expanded capability of Smartphones allows teens to not only use their phones for calling but also to access the internet and to take and share photos and videos which leads to some interesting teen activity.

Teens and Sexting

Because texting with cell phones has become a centerpiece in teen social life, parents and educators have become increasingly concerned about the role of smart cell phones in the sexual lives of teens and young adults. Press coverage over the past few years has focused on how teens are using, or misusing, cell phones as part of their sexual interaction and exploration. The greatest amount of concern has focused on "*sexting*" or the creating, sharing and forwarding of sexually suggestive nude or nearly nude images by minor teens.

A recent Pew research survey indicated the 4% of cell-owning teens ages 12-17 say they have sent sexually suggestive nude or nearly nude images of themselves to someone else via text messaging. 15% of cell-owning teens ages 12-17 say they have received sexually suggestive nude or nearly nude images of someone they know via text messaging on their cell phone.

Older teens seem much more likely to send and receive these suggestive images. For example, 8% of 17-year-olds with cell phones say they have sent a sexually provocative image by text while 30% have received a nude or nearly nude image on their phone.

The teens who pay their own phone bills are more likely to send "*sexts*." For example, 17% of teens who pay for all of the costs associated with their cell phones send sexually suggestive images via text while just 3% of teens who do not pay for, or only pay for a portion of the cost of the cell phone, send these images.

Among those teens surveyed, there seems to be three scenarios under which teens transmit suggestive or nude photos. The first scenario is teens exchanging images solely between two romantic partners. The second scenario is teens exchanging images between partners that are shared with others outside the relationship, and, three, is teens exchanging suggestive or nude photos between people who are not yet in a relationship, but where at least one person hopes to be.

Sexting seems to have caught the eyes of law enforcement officials and laws are now emerging, that to me, seem over the top. For example, there are some district attorneys that have begun to prosecute teens who create and share images with laws generally reserved for producers and distributers of child pornography. As I said, that seems a little over the top to me because many of these teens are simply experimenting with their growing sexuality, and I believe their transmission of nude or suggestive photos with other teens they may be romantically involved with has nothing to do with child pornography.

I'm not alone is this, for there seems to be a growing conflict between those that believe such enforcement is a heavy-handed response to a social problem best handled outside of the legal system in a way that treats minors as a special case best left to parents and principles. For example, recently in Pennsylvania, a local district attorney threatened to charge 17 students, who were either pictured in images or found with "provocative" images on their cell phones, with prosecution under child pornography laws unless they agreed to participate in a five-week after school program and probation. The parents of two of the girls countersued the DA with the assistance of the American Civil Liberties Union, who argued that the images did not constitute pornography, and that the girls could not be charged as they did not consent to the distribution of the images that pictured them. I'm not sure where this will wind up but obviously I come down on the side of common sense.

Teens and Driving

Cell phones have become increasingly important in everyday life so much so that many teens and adults text or call while they drive. I think most teens and adults realize this is dangerous but do it nevertheless. It has become so dangerous in fact that several states have already passed laws to ban all texting or talking with a handheld phone while driving.

Well, how dangerous is calling and texting while driving? According to the latest research from the National Highway Traffic Safety Administration, in 2008 alone, there were 5,870 fatalities and an estimated 515,000 people were injured in police-reported crashes in which at least one form of driver distraction was reported. Distractions among young drivers are of particular concern, as the highest incidence of distracted driving occurs in the under-20 age group. Research released in July 2009 by the Virginia Tech Transportation Institute (VTTI) that examined a variety of tasks that drew drivers' eyes away from the roadway, and suggested that text messaging on a cell phone is associated with the highest risk among all cell phone-related tasks observed among drivers.

Here are some interesting statistics.

1. In 2011 23% of automobile collisions involved the use of cell phones. That amounts to 1.3 million accidents.
2. It takes approximately 5 seconds for you to text while driving at 55 mph and in that amount of time you can go the length of a football field without looking at the road.
3. While driving, text messages make a crash up to 23 times more likely; dialing a cell phone makes an accident 2.8 times more likely; talking or listening on the phone makes an accident 1.3 times more likely, and reaching for a device makes an accident 1.4 times more likely.
4. 20% drivers of all ages admit to web surfing while driving.
5. Teens texting while driving spend approximately 10% of their time outside their driving lane.
6. 13% of teens aged 18-20 admit to texting or talking on a cell phone at the time of a crash.
7. 77% of teens say they are confident they can drive safely while driving; 55% of teens say it's easy to text while driving.

These statistics indicate a dangerous trend for our teenagers - a trend that needs addressing. As far as I could determine there are 39 states that prohibit drivers from text messaging. I believe Indiana, Kentucky, Virginia and North Carolina are four of those 39. I suspect this is one of those laws that will need to be more rigidly enforced.

I certainly think texting while driving is just too dangerous for any Oney, however, I'm not sure anything can be done to stop the use of cell phones for voice calls while driving. However, I would certainly encourage all Oneys, if they wish to make or receive a voice call while driving, to do so hands free through the use of Bluetooth. To be truthful, I am now just learning how to use that technology to make calls. However, until I fully master the art of Bluetooth I have sworn off making calls while driving – well almost.

Now The Darkside

In one of my previous missives dealing with demographics I briefly mentioned my distrust of Social Networks such as Twitter, Facebook, etc. In this, my last missive in this series on demographics, social networks and teens, I want to elaborate on the darkside of Social Networks and, make no mistake, they do have a darkside.

Humans are exceptionally creative in inventing and using tools for both good and evil and the use and misuse of a Social Network is no different. That is, Social Networks can be used for both the benefit and harm of the human race. For example, Social Networks help to spread democracy around the world by mobilizing the masses and making it easier to topple dictators and, simultaneously, they can be used by both people and governments to spread disinformation, by authoritarian governments to crack down on dissenters and for Intelligence Black Operations. Hey, what can I say, I love tools that have two edges.

Someone once described Intelligence as a hall of mirrors filled with people whose job is to lie. By that, he meant that nothing is ever what it seems. I always thought that a fairly good description, for Intelligence is basically a magician's trade whose craft is to deceive, create illusion and to provide disinformation.

In WW2 the Americans had a special group, the 23rd Headquarters Special Troops (the so called *Ghost Army*), whose job was to make armies appear and disappear in order to deceive the Germans as to the actual point of attack and by all reports, they were exceptionally effective. They were basically a suicide group because deception inevitably drew German fire. The tools they primarily used were audio deception (broadcasting over loudspeakers the sounds of an army on the move), radio deception (broadcasting fake radio traffic) and camouflage (the use of blow up rubber tanks, trucks and aircraft). My guess is that within the next several years we will see a movie on their activity.

Since WW2 the requirement to deceive is still there, but only the tools have changed so if you want to deceive, create illusion, or provide disinformation, for example, to undermine a regime, then what better way to do it than through a Social Network – and so we did.

Twitter - Cuban Style

ZunZuneo is the name of a "fake Cuban twitter" which permitted Cubans to broadcast short text messages to each other. At its peak, ZunZuneo had 40,000 users. The problem was it was not really Cuban but was actually created and run by Americans through a series of intermediaries (cutouts) to hide its origin. The U.S. State Department, working through USAID, actively worked to create a Twitter-like social network – ZunZuneo – to engage the local Cuban population in order to undermine the Castro regime. To make the fantasy real, the U.S. Government created an elaborate system of shell companies and foreign bank accounts to make sure that the Cubans bought into the whole system.

In 2009 and 2010, projects like ZunZuneo, were meant to be a major focus of U.S. diplomacy. Creative Associates, its original contractor, decided it was not technologically capable of building such a complex system, basically a scaled down version of twitter, so USAID hired Mobile Accord. In July, 2009, a representative of Mobile Accord flew to Spain and erected a series of shell corporations to hide ZunZuneo's U.S. ownership.

The creation of ZunZuneo is not unusual, for it is a stated US policy that there should be a single internet where all of humanity has equal access to knowledge and ideas. However, we are also realistic enough to recognize that the world's information infrastructure will become what we and others make of it so in 2010 Hillary Clinton, as the Secretary of State, stated that the diplomatic program of the United States is to create and fund social network-like software in nations that censored their media. ZunZuneo is one form that 21st-century statecraft would look like.

Unfortunately, this action was not well funded and USAID was paying tens of thousands of dollars in text messaging fees to Cuba's communist telecommunications monopoly, CubaCel. Payment to CubaCel was routed through a shell company in the Cayman Islands called MovilChat that was used to hide the program's money trail. By March 2011, ZunZuneo had 40,000 subscribers and started capping its membership, so as not to attract the attention of the Cuban government. It began looking for new leadership which could take over the ZunZuneo project, however, in mid-2012 the money ran out and the service went offline.

While it was active. Americans were using ZunZuneo as a vehicle to send text messages to Cubans. These messages were generally overtly political and poked fun at the Castro brothers. Typical of the messages was the following: *"THE BACKWARDS WORLD: 54% of Americans think Michael Jackson is alive and 86% of Cubans think Fidel Castro is dead."*

Well, I thought ZunZuneo was a good effort that simply did not go far enough but is typical of the efforts we and other nations are engaged in. As a disclaimer, information on ZunZero is now open source.

Dirty Tricks

The US intelligence, as shown by the example above, is finally coming into the 21ˢᵗ century through the old magician's trick of illusion but this time by the conjuring of information (I love that phrase because it projects the image of the magician at a keyboard). Glenn Greenwald, formerly of the Guardian Newspaper and now of The Intercept, recently acquired several Secret British briefings on how the UK, Canada, New Zealand, Australia, and the U.S. (they are sometimes called the *five eyes alliance)* discuss and exchange ways to exploit Twitter, Facebook, YouTube, and other social media as secret platforms for propaganda; that is, the conjuring of information. If you want to know more about the activities of the *five eyes,* then google the word **Echelon**.

But first some background. Part of good spycraft is to create an illusion. To do this, whether operationally or on-line, you must influence people, and in order to influence people, there are certain principles that have proven quiet effective. These principles for influencing people are all centered on the realization that people make decisions as part of a group, and when they make decision it is based upon an emotional rather than a rational response.

These principles, generally self-explanatory, are:

(1) The **Need and Greed Principle** relies on the human emotion to want more; that is, the more you lust after something the easier you are to deceive.

(2) The **Distraction Principle** makes use of the human emotion to turn our attention to movement and action by noticing such things as false police raids, dishes dropped, and ripped bodices. These type events are designed to draw attention away from the real action.

(3) The **Flattery Principle** relies upon the human emotion to have our ego stroked. Operatives make the other person look good by telling them how clever, intelligent, and attractive they are. Operators listen attentively and synchronize their voice, gestures, and body language to that of the target. Women operatives are especially attuned to this principle.

(4) The **Social Compliance Principle** plays on our tendency to cooperate with authorities, those we perceive to be above us in the work or social hierarchy, or those carrying out a familiar task for our benefit such as a police officer: "This is police business and does not concern you. Move along!" **Social Engineering** is based upon the Social Compliance principle.

(5) The **Consistency Principle** relies upon the strong human emotion to be consistent with prior acts and statements. No one wants to be perceived as a fake, a liar, or worse yet, a flip-flopper.

(6) The **Dishonesty Principle** relies on the fact that because you have done something illegal, no matter how small, you won't be able to go to the police for redress. Good operators start their target small then build to their objective. Well, remember the old adage: in for a penny, in for a pound.

(7) The **Herd Principle** relies on the fact that those who lead the pack run the risk of receiving the first bullet, so humans naturally favor following behind; that is, let someone else go first. The good operator will always get someone to go first – the Judas Goat – then the herd will follow.

(8) The **Deception Principle** plays upon our familiarity with devices, situations, and people to deceive us. The human brain has a tendency to fill in the blanks for us. For example, one of the classic cons is to put in place a false ATM and watch people line up to use it.

(9) The **Time Principle** relies on the fact that good decisions require time whereas bad decisions do not. You can more easily be deceived when the operative rushes you.

(10) The **Reciprocity Principle** relies on the human emotion that good deeds should be returned. If I do you a good deed then you owe me one. When that occurs you are now in the agent's debt.

Well, you have just had your first class in being an Intelligence operator. The employment of one or more of these principles allow an online (or offline) covert operative to influence the action of a person or a group. By the way, these are the same principles employed by con artists. The truth, I suppose, is that intelligence operatives are really government con artists.

In the covert online world, these principles are employed to inject false material onto the Social Networks/Internet in order to destroy the reputation of people and/or companies, and use social sciences and other techniques to manipulate online discourse in social networks to generate outcomes considered desirable to an operation. In order to achieve these ends a number of tactics are employed, many of them common to other intelligence operations but all based upon the principles enumerated above.

These tactics are:

(1) **Infiltration Operations** is the infiltration of an organization or activity by a covert operator to accomplish a particular action. For example, delete, add or modify information. For a good example, google *Operation Snow White* conducted by Scientology.

(2) **Ruse Operations** is a disinformation campaign designed to deceive the target as to the real intention of the operator. A good example of a ruse operation occurred during WW2 – Google *Operation Mincemeat.*

(3) **Set Piece Operations** is a false scene requiring extensive logistics and planning. You often see this in movies where an entire office has been set up to fool a target.

(4) **False Flag Operations** are covert operations conducted by governments, corporations, or other organizations, which are designed to deceive the public in such a way that the operations appear as if they are being carried out by other entities. For an example, google *Operation Northwoods.*

(5) **False Rescue Operations** is an operation in which an operative rescues someone who is shown to be in danger, thereby gaining their trust and making that person in his/her debt.

(6) **Disruption Operations** can take many forms. It was once explained to me like this: a good disruptor in an insurgency is not the man ready to fight the tough guy at the bar. He is the guy who apologizes to the tough guy, goes outside and slashes his tires. I always thought that was a pretty good explanation of a disruption operation and finally.

(7) **Sting Operations** are deceptive operations designed to catch a person committing a crime. A typical sting will have a female agent entrap a male target with compromising photos in order to blackmail him.

These are also generally self-explanatory and many of them should sound familiar to you. These operations are used singly and in combination in both covert off and online operations. The following are typical covert online operations.

For example, to **discredit an individual** you could set a honey trap with a female operative, plant a suggestive photo of your target on a social networking site or, better still, send a damning email/text to their colleagues, neighbors, friends or co-workers. If you just desired to harass an individual then turn off their electricity or water, order unwanted items in their names, change their credit scores, etc., and, finally, if you wanted to really sideline them for a while then order child pornography in their names, and anonymously notify the police of their criminal activity.

If you want to **discredit an organization** then you could leak confidential information to the press via blogs or to their competitors, post negative information about managers and employees on appropriate social media, ruin business relationships by posting incriminating items about business partners, etc.

It is amazing how creative covert online operators can become in order to destroy a reputation especially when using social media for that purpose.

An actual example of tactics used by the Brits is the *Ambassadors Reception* virus that was sent to specific targets, which would then encrypt itself, delete all emails, encrypt all files, make the screen shake, and block the computer user from logging on.

Another actual example is the use of on-line sexual "*honey traps*" to snare, blackmail, and influence targets. Most often, a male target is led to believe he has an opportunity for a romantic relationship or a sexual liaison with a woman, only to find that the woman is actually an intelligence operative bent on blackmail. The Israeli government, for example, used a "honey trap" to lure nuclear technician Mordechai Vanunu from London to Rome. He expected an assignation with a woman, but instead was kidnapped by Israel agents and taken back to Israel to stand trial for leaking nuclear secrets to the media.

One especially successful operation run by the Brits involved in-person surveillance. The Brits are always good at naming things so those individuals performing a surveillance function are called '*watchers.*' I love that name. The name given to the operation was "*Royal Concierge*" which is another great name. This operation exploited hotel reservations to track the whereabouts of foreign diplomats and send out daily alerts to analysts working on selected British soft targets. The British government used the program to try to steer its quarry to Signals Intelligence (SIGINT), friendly hotels where the targets could be monitored either electronically or by a watcher. By way of explanation, most hotels are under surveillance or bugged by intelligence agencies. It is not unusual to have a hard drive in a laptop copied when left unattended in a hotel room. The French are great at this.

Unfortunately, Der Spiegel, a German magazine, got wind of **Royal Concierge** and exposed it. Well, newspapers and magazines seem to spoil all the fun that is why I have always avoided them like the plague.

The Brits, however, seemed to take a different tack and decided to utilize reporters for their own benefit. Well, the Brits have been in this business for a long time and are quite sophisticated. They created an operation they named "*Credential Harvesting*" (another great name) to select journalists who could be used to spread information. The intent of the operation was to identify non-British journalists who would then be manipulated to feed information to the target during an interview. The journalist would, of course, be unaware that he is being used as an agent of influence. Really a sophisticated operation!

Finally, the Brits used a *Denial of Serv*ice (DoS) operation against the Taliban communications system; posted negative information to attack private companies, sour business relationships, and ruin deals in order to stop weapons transactions and, finally, they engaged in an operation against Iran by posting negative information to blog posts. I love the damn Brits and their operations!

By the way all of the operations described above are now open source thanks to Snowden who, from my perspective, is a traitor and not a whistle blower as some would claim.

As an aside British, MI5 and MI6, along with the Americans and Israelis engaged in an operation called *Stuxnet* in order to destroy Iranian centrifuges which were being used to make enriched uranium for the Iranian nuclear program. I have always thought this is one of the great intelligence operations of the 21st century. If you want to know more about this outstanding operation, then google *Stuxnet* and see where your intelligence dollars are going.

Well, enough dirty tricks. Hopefully, you see why you need to expose as little of yourself as possible on a social network. Better still, if you must belong to a social network, then become an intelligence operator and hide your true identity behind a false one.

References:

As always, I wish I could claim some originality in the research used in this letter but like so many other past letters I cannot. Instead I must stand on the shoulders of others in order to attempt to look at the darkside of social Networks. If you want to get a more detailed glimpse of the darkside of social networks here are some of my sources.

1. *Cuban Twitter* By the Associated Press
2. *Ghost Army Haunts Michigan Library* By Nancy Mattoon
3. *How Covert Agents Infiltrate the Internet to Manipulate, Deceive, and Destroy Reputations* By Glenn Greenwald
4. *Teens and Sexting* By Amanda Lenhart
5. *Teens and Mobile Phones* By Amanda Lenhart, Rich Ling, Scott Campbell and Kristen Purcell
6. *The Emerging Dark Side of Social Networks* By Dominic Basulto
7. Numerous other Articles

Part 4

Gun Control and School Security

Part 4 – Gun Control and School Security

Context for Gun Control Letters

Well, I am still visiting the gun stores and from all indications, the gun scare is over. Oh, you missed the big event? According to the NRA and Republicans, Obama was supposed to take away all our guns and leave us defenseless and at the mercy of terrorist and criminals. Because of that scare, when Obama was elected, the bullets and guns fairly leapt off the gun store shelves. Really great business for the gun manufacturers for whom the NRA and Republican now seem to be a shill. Well, we are six years into the Obama administration and, if anything, for the last several years the guns laws seem to have been loosened by the courts for which the NRA and Republican have taken full credit. Of course the NRA continues their shrill, strident tone while the Republicans have turned their attention back to reducing taxes on the rich.

OK, my rant is finished so back to the letters. As you may know gun control and gun safety is something I have always been interested in and I was recently asked by my nephew, JW, for my thoughts on gun control and school security. Attached is my analysis of both subjects. However, in order to better understand gun control, I have included an updated version of a letter I had previously written to JDWO in which I elaborated on the collective versus individual right to own a gun based upon a legal interpretation of the 2nd amendment. In addition, I have included my thoughts on the recent Ferguson, Missouri and Cleveland, Ohio shootings.

By the way, Obama has stated publicly that the 2nd amendment is an individual not a collective right. However, he has gone on to say that it should be applied with commonsense rules – and therein lies the rub for gun advocates. What constitutes commonsense rules? As always when an issue is unclear, people tend to ascribe the worst interpretation to a word's meaning. In my opinion, what Obama means by commonsense is that rules must be applied locally and not nationally.

By way of full disclosure I am a lifetime member of the National Rifle Association.

J.T. Oney

Letter 1 - The 2nd Amendment

I read with interest your essay on "Gun Control" and found it both informative and persuasive. I thought your analysis was excellent and your conclusion supported by facts. From your logic one can only draw the logical conclusion that gun control does not prevent violent crime.

You must remember though that logic does not always hold sway in these discussions for in many cases ideology reigns and ideology is always the prison of rigid minds and no amount of facts or logic will change an ideologue for in most cases their rigidity is rooted in emotion and not logic.

You are correct in your statement that the right to bear arms is hotly debated and the debate is primarily between those who believe this is a **<u>collective right</u>** (guns are only for the military, law enforcement, etc.) versus those who believe this is an **<u>individual right</u>** (that is, each individual citizen has a right to a firearm).

This was not always the case for it was only at the turn of this century that the collective argument was put forward. I'm not sure why this argument was advanced. Perhaps in the belief that the possession of arms does contribute to violent crime, perhaps in the belief that only a constituted authority should possess the means of force, perhaps…

Regardless of their rationale at the heart of this discussion lie two different interpretations of the founder's intention when they created the second amendment. That is, should the emphasis be upon "**a well-regulated militia**" (a collective right) or should the emphasis be upon "**the people**" (an individual right).

Well, what was the intent of the foundering fathers? I believe as you do that it was their intent that this was an individual right. Here's why but first some history.

<u>The Confederation</u>

When the founding fathers concluded that the only way to retain their rights as free born Englishmen was to dissolve the bonds to their mother country through an armed conflict (The Revolutionary War) they also realized that the new country would need a new government. The men at this time were regionally oriented and concerned primarily with the impact of independence upon their individual states. Therefore, they believed that each state should act as a sovereign nation with each state having the right to control tariffs, enter into treaties with foreign countries, form militias, etc. That is, each state should be its own "**Nation State**" and an **Article of Confederation** was all that was necessary to govern their interaction. Under the Articles of Confederation all power remained with the states with the central government receiving its budget, militia, etc., from the voluntary contributions of each state. One can easily see the problem that Gen. Washington faced in prosecuting the Revolutionary War - States contributed support unequally or not at all, and Washington was constantly begging monies to clothe and feed his men.

The Constitution

After the Revolutionary War it became obvious to the governing elite that some changes were needed if the young country was to survive, so the states sent delegates to a convention to be held in Philadelphia starting May, 1787. The purpose of the convention was to modify the Articles of Confederation in order to strengthen the confederation. The delegates from Virginia, led by Madison, and Pennsylvania, led by Morris and Wilson, however, had other ideas so they, in essence, hijacked the convention in order to dissolve the Articles of Confederation and create a Republic based upon a Constitution. The delegates met at the Pennsylvania State House during the hot summer of 1787 (May-September) and during that time created one of the world's unique documents: **The Constitution of the United States**.

The Constitution came about as a result of two major compromises on how best to distribute power. The first compromise related to the distribution of power between the decentralized states and a strong centralized Federal Government. Compromises were made which, unfortunately, were not fully resolved until the Civil War. Many of delegates knew this and were uneasy about many of the compromises, particularly slavery, but felt they had no choice if the Republic was to be founded.

The second compromise related to the distribution of power within the central government; that is, how should power be distributed between the Executive, Legislative, and Judicial branches of the government? The delegates knew this would be an ongoing battle as each branch jockeyed for power and, based upon the compromises, were satisfied that no branch would be able to gain the upper hand.

A major controversy left unresolved at the conclusion of the Convention was whether or not a Bill of Rights should be included in the constitution.

Bill of Rights

The Constitution was published and sent to each state for ratification. The adoption of the constitution in many states was a close run thing with the major controversy centering on the lack of a Bill of Rights. The discussion was divided into two camps: the **Federalist** and the **Antifederalist**. The Federalist maintained these rights were inferred in the constitution and need not be enumerated, for one could not enumerate all rights; to do so would require a book the size of the bible. The Antifederalist basically held that the constitution should not be adopted until it contained the more important rights of citizens, among these being freedom of religion, freedom of speech, right to a speedy trial, no warrantless searches, the right to bear arms, etc. During this discussion many of the philosophical foundations of our constitution were laid down with the publication of essays from both the Federalist and Antifederalist. It was subsequently decided that the Constitution would be amended to contain a "**Bill of Rights.**"

Individual or Collective Right

I think it is clear from the writing of the Founders that they believed the Militia was composed of individual citizens who would furnish their own Musket/Rifle, powder and ball. From their writings it is also clear they believed the citizens would use these arms to defend themselves, to defend their state when called upon, to hunt for food and for sporting purposes. However, there are valid arguments for both the Collective and the Individual positions, but the strongest and most appealing argument I have heard relates to the meaning of the word "**the people**" as used by the founders in the Bill of Rights.

As I have already indicated the 2nd Amendment states the following:
*"A well regulated Militia, being necessary to the security of a free State, **the right of the people** to keep and bear Arms, shall not be infringed."*

I have underlined what I consider the key phrase.

This same phrase is used at other places in the Bill of Rights. For example the 1st Amendment:

*"Congress shall make no law respecting an establishment of religion, or prohibiting the free exercise thereof; or abridging the freedom of speech, or of the press; or **the right of the people** to peaceably to assemble, and to petition the Government for a redress of grievances."* Again I've underlined the key phrase.

This same phrase is also used in the 4th Amendment. For example:

*"**The right of the people** to be secure in their persons, houses, papers, and effects, against unreasonable searches and seizures, shall not be violated, and no Warrants shall issue, but upon probable cause, supported by Oath or affirmation, and particularly describing the place to be searched, and the persons or things to be seized."*

The phrase *"**the people**"* is also used in the 9ᵗʰ and 10ᵗʰ Amendment.

Amendment Nine

*"The enumeration in the Constitution, of certain rights, shall not be construed to deny or disparage others retained by **the people**."*

Amendment Ten

*"The powers not delegated to the United States by the Constitution, nor prohibited by it to the States, are reserved to the States respectively, or to **the people.**"*

I believe the framers of the Constitution and Bill of Rights were very careful in their phrasing and wording since they had pledged their life and liberties to the cause of freedom. Therefore, their use of the phrases "the right of the people" and "the people" would have been consistent throughout both documents.

I once heard a Jesuit priest use the phrase **"Precision of Thought - Economy of Expression"** to describe the result of a good education. The founders were highly intelligent, educated people, and to think they would not use the same meaning for the same phrase within the Bill of Rights is illogical.

If that is true, and I think it is, then the meaning of "the People" and not "a well regulated militia" is at the heart of understanding the intent of the 2ⁿᵈ amendment. In the 1ˢᵗ, 4ᵗʰ, 9ᵗʰ and 10ᵗʰ amendments the phrase "the people" refers to individual citizens. It is illogical to assume that the same phrase in the 2ⁿᵈ amendment would have a different meaning. The 2nd amendment must, therefore, refer to an individual right of each citizen and not to a collective right.

Letter 2 - Gun Control

Thanks for the prodding. I've been meaning to write a letter on Gun Control since it has been all over the news but have been busy on the next book. However, because this subject, gun control, has been all over the news and with your prodding I decided to take some time and put in my two cents.

As always things have context so by way of full disclosure I'm sure you are aware that I am a life-time member of the NRA and fully support the right of individuals to have a firearm. I think the question now is not the possession of a firearm but how and what type firearm?

Before I talk about that issue, though, I think it worthwhile to provide some background.

The Second Amendment

The text of the Second Amendment is ambiguous and has been interpreted in two major ways throughout its history. The second amendment says, "***A well regulated Militia, being necessary to the security of a free State, the right of the people to keep and bear Arms, shall not be infringed.***"

Gun-rights supporters believe the second amendment guarantees an **individual** the right to bear arms. That is, it is an individual right. Hard-line gun-rights advocates such as the NRA portray even modest gun laws as infringements on the second amendment, and are rigidly opposed to anything remotely related to gun control, such as high capacity magazines or background checks. Their reasoning is that *any* gun-control measure, no matter how seemingly reasonable, puts us on the slippery slope toward total civilian disarmament. For these people, the Second Amendment is **all rights and no regulation**.

Gun control advocates on the other hand feel the Second Amendment is a **collective right** and only applies to state militias, that is, all tools of power belong in the hands of the state. These gun-control hard-liners support any new law that has a chance to be enacted even if that law is unlikely to reduce gun violence. For them, the Second Amendment is **all regulation and no rights.**

Author's Note: For a more detailed discussion of the Second Amendment see my previous letter.

That quick look at the second amendment brings us to the National Rifle Association (NRA). A reminder: I am a life time member of the NRA.

The NRA

Today, the NRA is the strongest advocate against gun control; however, that was not always the case. The NRA was founded in 1871 by George Wingate and William Church primarily to improve the marksmanship of American soldiers. They had been in the Civil War and knew firsthand the poor marksmanship of the average civil war soldier. I'm not sure much has changed in the intervening years. From my perspective, the marines seem to be the only branch of service that truly stresses marksmanship; that is, every marine is a rifleman.

In the 1920s and '30s, the NRA was at the forefront in legislative efforts to enact gun control. For example, Karl Frederick, the NRA president at that time, helped draft the **Uniform Firearms Act** which was a model then and now for state-level gun-control legislation.

Frederick's model law had three major elements. **First**, no one could carry a concealed handgun in public without a permit from the local police. **Second**, gun dealers must report to law enforcement every sale of a handgun. **Third**, the law imposed a two-day waiting period on handgun sales.

Interestingly, the NRA today condemns every one of these provisions as a burdensome and ineffective infringement on the right to bear arms.

During the 1930s Congress passed the **National Firearms Act of 1934**, which imposed a steep tax and registration requirements on weapons such as machine guns and sawed-off shotguns which were easily acquired by Chicago gangsters.

(Question: What is the Chicago typewriter? Answer: The Thompson submachine gun.) I always found it difficult to control the Tommy gun. Perhaps I didn't have enough practice. I found the grease gun even worse; I never was any good with it.

When this law was passed, the NRA supported it with some exceptions. For example, they successfully lobbied to have excessive taxes on handguns stripped from the final bill by successfully arguing that people needed such weapons to protect their homes. At that time though the NRA supported what they termed **"reasonable, sensible and fair legislation"**.

In the 1960s, with the assassination of President John F. Kennedy, Franklin Orth, NRA executive vice president, testified in favor of banning mail-order rifle sales.

All that, however, was about to change. In the 1960s and 1970s a growing number of NRA members, because of their fear of rising crime rates and especially their fear of the Black Panthers, were buying guns for protection. The NRA leadership seemed oblivious to this seismic change to such an extent that in 1976, Maxwell Rich, the executive vice president, announced that the NRA would sell its building in Washington, D.C., and relocate the headquarters to Colorado Springs, thereby retreating from political lobbying and expanding its outdoor and environmental activities.

Rich's plan resulted in an uprising among the NRA hardline gun-rights advocates. A palace coup was staged by Harlan Carter, a bulldog of a man and the former Border Patrol Director, who ran the NRA's recently formed lobbying arm, the Institute for Legislative Action. In May 1977, Carter and his allies staged a coup at the annual membership meeting in Cincinnati, Ohio. Carter was subsequently elected the new executive vice president and immediately began to transform the NRA into a lobbying powerhouse committed to a more aggressive view of the Second Amendment. The best way he felt to do that was by entering the political arena.

A sign of this new determination to influence electoral politics was evident in his 1980 decision to endorse a presidential candidate. For the previous 100 years the NRA has stayed clear of politics. The NRA had now entered politics with a vengeance.

Carter's stance for the NRA boiled down to the mantra, "No Compromise!" which was summed up by Neal Knox, the new head of the ILA, when he said, "It is nice to be loved, but better to be feared." That mantra and philosophy has been carried out by all subsequent leaders of the NRA to include its present executive vice president, Wayne LaPierre. This mantra and philosophy has been exceptionally effective.

From a number of peoples perspective, the NRA has gone from being reasonable to radical. For them, the NRA has basically become a Political Action Committee (PAC) which fronts for the gun and ammunition manufacturers using the Second Amendment as a cudgel against all who attempt to impose any gun control measure which reduces firearms and ammunition sales. Fear mongering does seem to sell weapons and ammunition.

They are now the big dog on the block and seem to take great pleasure in exercising their power through threats and intimidation. They have become masters of hard core politics.

I have my doubts about the radicalization of the NRA because it has moved away from what I believe to be its primary mission: teaching people how to shoot. I believe in the idea of the **American Rifleman** as exemplified by the Marine Corps where everyone is a rifleman first. Good riflemen need to be trained over years not one or two weeks. In order to strengthen the US, the NRA needs to get back to its primary mission of teaching marksmanship to Americans. The military needs more American Riflemen.

OK, enough about the NRA.

Effective Gun Control

Let me state right up front that, in my opinion, there is no such thing as effective gun control. Someone estimated that as of now there are approximately 310 million guns in the hands of the American public. To think that any law will result in these guns being turned in or to think that the Government would attempt to confiscate them is absolute nonsense. So from my perspective, gun control is a total misnomer. It simply cannot be done.

Well, can we end the killings with handguns? Right now we have between 8-9 thousand gun murders in the United States, primarily due to interpersonal conflict due to greed, revenge, jealousy, fear, etc. These are the things that make us human. Combine that with the fact that we have a culture of violence and we have a deadly combination that inevitably leads to violent confrontation.

I have always liked to blame the culture of violence on the English, for, from my perspective we are a direct reflection of 1500 and 1600 England. During this time, England was in constant turmoil with civil wars and their inevitable violence seemingly popping up every few years. Those who were persecuted, or on the losing side, needed somewhere to go and what better place than a new land. If you want a good example of this look at the Cavaliers in Virginia.

Of course it did not help things when in King Philip's War, 1675-78, between 5 and 10 percent of the English settlers of fighting age were killed fighting the Indians. As a result, laws at this time were passed requiring all able bodied settlers to keep firearms in their homes for their defense.

The mid 1700s saw the advent of the "Kentucky rifle," which became the long range symbol of the frontier. This was the time of Daniel Morgan and his Corp of riflemen who dressed in hunting shirts. Washington sent them hunting the British and they proved especially effective at killing the British Officers. This was also the time of Daniel Boone and the settling of the western frontier through constant warfare with the Indians.

We can't forget the 1800s when Sam Colt and the "Peacemaker" made every one equal; after all, God created man but Sam Colt made them equal. Frontiersmen after the civil war wore guns like noble men in the 18th century wore their swords.

The 1900s were filled with Chicago gangsters and their "Chicago Typewriter" while the literature and movies abounded with the heroic private eye and the snub nose revolver. Of course, we can't forget the five wars, terrorists and their AK 47, and finally mass slayings.

Whoever says we don't have a culture of violence needs their heads examined.

What can be done?

I suppose the question is really not what can be done, but what can be done effectively? Today, there seems to be four major gun control issues being discussed. First, is a ban on assault weapons. Second, is the size of available magazines. Third, is universal background checks while, fourth, is mental health. Let me comment on these issues in order.

First, assault weapons. There are an estimated 310 million firearms in the US (well, give or take a few million but, hey, that is the nature of guns). Approximately 3.7 million of these are AR-15 style rifles. I say AR-15 style rifles because we have to be careful in our definition as to what an **assault ri**fle is and what it is not. In my opinion an assault weapon has the capability of being fired in a fully automatic mode while most **assault style rifles** in civilian hands are semi-automatic. Let's assume for a minute that the 3.7 million figure is correct. Well, from my perspective, implementing assault gun control on AR-15 style rifles is already impossible. In addition, this particular issue will never pass congress for there are too many congressmen living in conservative congressional districts who want to get reelected. This has a 0% possibility of passing.

Second, magazine size. Someone once said, a hunter I suppose, that if you needed more than 3-5 rounds to kill your game, then they are not skilled hunters but a butcher and need to visit the range. From my perspective, I suppose the same could be said about civilian self-defense. That is, eight rounds should be enough to end a gun fight. If it takes more than eight rounds then someone has not been practicing. You cannot just strap on a gun and expect to win a gunfight. Bill Jordan once said there are no second place winners in a fight. To win, you need to practice daily. This has a 25% possibility of eventually passing probably at a ten or twenty round magazine limit.

Third is Universal Background Checks. I'm not certain there can ever be universal background checks. Background checks certainly make sense at licensed firearm dealers, at gun shows, etc. The problem arises when my cousin up the hollow decides to sell a weapon to his cousin across the hill. There is no way he will come out of the hollow, pay money for a background check then go back up the hollow and sell his weapon. From my perspective, Universal background checks are impossible; however, there are some loop holes that should be closed such as those at gun shows. There is a 25% possibility of eventually passing some additional background checks.

Fifth is mental health. I think everyone will agree, even the NRA, that keeping weapons out of the hands of the mentally unstable is a reasonable thing to do. The problem is how to do it? Any background check should also include a mental health check. However, logically, only those people which have legally been declared a menace will be listed in a data base. Those people still under a doctor's care are assured of a doctor client privilege and will not be listed. I think those that can legally be identified should be listed and checked as part of the background check but not everyone will be included. Even if this is included in a background check, it must be recognized that our mental health system, like our physical health system, is in shambles and is in need of repair. The Affordable Health Care Act is a partial fix but really does not go far enough or address the mental health system. In addition, adequate funding for this area will always be a problem. There is a 50% possibility of including some categories of the mentally unstable in background checks.

There are some who, in addition to the measures listed above, advocate that gun owners be licensed similar to a driver license, a pilot license, etc. On its surface this appears to make sense because it would, for example, require the individual to be fully trained in order to properly operate the weapon. The problem, however, is that will not prevent criminals from acquiring weapons. The biggest problem, however, is that the Second amendment guarantees an individual the RIGHT to own a weapon. This idea is a nonstarter.

Will additional laws fix the problem?

The answer is obviously no. The only thing it may do is to reduce the risk of murders and mass killings. Because of our culture of violence, the risk of these things occurring will never be zero. In my opinion the real onus on controlling gun violence lays the same place as a proper education, and that is with the family. It is a family responsibility to assure that the son is properly trained in the use of a weapon and, most importantly, the responsible use of a weapon (for whatever reason a female does not seem prone to gun violence; I suspect this is due to culture). If the family has an unstable child, then it is their responsibility to assure it is recognized, receives treatment, and that he/she does not have access to weapons.

To think that a culture of violence can be legislated away is the height of foolishness, but I suppose legislatures need to be seen as doing something even if it has little or no effect. I suppose that is the nature of politics.

As soon as I have time I'll do another missive on School Security. If you don't mind, I'll pass this along to the family.

Letter 3 - School Security

Well, I have finally found the time to respond to your inquiry dealing with school security and, with your concurrence, will forward the letter to the rest of the family in hopes that they will find the response informative but annoying. But first, some background.

Background

School incidents have been a recurring theme since the very founding of America and the need for school security has been discussed since the very first incident occurred before this was a nation.

The first known school shooting in the US was the Enoch Brown School Massacre which took place on July 26, 1764, in what is now Franklin County, Pennsylvania, when four Lenape American Indian warriors entered a log schoolhouse of white settlers and shot and scalped the schoolmaster, Enoch Brown, before turning their tomahawks on the children and killing nine students.

The most deadly attack on a school occurred in May, 1927, in Bath, Michigan, when the school care taker, Andrew Kehoe, detonated 600 pounds of dynamite that he had placed inside Bath Consolidated School. The explosion killed 45 people, including 38 elementary school children and injured at least 58 more. Kehoe, a local farm owner who was also the school's caretaker, had planted the bomb at the school because he was angry about property taxes used to fund the school. He burned down his farm the same day, and then committed suicide by blowing up his car, killing himself and five other people.

In my opinion whatever is done to secure the schools must be done at the local level. There is simply too much resistance by lobbies for anything to occur at the federal or state level. I have always thought that in a democracy, change must come from the bottom up and not from the top down and I believe that is the case with school security.

When we look at securing the school we must all remember that there is not just one threat to school security but a continuum of threats which range from drugs, weapons, and gangs to bomb threats and school shootings.

All risks to school safety, however, are not equal, some events have a higher risk than others, and risks are unique to each school; therefore, each school will need to perform a risk assessment and prioritize their risk reduction measures against the identified risk factors. Neither a one-time school security assessment nor a common security template can be developed that encompasses every school, for each school is different. A school by school assessment and an individual security plan will need to be prepared.

As I indicated schools are faced with a continuum of threats. Some pose a higher risk than others. For example, the high risk threats are activities such as athletic events, dances, a school's first day, class changes, and the opening and close of the school day. Unfortunately, high risk threats also include irate parents or disgruntled employees.

From my perspective, however, the three greatest threats to school security are (1) inconsistent school leadership by the school board, superintendent and school principal, (2) complacency on the part of school staff, students and parents with regard to reporting incidents, failing to challenge strangers and parents or staff failure to follow proper entry and visitor procedures and (3) inadequate funding for security.

A knee-jerk reaction, which is what has taken place in the past, to a security incident cannot properly address school security. For example, in the past, funding has been on an anecdotal basis. That is, if a high priority security incident occurred then funding was provided. That will not do when it comes to school security. Long term stability in both policies and funding for school safety must be provided if schools are to be properly secured.

Defense in Depth

There is no one solution to school security as some would propose. I believe that school security, like any other type security, must be planned and implemented in-depth. Think of in-depth school security as a series of concentric rings encircling the school. Each ring is a security layer surrounding the school which provides a different means for securing the school. Each layer provides a specific type of security.

The objective of this type of in-depth security is to reduce the risk of a school shooter to a minimum by having the shooter needing to penetrate each layer of security before he/she reaches their objective. Unfortunately, no security can ever reduce a school shooting to zero. A determined individual willing to sacrifice himself will find a way through any defense no matter how well thought out or implemented. Let's now look at each of those security layers.

The **first ring**, the most internal concentric security ring, is inside the school itself. This is where you need a **permanent armed presence**. The inner most security ring is the most critical for that is the location where force-on-force will occur with the winner determining whether or not students are killed.

The **second concentric security ring**, moving outward, is the school entrance and the perimeter of the building. This is where **technology** can help. This includes such things as barriers, traps, fencing, cameras, alarms, shielded hinges, locks, lighting, etc.

The **third concentric ring** is related to **personnel and administration;** that is, school policies. This includes such things as policies related to security assessments, badges, background checks, psychological assessment of students and staff, lockdown procedures, incident indicators, etc.

The fourth **concentric security ring** relates to county/city policies and first responders. This includes security funding, police, fire, security organizations, training, school interface, hospitals, etc.

In order to keep this missive short, I will make recommendation related to the concentric rings but concentrating mostly on the inner most security ring.

But first a caveat. As you know I am a life time member of the NRA and have some disagreement with their shrillness and rigid ideology of "no compromise." However, they recently had Asa Hutchison produce a report stressing an armed presence in the school. As usual I have a problem with their conclusion regarding the arming of teachers and staff. I do agree, however, with their recommendation related to **School Resource Officers**.

With that said, here is my analysis and recommendations.

Arm the Teachers/Staff

It has been suggested by the NRA and several of our citizens particularly those who are gun-rights advocates that we should arm our teachers and staff. On the surface, this sounds worthy of study; however, as always the devil is in the details. Most teachers I know prefer to be armed with textbooks rather than with guns and, as a college professor, I certainly fall into that category.

Arming teachers will require the school board to take on a significant increase in responsibility and liability which I believe exceeds their expertise, knowledge, experience and professional capabilities. As you know, I support the right of our citizens to carry a weapon; however, giving this responsibility to teachers is asking them to perform actions in a public capacity that is outside the scope of their professional training. I believe a better alternative is to place an armed School Resource Officer at the high school and here the NRA and I are in agreement.

School Resource Officers (SRO)

We need to create a permanent position of a School Resource Officer in each school. A number of communities have already proven the advantage of placing a law enforcement officer in the school system. Unfortunately, many of these programs simply employ cuff-and-stuff methods and are only focused on arresting students. The SRO officer needs to be especially selected and trained so that he/she can perform more tasks associated with prevention than with arrest and prosecution.

Each school that employs an SRO will need to establish a Memorandum of Understanding (MOU), or an "interagency agreement," between the appropriate law-enforcement agency and the school district that specifically spells out their duties and responsibilities.

The SRO program should emphasize the importance of collaboration between school officials and local law enforcement by promoting a community-based approach to school violence. The National Association of School Resource Officers (NASRO) has divided the responsibilities of SROs into three areas, referred to as the "triad" concept of school-based policing: (1) educator, (2) informal counselor and (3) law-enforcement officer. In addition to their training as law-enforcement officers, each SRO should receive specialized training in teaching and counseling.

The benefits of SROs go beyond enhancing school safety by protecting students, teachers and administrators. Several communities have reported that placing SROs at schools has reduced the burden on patrol officers and road deputies who no longer need to respond to individual problems at local schools. They have also helped improve the image of police officers among youth and fostered better relationships between juveniles and police.

Unfortunately, funding the SRO will be a continual problem. Logically, funding for the SRO should be built into the local sheriff or Police Department. Funding from the state or federal level is simply too inconsistent because of the state and federal politics.

The Department of Justice's Office of Community Oriented Policing Services (COPS) did offer up a $60 million grant program which was intended to provide communities with the resources necessary to tackle crime and violence in schools. Following a wave of school shootings in the late 1990s, which included the Columbine massacre, COPS introduced a new program, called Cops in Schools (CIS), which awarded funding grants for schools to hire specially trained community officers. This grant provided for more than 6,500 SROs around the country. As usually happens in these type programs, politics caught up with it and the funding for the program was cut in FY2006.

As is always the case, state and federal budget constraints and shifting priorities have meant a decline or termination of key school safety programs. From my perspective, reliance on state and federal funds for school security funds is short sighted and foolish.

However, for most school systems because of funding constraints, I believe a combination of School Resource Officers at the high school and School Security Officials at the elementary school systems will need to be provided. I believe a Police Reserve or Reserve Deputy Squad should be organized to handle special high threat events at the school such as dances and athletic events. They should also be the source for the School Security Officials at the elementary school.

Recommendations for the Security Rings

The following recommendations related to the school security rings are not all inclusive but I believe are the major ones needed to properly manage and control school security. They are not meant to be all inclusive but merely representative and to cross concentric ring boundaries.

First, the school board should create a policy requiring the establishment of security guidelines by each school building.

Second, a County/City Crisis Team and a Building Crisis Team for each school should be formed. This would, of course, include identifying the members and their responsibilities.

Third, each school should develop a Threat Assessment Team, which will work in coordination with mental health professionals to develop preincident indicators in order to identify students or outside persons exhibiting threatening behavior and posing a risk to the school.

Fourth, a Continuity of Operation Plan (COOP) should be created by the County/City Crisis Team. If a school is inoperable for a week, a month, or a year, then plans need to be in place to continue the student's education. Their education is too important to be interrupted on a long term basis.

Fifth, the County/City Crisis team should establish an Emergency Operation Center (EOC). This would be a place for the Crisis Team to assemble in order to coordinate their response to an emergency situation. Rushing to the emergency site, and attempting to make decisions in an emotionally charged atmosphere, merely adds to the confusion.

Sixth, two Parent-Student Reunification Sites need to be established. The first site, for small-scale incidents, should be adjacent to the school building while the second site, for large incidents, should be located off-site. School administrators often underestimate the overwhelming number of parents that flock to the school in an emergency and the difficulty in releasing the students to their parents in a timely manner.

Seventh, the County/City needs to develop an interface between the County/City Incident Command System for both the County/City Crisis Team and the Building Crisis Team. It is important in creating this interface to assure a smooth handover of control from the Building Crisis Team to the arriving first responders and emergency personnel.

Eighth, a Joint Information Center (JIC) needs to be created where the Public Information Officers (PIO) from the schools and the first responder organizations, such as the police and fire, can formulate and disseminate information in a unified manner.

I believe this area is so important that I want to elaborate on it.

Public Information

Communicating with the media during an incident is one of the most important and frustrating issues in managing the crisis. During a crisis the media will be in an information feeding frenzy and if the school and public officials don't talk *with* them then the media will talk *about* them.

I believe the local new media are an exception to my statements and should be handled separately. They are invested in the local community, know everyone, and will have the best interests of the community in mind when reporting the news.

Well, based upon past experience, here is my rant.

You can count on the media to not only flock to the school during a crisis but long after the crisis is over. Typically the news cycle will run through four stages, and during all these stages, officials would be wise to talk to the media.

First, will be the **Breaking News Cycle** where little is known, but the competition for facts among the competing news organization will be fierce to get it out first. During this cycle the media mob will feed with abandon and if officials do not feed them they will feed on the officials. The worst thing one can say during this period is "No Comment" or "This is an isolated incident." These comments are interpreted by the news media that the officials are either incompetent, lying, or both.

Second, will be the **Investigation Cycle**. This cycle will be when the police, fire, or school investigates the incident. The news media will want to know what happened, and, in most cases, will request access to the building, students and teachers.

Third, will be the **Analysis Stage** in which the news media will provide ongoing analysis of the developing facts by soliciting the opinions of experts. Everybody knows what an expert is, right? He is an idiot with a briefcase three miles from home whose only desire is five minutes of fame.

The fourth and final stage will be the **<u>Grief Stage</u>** in which the media will focus on the emotional impact of the incident on the family. This stage will include the funerals and memorials. For the news media, everyone is a spokesperson and the more emotional the better. There is an old saying in the news business, "**If it bleeds it leads. If it cries, it flies.**" The news media is a business that needs to earn money, and because of the competitive nature of the news organizations, the more dramatic the news the better.

The news media must be fed, and it is ultimately the responsibility of school or public officials to feed them by being accurate, timely, and redundant in their information dissemination to the news media.

Finally, for those really interested in school security, there is a wealth of information in the reference section of the NRA SHIELD report by Asa Hutchinson. I would encourage everyone to look closely at the Best Practices in that reference section.

Letter 4 - The Ferguson Shooting

Subject: An Open Letter to a Law Enforcement Officer

My family and I recently had an interesting discussion about the shooting by the police in Ferguson, Missouri and Cleveland, Ohio. I'm sure you stayed informed of both. As you recall a Ferguson Police Officer named Darrin Wilson engaged in a confrontation with Michael Brown which resulted in the death of Brown. In Cleveland, Ohio, Police Officer Timothy Loehmann unfortunately mistook a pellet pistol for a real one and shot and killed 12 year old Tamir Rice. Both are unfortunate incidents in which the officers, the victim's family and the communities will have to live with these tragic events for years to come.

You are a Law Enforcement Officer and are paid to protect the public, and, as such, you are the public's first line of defense. You were especially selected and trained for one mission and that is to protect us, the public. Don't get me wrong. I will not need you all the time, for I fully intend to protect myself and my family when possible. After all, I was raised in the mountains, believe in the right of self-defense, own a gun, and know how to use it. There will be times, however, when we need help, and when we call, we expect you to be there prepared to give your life in defense of our safety.

I know that is tall order but that is your job and that is why we pay you. I wish we could pay you, the teachers and firemen more but we can't, at least not right now. I know you deserve more pay, a lot more, but unfortunately the resources are just not there. Nevertheless, even with the marginal pay you receive, I expect you to do your job of protecting me and my family. That is what you swore to do and I expect you to keep your word.

I know that you, as a Law Enforcement Officer, have been under the microscope since the shootings in Ferguson and Cleveland, and I also know that your training is currently being scrutinized in hopes of improving your performance. If that is so, and it probably is, then don't take it personally since, truthfully, that is how bureaucracies work. The higher ups are going to cover their butts and everyone knows and expects it.

In addition, the pundits are piling on and seem to relish pointing out the actions of both officers, and you are getting tarred with the brush of using too much force, profiling, prejudice, discrimination, etc. Again, don't take it personally, that is simply what pundits do. Their job is to criticize you, many times unfairly, for being gun happy without their ever giving a thought to the many correct life and death decisions you make on a daily basis.

Again, don't get me wrong. I don't feel sorry for you nor should you feel sorry for yourself. As my Mom would say, "You chose this profession, now live with it." You make life and death decisions every day that, unfortunately, can result in the death of a citizen if you make the wrong decision or result in your death if you make the wrong decision. Either way you are wrong or dead. Again, don't get me wrong, you chose this profession and knew your career choice would put you in harm's way and when you put yourself in harm's way then bad things happen and you need to learn to live, or die, with the results.

What I would like to do, however, in this open letter is offer some advice that will hopefully keep both you and me safe. In giving this advice just remember that you are not alone. I support you and will attempt to be there when you need me. After all, if I hire and pay you then I need to support you. Occasionally, though, I will need your help and when that help arrives I want it to come with the knowledge that it will employ the best tactics and training possible.

We both realize that tactics and training for the Law Enforcement Officer is intended to give him an edge, so here is some advice that may allow you and the citizens you protect to go home at night.

1. **<u>Distance creates safety.</u>** Distance from a suspect or assailant not only creates safety but allows for more reaction time when confronting a dangerous situation. The closer you are to a suspect the more confrontational a situation can become and the shorter the reaction time necessary to resolve the situation. In the Cleveland incident, it may have been more tactically sound if both officers had been farther from the 12 year old boy giving them more time to assess and perhaps defuse the situation. In the case of Ferguson, it may have been more tactically sound if Officer Wilson had

backed off after the initial confrontation and waited for his friends rather than escalating the confrontation.

2. **Bring Friends**. When you are engaged in a confrontation, or expect to be engaged in a confrontation, it is always best to have some friends along with shotguns. Nothing defuses a situation faster than the sound of a shotgun being racked or being confronted by overwhelming force. Too often a younger, inexperienced officer will let their ego get the better of their judgment and want to go mano a mano and then talk about it over a beer whereas the more experienced officer will call for his friends to come support him and then discuss the situation from a position of strength. The outcome in the Ferguson shooting may have been different if Officer Wilson had waited for his friends. I'm sure the tactic employed by the responding officers in Cleveland of driving close to the victim will be reviewed.

3. **Badge Heavy.** As a Law Enforcement Officer you should never go badge heavy and by this I mean rely on your badge and bullying to resolve a situation. You, as a sworn Law Enforcement Officer, have the force and power of the state behind you. You represent the point of the public spear in the use of force, deadly force, and when required the state can bring overwhelming force to a situation. Individual citizens cannot match that force and know it; therefore, there is no need for you to engage in using your badge to bully citizens. Unfortunately, younger officers just out of training or with little experience become aware of and enjoy the power that their badge represents. Badge heavy officers should always be paired with older, more mature officers who realize, as Shakespeare would say, that "**Faire and softly goeth far**".

4. **Lower Emotions**. When you arrive at a scene you are facing the unknown, your adrenalin is flowing, and you are running on high and cranked for action. This is natural and as it should be, for we are all humans and conditioned by nature to either fight or flee. Unfortunately, when you arrive on the scene you are facing another human who has also been conditioned by nature to either fight or flee. After you have stabilized the scene,

emotions can still escalate and get out of hand. You should expect your commands to be obeyed and the average citizen will willingly do that because you have earned their trust. Unfortunately, emotions will sometimes get in the way of citizens quickly acting upon your commands no matter how loud or authoritatively it is given. This, unfortunately, can lead to an explosive situation because you have come to expect your commands to be obeyed and when they are not, your natural reaction will be to escalate the continuum of force to enforce your commands. This is the point at which **'calmer heads must prevail**.' Emotions must be lowered and this is most often done by employing a lower, less emotional, and confrontation tone. There is a time for talk and a time for action and knowing the difference saves lives. Unfortunately, knowing the difference comes only with experience and there is the rub. Would the outcome in Ferguson have been different if the situation had not escalated? Perhaps, but we will never know.

5. **Shooting to Wound.** How many times have you heard someone say, "Well, he should have shot to wound." That person has either been watching too much TV, has little or no shooting experience or both. Military Professionals may expend up to 10,000 rounds a month in practice. You as a Law Enforcement Officer do not. Because of time and money constraints, you are lucky to get to the range every three months and even then the amount of ammunition provided is limited. You punch holes in a stationary target at specific distances to qualify in order to meet the legal requirements specified by your department in expectation of going to court after using your firearm. You are trained to fire at the major part of the body and to kill, not to wound. The shooting techniques you employ is probably sufficient for legal purposes, but other professionals question whether or not it is sufficient for a gunfight where you are frightened, the adrenaline is flowing, you are shaking, you are moving, it is dark and you are looking for cover. You were probably taught '**in a fight front sight**' but you are now looking at the shooter, not the front sight, because that is where the threat is. You are shaking so bad it is a wonder you can hit anything. To ask a police officer to shoot to wound is totally impractical and, not to put too fine a point on it, the height of idiocy.

6. **Police Militarism.** You should have the best equipment and training the public can provide. If I have asked you to put your life on the line then that is the least I can do. After 911 it became apparent you were ill equipped to support a counterterrorism function; therefore the government began to provide you with military equipment to include heavy vehicles. Unfortunately, little or no training or guidance on when or how to employ the equipment came with it. Since you want to bring overwhelming force to bear on demonstrations or riots, what better way than to show up with an armored vehicle. After all, one of the basic doctrines of riot control is intimidation. OOOps, you forgot how a bulky armored vehicle looks on the front page as you confront demonstrating American citizens. You now realize you look like a black booted thug and finally come to your senses when the public, in alarm, begins to scream, **"this is not Tiananmen Square."** Well, you realize you need to regroup and rethink the use of counterterrorism equipment. However, you are going to be faced, sooner or later, with terrorist activity in your area so there is every reason for you to have military equipment, but for use on terrorist and not on your fellow citizens. You will need to develop rules for employment and that deployment must be continually practiced and when employed it should be under the control of a senior experienced sergeant. Some good advice I once heard was that **"heavy weapons must have a very narrow focus!"**

7. **Police Body Cameras.** Well, after Ferguson and Cleveland, it was inevitable that the proposal be advanced that you be required to wear a body camera. How many times have you heard that the crime scene or interrogation should have been captured by video because it does not lie? I have been asked my opinion on this several times and I think the idea should be explored but with caution. One caution is this. When you turn that camera on your action and the action of your opponent will change for the focus is now on the camera and your realization that the confrontation will be judged by your superiors or by a court. Therefore, you may begin to act cautiously, and a cautious officer may hesitate, and to hesitate may mean you do not go home to your family at the end of the day. Your mission is to

support the public but yet, at the end of the day, be able to go home, and anything that prevents that from happening should be handled cautiously. Don't get me wrong, there will always be one of you who is first through the door. Just make sure everyone realizes the consequences. My second caution is that in many cases there is no context for the scene captured on camera. For example, it may show the perpetrator getting the crap beat out of him but does not show the reason for it or what happened prior to the scene captured on camera. The third caution is the public's right to privacy. When the camera goes on it captures things in an indiscriminate manner and in some cases scenes or individuals are captured without their consent. Unfortunately, cameras, like witnesses, do, in fact, lie and should be used cautiously.

8. **Witnesses Lie.** Perhaps I should rephrase that to "**witnesses are unreliable**." My first experience with this came in a class room when the instructor was interrupted by a gunman who appeared at the door, fired three shots at the instructor then vanished. After order was restored and the instructor picked himself up off the floor, the students were asked to write a description of the gunman. The result was ten students with ten DIFFERENT descriptions of the gunman. We see events through the prism of our culture and value system. We don't deliberately lie; it's just that we have difficulty seeing what really happened, because, in most cases, our brain completes what we expect to see. This is why you need as many witnesses to an event as possible and even then you will rarely get a consensus on the truth. A good example of this is Ferguson where different people saw the same shooting but described it differently. It is an axiom that a good observer must be trained and the average person is neither trained nor reliable.

9. **I look for Trouble.** I have often thought that the proper description of your job is, "**I Look for Trouble.**" You, on a daily basis, deal with the underbelly of society. As a result both your divorce rate and drinking is higher than it should be. Because you are constantly dealing with the worse elements of society you quickly become jaded, suspicious of your fellow

man and begin to associate only with the people you trust which are your fellow officers. I always thought this was natural and to be expected. Because of this you must constantly remind yourself that you are part of the civic body and are paid and work for the people. I always thought we were lucky in the mountains because our deputy sheriffs grew up in the county, was known and respected. Unfortunately, that is not always true of major police departments in urban areas who can easily become a community unto themselves and are viewed as such, and because of this, can be viewed with suspicion by elements of the public.

10. **Training.** The real estate folks have three things to say about the importance of property: Location, Location, Location. Borrowing from this I have three things to say about your tactics: **Training, Training, Training**. You, like the military, must constantly train. Most of us who come from the hills and played sports remember the coach constantly reminding us that 'how we practice is how we play' and we practiced constantly because we needed to react instinctively. When you are faced with a dangerous situation you will react according to your training because practice becomes instinct which is what is required when instantaneous decisions must be made. If you are trained to '**shoot first and let God sort it out**' then that is exactly what you will do. If, however, you are taught to use time, distance, your friends and cover then that is exactly what you will do. The public and I expect a well-trained law enforcement officer employing sound tactics to protect us.

I know this advice is just common sense but it is always good to occasionally be reminded of obvious things. Thanks for listening. I look forward to your continued professional help and promise that I will, in turn, support you.

Part 5

The Torture Debate

Part 5 – The Torture Debate

Context for the Torture Letter

Torture has been a constancy among humans since time immemorial. We have used it to gain pleasure, as part of an execution, for revenge, and to acquire information. For whatever reason, we seem to enjoy inflicting pain on others. That seems to be especially true if the 'others' do not belong to our 'tribe'. I suppose the attitude of "we" versus "they " has simply become part of our DNA.

The discussion on torture has once again raised its ugly head with the release of the Intelligence Committee report on the use of torture by the CIA. The democratic congressional committee members in outrage, whether feigned or not, indignantly released the report.

The public seemed to yawn for the report was received with mixed reviews. That is, about half the people were outraged while the other half seemed to accept the necessity of torture by the CIA.

I fall somewhere in between. That is, I do not believe in torture as a national policy but do believe that in highly selective instances a case can be made for the necessity of torture.

What do you think?

J.T. Oney

Letter 1 - The Torture Debate

I have always found the debate relating to torture fascinating for it seems to be a constantly recurring theme throughout history. That is, torture has always been used by various nation states, culture, or tribes as a method of interrogation, punishment, coercion or execution. For example, it was quite common until the 1700s for criminals to be tortured to death rather than being executed.

I have never been convinced that societal execution was ever a good form of criminal deterrence but it does seem to satisfy our natural instinct for revenge.

Because of constant practice man has always been really creative when it comes to torturing their fellow man. Some of the more creative methods have been boiling to death, flaying, crucifixion, impalement, crushing, burning, sawing and necklacing. Even stoning still seems quite popular in some fundamental Islamic communities.

(Note: If you don't already know, Necklacing is the placement of a rubber tire filled with gasoline around the neck of an individual then lighting the gasoline.)

Being human we all have our favorites. My favorite torture is *Scaphism*. Never heard of it? I first ran across it in doing research on Plutarch, a 1st century Greek historian, and when it came to torture the ancient Greeks were really creative. Let's see what you think!

Plutarch writes in his biography of Artaxerxes that Mithridates was sentenced to death by scaphism for killing Cyrus the Younger. Mithridates was put into a box tailored especially for him (two small, modified wooden boats placed top-to-top). His entire body was covered with honey with his arms, feet and head left sticking out of the box. Various insects were then allowed to feed on him. Plutarch says it took him seventeen days to die. Now I found that the height of creativity in torture!

The Spanish Inquisitors were also quite expert in torturing the heretics in order to get them to recant and once again become faithful, believing Christians. The Inquisitors seemed to have two favorite torture methods, the ***Strappado a***nd the ***Heretics's fork.*** Never heard of them? Well, in their version of the Strappado the hands of the heretic was tied behind his back with a rope then looped through a pulley and the heretic slowly lifted until he confessed and converted. This technique proved quite a successful conversion technique.

The Heretics Fork was an iron bar with a fork at both ends placed between the breast bone and throat just under the chin and secured with a leather strap around the neck. This resulted in sleep deprivation since the individual could not go to sleep without his head coming forward resulting in great pain. This technique also proved quite successful in converting the heretics.

In the 1300, 1400 and 1500s the British were quite violent and, through long practice, became very accomplished at torturing their prisoners. Their favorite method for traitors seemed to be ***Hanging, Drawing and Quartering***. This was rather gruesome since it involved hanging the prisoner until he was near death, taking him down then disemboweling him while still alive and, finally, quartering him. William Wallace, the hero of Braveheart, was one of those who had various parts of his body scattered to England's four corners. Even the Scotts got into the act and became notorious for playing field hockey with English heads. As an aside it is interesting that our own rather violent culture can be traced directly to this English period.

The word ***torture*** comes from the French and they seemed to have liked the **Iron Maiden** which consists of an iron cabinet, with a hinged front, which could enclose a human being. The cabinet's back and hinged front had spikes that penetrated the body when closed. If the victim did not confess or provide the required information it took about two days for them to die.

It was in the 1700s that the use of torture began to decline. For example, Napoleon realized the futility of torture and forbid "...*the use of torture which is contrary to reason and humanity.*" His rational was that ":..*the wretches say whatever comes into their heads and whatever they think one wants to believe*". This observation is as true today as it was then.

During World War Two both the Germans and the Japanese forgot Napoleon's dictate or, perhaps, just relished their ability to torture and kill people.

The Nazis killed approximately 6 million Jews and 20 million Russians. I love this word approximately– give or take a million of so - when applied so casually to a body count.

The Japanese, not to be outdone by the Germans, killed approximately 30 million. They employed torture extensively on prisoners in their effort to gather military intelligence. One Japanese officer stated afterward that: *"The major means of getting intelligence was to extract information by interrogating prisoners. Torture was an unavoidable necessity. Murdering and burying them follows naturally."* Well, the Japanese were a rather cold bloodied bunch.

This historical review of use of torture brings us to the current issue of torture by the CIA. Historically, there are a number of reasons why torture is used. As I indicated previously torture can be used as an act of revenge, as part of an execution, for religious conversion, or to acquire information. My comments here will be restricted to the use of torture to acquire information.

After 911 fear was rampant throughout the land to include both the Executive and Legislative branches of government. Because of this, the CIA was tasked to provide security to our country by finding those terrorist responsible for attacking the US and preventing a reoccurrence *"by any means necessary."* The men and women at the CIA are not dummies and realized this implied the use of harsh interrogation techniques, possibly torturing prisoners, so they asked for and were provided with legal justifications for the use of *"**Enhanced Interrogation Techniques (EIT)**."* Euphemisms such as this are quite interesting because they are commonly used when people want to distance themselves psychologically from their actions.

The CIA, in an honest attempt to secure the safety of the country, became the latest in a long line of agencies and governments to employ torture to extract information from individuals, in this case those captured in the *"**War on Terror**."* Senior government executives defended these techniques as necessary to keep Americans safe and indicated the techniques employed was not torture since there was no long term physical damage to the victim.

There were two major techniques employed by the CIA or their contractors to extract information from prisoners. These were **Waterboarding** and **Hypothermia**.

In Waterboarding the prisoner is bound to an inclined board, his feet raised with his head slightly below the feet. Absorbent material is wrapped over the prisoner's face and water is poured over it thereby inducing a drowning effect on the prisoner. Depending upon the prisoner, it may take 5-6 times before the subject will answer questions or at least say anything he thinks you want to hear.

As an aside some Special Operations forces are subjected to Waterboarding in order to increase their ability to resist torture and become knowledgeable of the method.

In Hypothermia the prisoner is typically left to stand naked in a cell kept near 50 degrees Fahrenheit, while being regularly doused with cold water in order to increase the rate at which heat is lost from the body. A water temperature of 50 °F leads to death in about one hour so most prisoners have difficulty withstanding this form of interrogation.

I found these techniques rather tame in comparison to those used by the Spanish, English, and French during the middle ages.

The CIA torture report recently released by the Senate Intelligence Committee highlighted the approved techniques designed to elicit information from terrorist prisoners. The rationale for the CIA in using these techniques was to gain actionable intelligence and to detect and prevent future terrorist activities that might harm the US. One simply has to recall the fear permeating the government at that time to understand how senior government executives tolerated a variety of steps, that now look questionable, in order to protect us from further attacks. Make no mistake, senior executives in the Legislative and Executive Branches, to include the President, knew about these techniques even though many now distance themselves from it.

We cannot make the fact that we used torture on prisoners go away because it is true and, to be truthful, I have some sympathy for the CIA men and women who took this action to protect the United States.

An opposite view of torture is taken by Senator Feinstein, current Chairwoman of the Senate Intelligence Committee, who indicated we need an ethical roadblock against future torture, and hopes the release of the report on CIA torture will be one action allowing us to build that roadblock. She said she fully realizes the release of the investigative results will cause a furor among various countries, because it damages the US as an international ethical symbol, and that foreign governments such as Russia, China and Iran will point to the US as being morally and ethically bankrupt.

In addition, some opponents of the release of the torture documents proclaim that it will give terrorists reason for continuing to use torture as a means of coercion. I'm not convinced of this because anyone who has observed the extremism exhibited by ISIL must realize they need little or no incentive to commit violence and torture. Again, to be truthful, I have some sympathy for Senator Feinstein's perspective.

The torture debate, as it should, will continue to rage for the foreseeable future. The latest iteration is Dick Cheney's book, "*In My Time, A Personal and Political Memoir*," in which he continues his support for enhanced interrogation techniques once more arguing that they were necessary for our security and that one cannot equate these techniques with torture. I suspect what Cheney is looking at a definition of torture based upon the severity of pain inflicted and not a definition based upon intent. Typically, countries that practice torture use this restrictive definition of torture and make the severity of pain the most important criterion of the definition because the threshold of pain can be increased while officially denying it is torture.

The current debate about torture seems to boil down to these questions: one, is torture effective in gaining intelligence and, two, is torture under all circumstances morally unacceptable?

The current CIA director seems to feel that question one is unknowable and within the parameters used by the CIA, I suppose a case can be made that information could have been better obtained through less coercive means. However, I'm not entirely convinced that useful information cannot be gained through torture. There are knowledgeable analysts who seem to feel that the validity of information obtained through torture depends upon how soon after a violent action has occurred that torture is applied. That is, if torture is applied immediately while the subject is still in a state of confusion, shock or disorientation then valid intelligence can be obtained. However, they seem to feel that the longer after an incident the application of torture is applied then the less valid the acquired information. There seems to be a certain amount of logic to this view although evidence seems to be through analogy only.

As far as the second question is concerned an argument can be made that torture under any circumstances is morally unacceptable simply because it violates the Christian tenet that we should treat others as our brother. The problem I have is the difficulty in viewing or treating extremist and terrorist as my brother. If someone is intent on killing me, my family, or causing mass casualties then where is the morality in that? Because of my morality, am I obliged to turn the other cheek under those circumstances or do I compromise my ethics and revert to my base nature?

Because of our mountain heritage we each know the answer to that question: we do whatever is necessary to protect our family.

Consequently, I can easily visualize a unique set of circumstances in which torture might be necessary; therefore, I am not fully convinced that torture under ALL circumstances is unacceptable. In my opinion, if the senior, on-site intelligence agent believes that someone has critical, time sensitive information, and feels that torture is one of the ways that should be employed to acquire that information, then, for me, torture becomes an acceptable tool to be used.

Some people view the world as either black or white, torture or no torture. Unfortunately, I view the world as gray, and from my perspective as long as terrorism exists, fear will be its handmaiden, and, in fear, a population will commit or forgive excesses to include torture. During the time under discussion, fear for another mass casualty event resulted in responsible people authorizing coercion, therefore, I can understand why the CIA used torture.

Torture by nature is a messy business and many at the CIA were unhappy with its application but they did it anyway. Yes, I can hear someone now pointing their finger and saying – they followed orders just like the Nazis at Nuremberg. Those pointing fingers are from the same people, siting comfortable and secure in their homes, who now blame the CIA and call for their prosecution. I have difficulty understanding or sympathizing with that perspective.

It must be realized, however, that torture as a **NATIONAL** policy has no place in a society that wishes to retain any semblance of morality or standard of ethics. However, as long as there are extremists or terrorists abroad in the world willing to commit any atrocity, then, realistically, torture will continue to remain a tool in the senior, on-site intelligence officer's interrogation toolkit whether authorized or not. That is as it should be.

Part 6

The Strange Case of Amanda Knox

Part 6 – The Strange Case of Amanda Knox

Context for the Amanda Knox Letter

The Amanda Knox case may appear out of context when compared to the other letters in this volume but nevertheless I found the case so strange and interesting that I decided to include it as a lesson learned for all Oneys.

Amanda Knox was one of the most naïve individuals I have ever read about. I really would have liked to have met her to determine for myself if she was really as naïve as she appeared. I suspect she was, indeed, naïve prior to the trial and imprisonment but after these traumatic events I cannot help but believe that she has lost her innocence and trust in authority.

I have followed the case with interest and looked at the YouTube videos of her interviews and those of the Italian Public Minister, Giuliano Mignini, who is firmly convinced of her guilt and appears willing to go the extra mile to see her in prison.

After reading ***The Strange Case of Amanda Knox*** you might consider viewing several of the YouTube videos about the case. I believe you will also find them exceptionally interesting.

J.T. Oney

Letter 1 - The Strange Case of Amanda Knox

The Murder

On the night of November 1, 2007, the killer plunged the knife two times into the neck of Meredith Kercher, a student from London attending college in the Italian city of Perugia. Still, Kercher would not die. The killer then found a soft spot in her neck and sawed the knife back and forth leaving a gash three inches long and three inches deep. Still, Kercher would not die. At least not for another ten minutes, for the killer had missed the carotid artery. As Kercher lay in agony bleeding on the bed, the killer used three white towels to sop up the blood. After Kercher was dead, the killer threw a cover over her and left the room, leaving bloody fingerprints and foot prints in exiting.

Amanda Knox, who had been staying with Raffaele Sollecito, her boyfriend of one week, returned at 10:30 a.m. on November 2nd, to the cottage at 7 Via Della Pergola that she shared with Kercher and two Italian girls. The Italian girls were on vacation and Kercher's door was closed so Amanda decided to take a shower. As she blow-dried her hair she noticed blood in the sink and that someone had used the bathroom since feces was still in the commode. She began to suspect an intruder and went to tell her boyfriend who returned and attempted to enter Kercher's room but was unsuccessful.

Sollecito called the *carabinieri* (the Italian military police with responsibility for policing both the military and civilian populace; there is no such thing as *posse comitatus* in Italy) and the couple went outside to wait. Soon two officers arrived, not from the *carabinieri,* but from the postal police who have responsibility for investigating such things as Internet fraud and stolen phones but not murders. They had recently recovered a cell phone from a rosebush half a mile away that was registered to Filomena Romanelli, one of the Italian students, at 7 Via Della Pergola. Knox and Sollecito explained to the bewildered officers that there had been a burglary, and invited them into the house.

The four people now in the house were soon joined by four others, Romanelli, her boyfriend and a third couple. Now everyone is traipsing through the house busily contaminating the evidence. The postal police refused to break into Kercher's bedroom, claiming respect for the girl's privacy. Romanelli, however, insisted and one of the boyfriends kicked down the door and the body was discovered.

Amanda Knox's stepfather describes her as "dumb as a rock" when it comes to "street smarts" and so naïve she did not hesitate to talk to strangers in parks. The two Italian roommates called their lawyers, Kercher's British friends fled the country, while Knox's mother asked her to fly home, but Knox refused saying she wanted to see Kercher's family when they arrived in Perugia and she also wanted to help investigators find the killer.

Yep, dumb as a rock for she was later convicted of murder and sentenced to twenty-six years in jail.

But everyone knew there were real problems with the case. For example,

1. Really incompetent police work,
2. Gross evidence contamination,
3. Mishandling of evidence,
4. The lack of any physical trace of Knox in Kercher's bedroom,
5. The prosecution's failure to establish motive or intent
6. The fact that the prosecutors did not immediately drop the case against Knox and Sollecito after the bloody fingerprints and footprints came back matching a 20-year-old petty thief named Rudy Guede.
7. Finally, there was Italy's judicial process with a carnival atmosphere. One author described the lawyers and defendants constantly "interrupting the proceedings with groans and catcalls and wild gesticulations, while the press in the gallery yammers away like the kids in the back of the classroom."

The police needed help and who better to get it from than Amanda Knox herself. Yes, indeed, both dumb as a rock and a naïve as a five year old. What better combination to land her in jail.

In order to briefly see how this miscarriage of justice could occur I need to briefly review the difference between Civil Law and Common law.

Some Civil and Common Law Background

Common law is a peculiarly English development and since the United States is a former English colony our judicial system is primarily based upon Common Law. Before the Norman Conquest, different rules and customs applied in different regions of England. But after 1066 (remember the Battle of Hastings?) monarchs began to unite both England and its laws using the King's Court. Justices created a common law by drawing on customs across the country and rulings by the various monarchs.

Because it is an English development, Common Law systems are found only in countries that are former English colonies or have been influenced by the Anglo-Saxon tradition, such as Australia, India, Canada and the United States.

Common Law is based primarily upon precedent which means the judge's decision is normally based on previously determined court cases; that is, the judge will normally pick the case(s) most similar to the present one and base his/her decision on those cases. Common Law is highly adversarial in that the prosecutor and defense appear before the judge and argue the merits of the case with the Judge serving as an arbiter.

Under United States law, elements of a crime are things that must be proven to convict a defendant. Before a court finds a defendant guilty of a criminal offense, the prosecution must present evidence that is credible and sufficient to prove beyond a reasonable doubt, even when opposed by evidence presented by the defense, that the defendant committed each element of the particular charged crime. The component parts that make up any particular crime vary depending on the crime.

Things that are considered in a crime are such things as (1) the intent, (2) the occurrence of an act (conduct), (3) the criminal intent must precede or coexist with the criminal act (concurrence), (4) and actual harm must have occurred (causation) which is perhaps the most difficult element to prove.

In common law, conduct could not be considered criminal unless a defendant possessed some level of intention with regard to both the nature of his alleged conduct and the existence of the factual circumstances under which the law considered that conduct criminal.

In US courts for criminal cases, the prosecution must prove the defendant's guilt **<u>Beyond a Reasonable Doubt</u>**. This is a high standard of proof and is based upon the elements of a crime.

In a Common Law court, the judge, in his court, is faced with the issue of whether his court should hear a suit on the particular facts related to the case. He will not rule on hypothetical facts but wants particularities. He may be aware that one party is a hardened criminal while the other an honest man, but he must judge on the facts of the case and not their previous actions or conduct.

From a procedural standpoint, a crime is reported and the police investigate and establish the facts of the crime which is brought to a prosecutor, who makes a determination as to whether or not the facts warrant prosecution. A warrant is then issued and the case brought before a judge and a jury. The jury decides on the facts of the case while the judge determines the appropriate sentence based on the jury's verdict.

The difference between Common and Civil legal traditions lies in the main source of law. Although Common Law systems make extensive use of statutes, previous judicial cases are regarded as the most important source of law, which gives judges an active role in developing rules. For example, the elements needed to prove the crime of murder are contained in case law rather than defined by statute. To ensure consistency, courts generally abide by precedents set by higher courts examining the same issue. For example, the Supreme Court is the highest court in the land and is considered the final arbiter in establishing a law as the law of the land.

Lawyers in Civil Law jurisdictions like to think that their system is more stable and fairer than Common Law systems, because laws are stated explicitly and are easier to discern; that is, laws are codified by legislation. But Common Law lawyers take pride in the flexibility of their system, because it can quickly adapt to circumstance without the need for Parliament to enact legislation. In reality, many systems are now a mixture of the two traditions, giving them the best of both legal worlds.

Well, back to **Civil Law** which dominates the European continent. It must be remembered that Roman Law held sway on the European continent from about 449 BC until about 1804 when the continent made the transition from Roman Law to Civil Law with the publication of the French civil code.

In the course of the 19th century, many European states either adopted the French model or drafted their own codes. Civil Law systems have become more widespread than Common Law systems. For example, the CIA World Factbook lists 150 Civil Law countries and 80 Common Law countries.

As I indicated previously, Civil Law is codified. Countries with Civil Law systems have comprehensive, continuously updated legal codes that specify all matters capable of being brought before a court, the applicable procedure, and the appropriate punishment for each offense.

Such codes distinguish between different categories of law: (1) **Substantive Law** establishes which acts are subject to criminal or civil prosecution, (2) **Procedural Law** establishes how to determine whether a particular action constitutes a criminal act, and (3) **Penal Law** establishes the appropriate penalty.

From a procedural standpoint, a "**Public Minister**" often brings the formal charges, investigates the matter, and prosecutes the case. That is, this individual is both the prosecutor and the lead criminal investigator but working within a framework established by a comprehensive, codified set of laws.

OK, enough background. Back to the Amanda Knox case.

The Investigation

Knox had several disadvantages from the start: She was American and, despite majoring in Italian at the University of Washington, could barely speak the language. Her poor comprehension may have contributed to her second problem: her inability to realize that she was, from the first day of the investigation, suspected of murder. Most damaging, however, was her obstinate faith in the kindness of strangers especially the police and prosecutor.

Giuliano Mignini, was assigned to oversee the murder investigation. Mignini's official title is "**Public Minister**," a hybrid of detective and district attorney. The Public Minister leads the investigation, giving directions to the police under his care, and serves as lead prosecutor during the trial. This arrangement, of course, means that the police often find themselves under guidance to look for evidence that supports the prosecutor's hypotheses. This is especially true in high-profile cases when there is enormous pressure to explain quickly what happened. That is, create a theory of the crime then look for facts to support that theory. I obviously prefer an investigative process where the police follow the facts rather than a preconceived theory.

When Mignini arrived at the crime scene he asked the chief forensics expert, Patrizia Stefanoni, whether she had taken Kercher's body temperature, a reliable indicator of time of death. Stefanoni said she was worried that doing so might contaminate the body and advised that they wait until other testing had been done.

This oversight became crucial to the case because the temperature was not taken until November 3rd, twenty-four hours after the death, at which point the death was set between 8 p.m. and 4 a.m. The failure to make a more exact estimation proved critical because if Kercher died after 9:30 p.m., Amanda Knox and Raffaele Sollecito would have had an alibi: They were seen at Sollecito's apartment at 8:45, and Sollecito's computer showed activity as late as 9:10.

From the beginning of the investigation, Magnini suspected that both Knox and Sollecito had committed the crime primarily because he was fascinated by the erratic conduct of Amanda Knox. She was extremely unconvincing in the role of someone who may be innocent.

There were a number of things disturbing to the investigators. One was a video that appeared on YouTube soon after the body was discovered. Filmed by paparazzi who quickly materialized at the "house of horrors," the video showed Sollecito consoling a pallid, dazed Knox outside the cottage. Sollecito rubs her arms and gives her three kisses.

In addition, officers later complained that Knox, after being brought to the police station for questioning, had started doing cartwheels and splits in the waiting room. Convinced that she was psychotic, the guards begged her to stop, explaining that such behavior was "inappropriate." Another detective also complained when he saw Knox sitting on her boyfriend's lap while awaiting interrogation.

Mignini's theory of the crime was beginning to take shape. He was beginning to think that Kercher had been slaughtered as part of a sexual satanic ritual between Knox, Sollecito and Kercher. He thought Knox was smart enough to avoid saying anything inculpatory, but stupid enough to draw attention to herself. He believed that Sollecito, the spoiled computer geek, was weaker and had been manipulated by Knox so they turned their focus onto him, hoping that he would break.

On Monday night, November 5, 2007, Sollecito was asked by the police to return to the station for yet another interview. Knox, as usual, accompanied him. During Sollecito's interview, investigators accused him of covering up for Knox. He asked for a lawyer and to speak with his father but both requests were denied. "Confused and nervous," as one of the officers described him, Sollecito finally stated that Knox could have left his apartment for several hours on the night of Kercher's murder while he was asleep.

For the investigating team that was as good as an admission of guilt, therefore, Knox was brought to the interrogation room and for the next six hours underwent an extensive interrogation. At 5:45 a.m. on 6 November, after breaking down in tears and screaming Lumumba's name ("He's bad, he's bad"), Knox signed a confession. Written in Italian, it declared that Knox had accompanied Lumumba to the house on the night of November 1st. She had been standing in the next room while Lumumba stabbed Kercher to death. When Knox signed the confession, the interrogators started congratulating one another.

That morning, November 6th, the police announced that the killers had been found, and both Knox and Sollecito, whose shoe print the police initially believed matched one found at the scene, found themselves in an Italian jail.

Patrick Lumumba, the Congo-born owner of a bar in Perugia where Knox worked and, who was wrongly accused by Knox of being the murderer, spent two weeks in jail before an alibi secured his release.

Two weeks after the confession, a strange twist occurred when the forensics lab reported that the DNA evidence and fingerprints at the crime scene did not match Knox, Sollecito or Lumumba, but instead matched a fourth person, Rudy Guede.

Guede, who had been friends with the boys who lived downstairs from Knox and Kercher, and had met the girls in passing, fled the country after the murder. When the bloody fingerprints in the cottage were identified as his, Guede became the subject of an international manhunt. He was apprehended in Germany and admitted to being at the murder scene, but he claimed Kercher was killed by a mysterious intruder. Guede, at that time, told the police that Knox and Sollecito were not involved.

Both Knox and Sollicito believed that Guede's arrest and statement would destroy the case against them, but the prosecutors simply slotted Guede in the place of Lumumba, who had a solid alibi.

The Never Ending Trial

The trial, held in a subterranean chamber of Perugia's courthouse, would play to a packed gallery for its entire 11-month run where Mignini suggested that the victim had been slaughtered during a satanic ritual and in his closing argument, he went so far as to refer to Knox as a sex-and-drug-crazed "she-devil."

The Prosecutors claimed that Kercher was held down and stabbed after she rejected attempts by Knox, Sollecito, and Rudy Guede, to involve her in a sex game.

In December, 2009, Amanda Knox was sentenced to 26 years and Raffaele Sollecito to 25 years for the crime, which prosecutors said was a case of rough sex that got violent. Both Knox and Sollecito immediately appealed the sentence.

The Italian appeal process in Italy is more lenient than the American model. For example, in Italy, the appeals judge is allowed to retry the entire case. To the enormous relief of the Knox family, Judge Claudio Hellmann began the appeal with an assertion of reasonable doubt. "The only thing we know for certain in this complex case," he declared, "is that Meredith was murdered."

Hellmann ordered new analyses of the DNA tests by independent experts, a request that was refused during the original trial. There were indications that the readings on the knife and the bra clasp found at the crime scene would be ruled too weak to satisfy international forensics guidelines.

Separately, during his appeal process, Guede, who had been convicted in a separate trial of murdering Kercher and sentenced to 30 years, changed his story multiple times. In a final reversal, he claimed that he was at the murder scene with Knox and Sollecito and for that admission the judge reduced his sentence to 16 years. Go figure!

In October, 2011, after four years in jail, the convictions of Knox and Sollecito were overturned for "lack of evidence" primarily because the independent forensics experts said the crime scene DNA evidence had been contaminated by the police.

Knox immediately returned to Seattle where she signed a contract for four million dollars to write a memoir of the events tentatively entitled, *Waiting To Be Heard*. Well, maybe she is not so dumb after all, or maybe prison life increased her intelligence or maybe, just maybe, she lost her innocence.

Under Italian law, the appellate court can issue an acquittal verdict that the prosecution can still appeal to Italy's Supreme Court of Cassation. The prosecution did appeal in this case, and in March, 2013, the Supreme Court of Cassation overturned the appeal court's decision, arguing that "too many questions remained unanswered" and sending the case back down to an appeal court. Italy's Supreme Court gave as its reason that the jury that acquitted them didn't consider all the evidence and discrepancies in testimony needed to be answered.

Knox and Soliccito were then tried in absentia in a Florence court presided over by Judge Alessandra Nencini. But in this latest trial in Florence, the prosecution changed tactics, saying that the murder was a result of simmering tensions between Knox and Kercher over cleaning and standards of hygiene. Despite the ruling of the Supreme Court, there was little difference in the evidence or details of the case presented at the second trial. After a four month trial they were again found guilty. On January 20, 2014 the judge again sentenced Knox to 26 years, and Sollecito to 25 years.

Remember that Italy's judicial system is based on Civil Law which does not prevent double jeopardy. Despite this verdict, the case is not necessarily closed. It is expected that both Knox and Sollecito will appeal the sentence and under Italy's three-strike trial system this could also mean the case would continue with no immediate outcome.

As an aside, if it seems the Italian Court system presents a depressing picture considering these figures from a Reuters Analysis. There is a backlog of around nine million cases, 5.5 million civil and 3.4 million criminal. The state paid 84 million euros in compensation for miscarriages of justice and legal delays in 2011. There were nearly 50,000 such claims compared to 3,500 in 2003. Another 46 million euros was paid out to people unjustly thrown in jail.

Where do we go from Here?

There is a valid extradition agreement between Italy and the United States. If the Italian judicial system issues an extradition order then the State Department will decide if the request is proper and, if it is, the extradition request would go to the Justice Department, which would check to see whether the request established probable cause that Knox committed the crime and this is a relatively low bar to clear.

If the request clears that hurdle, it will go to a federal judge, but the issue to be addressed would be narrow: Did Italy follow all the rules and make a legitimate request? This is not an opportunity to retry the case in an American Court. If the request is found to be legitimate then Knox could be extradited.

To be clear, from my perspective, this will primarily be a political decision not a judicial one because she has been found guilty in the first trial and we have an extradition agreement with Italy. Because of public outrage over the perceived miscarriage of justice in a flawed judicial system, it will take an act of courage to extradite her; therefore, I suspect this extradition request will go into a bureaucratic black hole and remain in limbo for several years as the appeals process works its way through the judicial system. This will, of course, also leave Amanda Knox's life in limbo which is unfortunate but at least she can be consoled with her four million dollar advance fee. While all this is taking place, the Government will publicly agree to extradite her but only after she has exhausted all her legal rights.

Well, is Amanda guilty, the victim of a flawed judicial process or the victim of her own naiveté. I'll leave you to answer that question.

There are, however, some things all Oneys should take away from this case:

1. Have your lawyer on speed dial. At the site of an incident tell the police officer what you observed. Don't speculate. If you are called to the Police Station for interrogation then Lawyer up. A favorite police tactic is to question your innocence if you lawyer up. Ignore them and talk to them through your Lawyer.
2. Your observed conduct has consequences. While waiting to be interrogated, don't do cart wheels or splits in the waiting room and don't

sit on your boyfriend's lap. The judge may not take conduct into consideration but the police certainly do.

3. The police investigators should let the facts lead them to a conclusion. Prosecutors do not operate in that fashion. They hypothesize then gather or look for evidence to support that hypothesis. Be aware that some police also operate in that fashion so don't let your conduct or mouth give a false impression which leads to an erroneous hypothesis.

4. If you decide to be interrogated without a Lawyer, don't let the interrogators see you sweat. Be calm and rational in your answers. Interrogators will ask the same question ten different ways in an attempt to find a thread on which to pull. If you start becoming confused then ask for coffee, water, something to eat, etc. Finally, realize how stupid you were and ask for a Lawyer.

5. High profile cases are tried in the court of public opinion. Get your story out first and make yourself the victim. Talk to your Lawyer about a publicity campaign.

6. Finally, don't get involved in an incident that puts you under the purview of the Italian judicial system. If it does happen, either leave the country or lawyer up but don't be as naïve as Amanda Knox.

Update to the Amanda Knox Story

In March 2015 Amanda Knox was cleared once and for all by the Italian Supreme Court in the 2007 murder of her British roommate, Meredith Kercher. Her Italian lawyer, Carlo Dalla Vedova, announced the verdict to reporters in Rome, where the Court of Cassation ruled after 10 hours of deliberation. Amanda Knox received a $4 million advance for her book but that money, however, has gone to pay legal fees. At a last newspaper reporting the family is now reported to be penniless.

This story may, however, have a happy ending for Amanda Knox since she is currently engaged to rock musician and transplanted New York native Colin Sutherland.

++

In doing the research for this letter I ran across this discussion on Common Law Elements of a Crime which I found exceptionally interesting. I hope you do as well.

April 1, 2008 - **News Flash** - The medical examiner viewed the body of Ronald Opus and concluded that he died from a shotgun wound to the head. Mr. Opus had jumped from the top of a ten-story building intending to commit suicide. He left a note to that effect, indicating his despondency. As he fell past the ninth floor Opus' life was interrupted by a shotgun blast, passing through a window, which killed him instantly.

Neither the shooter nor the decedent was aware that a safety net had been installed just below, at the eighth floor level, to protect some building workers and that Ronald Opus would not have been able to complete his suicide the way that he had planned. "Ordinarily," the medical examiner continued, "a person who sets out to commit suicide and ultimately succeeds, even though the mechanism might not be what he intended, is still defined as committing suicide." The fact that Mr. Opus was shot and killed on the way to what he thought was a certain death, coupled with the fact that the fall clearly would not have, in fact, caused his death because of the safety net, prompted the medical examiner to feel that he had a homicide rather than a suicide on his hands.

An elderly man and his wife occupied the room on the ninth floor from where the shotgun blast had emanated. They were arguing vigorously, and he was threatening her with a shotgun. The man was so upset that when he pulled the trigger he completely missed his wife, and the pellets went through the window striking Mr. Opus. When one intends to kill subject "A" but accidentally misses and kills subject "B" in the attempt, one is guilty of the murder of subject "B" under the state's view of the so-called "transferred intent" doctrine.

When confronted with the possible murder charge, the old man and his wife were both adamant. They both said that they thought the shotgun was unloaded. The old man said it was his long-standing habit to threaten his wife with the unloaded shotgun. He had no intention, whatsoever, to intentionally or knowingly murder her. Therefore, the killing of Mr. Opus appeared to be an accident and certainly not grossly negligent conduct.

The continuing investigation turned up a witness who saw the old couple's son loading the shotgun about six weeks prior to the fatal accident. It transpired that the old lady had cut off her son's financial support, and the son, knowing the propensity of his father to use the shotgun threateningly, loaded the gun with the expectation that his father would shoot his mother. Since the son was aware of his father's habit and wanted his mother dead, he was guilty of the murder by using an innocent agent (his father) to accomplish the result, even though the son didn't actually pull the trigger. The case now becomes one of murder on the part of the son for the death of the unintended victim, Ronald Opus.

Now comes the exquisite twist. Further investigation revealed that the son was, in fact, Ronald Opus! He had become increasingly despondent over the failure of his attempt to engineer his mother's murder. This led Ronald Opus to jump off the ten-story building, only to be killed by the shotgun blast passing through the ninth story window. The son actually murdered himself! So, the medical examiner closed the case as a *suicide*!

OK, now for another twist. This case did not actually occur but was used by a law professor as a vehicle for discussing the elements of a crime.

FINIS

22421753R00170

Made in the USA
San Bernardino, CA
06 July 2015